ASGARD AND THE GODS

THE TALES AND TRADITIONS OF OUR NORTHERN ANCESTORS

FORMING A COMPLETE MANUAL OF NORSE MYTHOLOGY

ADAPTED FROM THE WORK OF

DR. W. WÄGNER

BY

M. W. MACDOWALL

AND EDITED BY

W. S. W. ANSON

Editor of Dr. Wägner's "Epics and Romances of the Middle Ages"

WITH NUMEROUS ILLUSTRATIONS

ARDVA·QVÆ·PVLCRA

LONDON

SWAN SONNENSCHEIN & CO., Lim.

PATERNOSTER SQUARE

1902

FIRST EDITION, *October*, 1880; SECOND EDITION, *August*, 1884; THIRD EDITION, *October*, 1886; FOURTH EDITION, *March*, 1889; FIFTH EDITION, *September*, 1891; SIXTH EDITION, *November*, 1894; SEVENTH EDITION, *October*, 1902.

WODAN'S WILD HUNT.

PREFACE.

—◆◆◆—

A COMPLETE and popular English account of the
religious beliefs and superstitious customs of the old
Norsemen, suited to our younger readers, has hitherto
been left unwritten. The editor feels sure that our elder
children can easily be brought to take a beneficial interest
in a subject of such great intrinsic worth to all of us, and
has therefore brought out the accompanying book.

Our old ancestors were a hardy, conservative race, and
tenaciously held by the treasured relics of their former beliefs and customs long after they had been shattered by the
onset of Christianity. They retained their primitive Odinic
belief as late as A.D. 800, and we therefore possess it in a
very complete state, far more so than any other European
system of mythology. We English have to this day inherited this conservative trait of their character, and are
still continually in every-day life coming across new and

unexpected remnants of our earliest beliefs. Paragraphs in the newspapers, containing reports of police trials, etc., very frequently bring forward new and as yet undiscovered superstitions, which clearly hark back to the once popular and all-extensive faith of the North.

Who would think, for instance, that in the time-old May-day festivals, we should discover traces of the oldest celebrations of the triumph of the Summer Odin over the Winter Odin, or that through the baby rhymes and nursery sayings of to-day, we should be able to trace the common creed of a nation of thousands of years ago ? To him unused to this kind of research, such things will appear impossible ; but we think our book will considerably extend the sceptic's line of vision, if indeed it does not convert him to an ardent student in the field he has before made light of.

With regard to the translation of the passages quoted from the Old Norse, Icelandic, etc., the original metres, alliterative poems, etc., have been imitated as accurately as possible, though it must be confessed that in one or two places the effect appears somewhat weak and laboured, a result that might have been anticipated, and one which it is hoped the reader will overlook.

With reference to the orthography adopted : in most cases the proper names have been anglicized in form, according to established rules, as far as has been possible. Let us take a few instances :—

The Icelandic nominatival *r* has always been dropped, as in the words Ragnarök*r*, Thrym*r*, etc.

In the case of reduplicated letters, the last has been eliminated, unless an alteration in sound would have been thereby occasioned, *e.g.*, Jotun has been adopted instead of Jotun*n*, Gunlöd instead of Gun*n*löd, etc.

W has been throughout used in place of V, since scholars have pretty generally decided that it more nearly represents the original pronunciation than the English V ; thus we spell Walhalla, Wiking, Walkyries, etc.

Many words have -heim affixed to them : -heim means abode, dwelling, and is the same word as the English *home ;* as instances, Nifelheim, the dark home ; Jotunheim, the home of the Jotuns, giants, etc.

The suffix -gard appended to a word means *place* (English yard, ward, gard-en), and is found in such words as Asgard, the place of the Ases, the gods ; Midgard, the middle place, the earth ; Utgard, the out or lower place.

W. S. W. ANSON.

October 1*st.* 1880.

PREFACE TO THE SECOND EDITION.

THE rapid exhaustion of the first edition of this work has called for its immediate reprint ; and the book is therefore issued in its second edition with but very slight alterations.

We have to thank our kind reviewers for their favourable *critiques* of our work, and to hope that they will extend it to Dr. Wägner's new volume, which we are about to bring out, forming a continuation of the present work, and dealing with the Epics and Romances of the Middle Ages, of the Teutonic and Carlovingian cycles. The two books together will, we believe, constitute a fairly complete treatise of the mythical and traditional lore of the Germanic race.

W. S. W. A.

April, 1882.

CONTENTS.

PART THIRTEENTH.

Loki's Condemnation.

PART FOURTEENTH.

Ragnarök, the Twilight of the Gods.

LIST OF ILLUSTRATIONS.

INTRODUCTION.

JUST as in the olden time, Odin, the thoughtful god, gave his eye in pledge to the wise giant, Mimir, at Mimir's Well, for a draught of primeval wisdom, so men, longing for knowledge and loving the history of old Germany, sought for the great goddess Saga with untiring diligence, until at length they found her. She dwelt in a house of crystal beneath the cool flowing river. The eager enquirers went to her, and asked her to tell them about the olden times, and about the vanished races which had once ruled, suffered, fought and conquered, in the north of Europe. They found the goddess sunk in dreamy thought, while Odin's ravens fluttered around her, and whispered to her of the past and of the future. She rose from her throne, startled by the numerous questions addressed to her. She pointed to the scrolls which were lying scattered around her, as she said : "Are ye come at last to seek intelligence of the wisdom and deeds of your ancestors ? I have written on these scrolls all that the people of that distant land thought and believed, and that which they held to be eternal truth. I went with these mighty races to their new homes, and have faithfully chronicled their struggles and attainments, their deeds, sufferings and victories, their gods and their heroes. No one has inquired for these documents in the long years that are past ; so the storms of time and the glowing flames of Surtur have caused the loss and destruction of many of them. Seek out and gather together such as remain. Ye will find much wisdom hidden therein, when ye can read the writing and understand the meaning of the pictures."

The men sought out and collected as many of the scrolls as they were able. They arranged them in order, but found, as Saga had told them, that very many were lost, and others only existed as fragments. In addition to that, the runic writing on the documents was hard to read, and the true meaning of the faded pictures uncertain. Nevertheless, they allowed no difficulties to terrify them, but courageously pursued their work of investigation. Soon they discovered other records, or fragments of records, which they had supposed to have been lost. What the storms of time had scattered in different directions, what ignorance had cast aside as worthless, they brought to the light of day, often from hidden dusty corners and from the cottages of the poor. They arranged their discoveries in proper order, learnt to read the mystic signs on the documents, and the veil fell away before their increased knowledge. The old Germanic world, with its secrets and wonders, and the views of its ancient people regarding their gods and heroes, which were formerly lost in the darkness of the past, were now visible in the light of the present. We intend to give, in the following pages, the treasures that were thus rescued from oblivion, and to interweave with them many scraps of information which are rapidly dying out and being forgotten. We have endeavoured to make the book as interesting as possible, to induce both the young and the old to examine of what Teutonic genius was capable in the early dawn of its history, a history which in modern times has shown its descendants crowned with immortal laurels on many a blood-red field of battle. The religious conceptions of the most famous nations of antiquity are connected with the beginnings of civilization amongst the Germanic races. If we unflinchingly follow out the traces of a common origin, in spite of the difficulties in our way, we shall often find that the gods of the heathen Asgard, and the tales about them, though apparently dissimilar, really have their basis in the customs and opinions held in the country in which they all had their birth, and that in their early stages they were more or less connected. Although in Central Asia, on the banks of the Indus, in the Land of the Pyramids, in the Greek and Italian peninsulas, and even in the North, whither Kelts, Teutons and Slavs wandered, the religious conceptions of the people have taken different forms, yet their common origin is still perceptible. We point out this connection between the stories of the gods, and the deep thought contained in them, and their importance, in order that the reader may see that it is not a magic world of erratic fancy which is opened out before him, but that, according to Germanic intuition, Life and Nature formed the basis of the existence and action of these divinities. Before we proceed to study each individual deity in his fulness and imposing grandeur, let us, for the better understanding of the subject, rapidly pass their distinguishing characteristics in review.

The Myths and Stories of the Gods of Norse antiquity come first in order. We shall see, as our work goes on, that their origin is to be found in the early home of the Aryan races in the far East, when the spirit of man in the childhood of the world bowed down before those phenomena of surrounding nature which exercised a decisive influence on the struggles and life of humanity. Our ancestors, like all other primitive folk, believed firmly in the personality of these phenomena. All occurrences in the external world, the causes of which were unknown, and all facts of mental perception gradually assumed a human form in the mind of the people. During their wanderings these were as yet vague; but after their settlement in their new home they got further developed by wise seers and bards into typical forms; and then, as time went on, increased in number, until at length they faded away as the old faith died out, or was thrust aside by a new religion. Besides this, we find that many mythical figures arose from the Teutons being brought in contact with other nations; others again, and these the greater number, were due to the idiosyncrasies and characteristics of the Germanic race, and to the climate and mode of life pursued in their new home. Next come the myths about the creation of the world, the gods and their deeds.

The Gods, their Worlds and Deeds.—In the abyss of immeasurable space the ice streams, Eliwagar, roll their blocks of ice; the heat from the South creates life in the frozen waters, and the giant Ymir, the blustering, boisterous, erratic, untamed power of Nature, comes into being. At the same time as the clay-giant, arises the cow, Audumla. She licks the salt-rock, and then the divine Buri is born. His grandsons, Odin, Wili, and We, conquer and kill the raging Ymir, and create the world out of his body. The giant's children are all drowned in his blood, except Bergelmir, who saves himself in a boat, and becomes the father of the giants. The flood is here described, and the giants are to the northern mind what Ahriman, the Principle of Evil, was to the Iranian. The gods point out to the sun and moon, day and night, the courses they must follow in chariots drawn by swift horses, after having completed which they are allowed to sink into the sea to rest. The deities created the first men out of trees—Ask (the ash), and Embla (the alder). Odin gave them life and soul, Hönir endowed them with intellect, and Lodur with blood and colour.

In the dark caverns of the earth the Black-Dwarfs, or Elves of Darkness, creep about and make artistic utensils for the divine Æsir, the Ases, by whom they were created. The Elves of Light on the contrary, have their dwelling-place in the heavenly realms. The latter are pure and good, while the former are often wily and treacherous, but still are not bad enough to be the companions of the wicked giants (known as the Jotuns), who continually fight against both gods and man. As we learn from the myths which follow, two horrible monsters are allied with these giants, and they are to help to decide the Last Battle. They are the Fenris-Wolf and the Midgard-Snake, which latter, lying at the bottom of the sea, encircles the earth (the dwelling-place of the living); and they are abetted by direful Hel, the goddess-queen of the country of the dead.

Hidden or chained in the depths out of sight, these monsters await their time. In like manner dark Surtur, with his flaming sword, and the fiery sons of Muspel, lie in ambush in the hot south country. They are preparing themselves for the decisive battle, when heaven and earth, gods and man, are all to pass away.

Odin; Wodan, Wuotan.—The scene changes; the separate figures of the gods stand out in their characteristic forms as northern imagination and Germanic poets have created them in the likeness of their heroes. First of these is Wodan, the Odin of Southern Germany, the god of battles, armed with his war-spear Gungnir, the death-giving lightning-flash, and followed by the Walkyries, the choosers of the dead, who consecrate the fallen heroes with a kiss, and bear them away to the halls of the gods, where they enjoy the feasts of the blessed. In the very earliest times all Germanic races prayed to Wodan for victory, as we shall see further on. He it is who rushes through the air in the midst of the howling storm, with his tumultuous host, the Wild Hunt, following after him. In the arms of Gunlöd he quaffs Odrörir, the draught of inspiration, and shares it with the seers and bards, and with those warriors who, for the sake of freedom and fatherland, have thrown themselves into the fiery death of battle. Trusting in his wisdom, he goes to Wafthrudnir, to take part in that contest in which the fighting consists of the clash of intellect against intellect in enigmatical speech, and he is victorious in this dangerous combat.

Later, he invents the Runes, through which he gains the power of understanding, penetrating and ruling all things. Thus he becomes the Spirit of Nature,—he becomes Allfather.

Frigga, or Freya, and her Handmaids.—Next to Odin appears Frigga, the mother of the gods, seated on her throne Hlidskialf Amongst the Germans she was looked upon as the same as Frea, the northern Freya, and was worshipped as the all-nourishing mother Earth. Three divine maidens form the household of the goddess; her favourite attendant Fulla or Plenty, helps her to dress, and carries her jewel-case after her; the undaunted horse-woman Gna, bears her orders to all parts of the nine worlds; and the faithful Hlyn protects her votaries. Frigga holds council with her husband regarding the fate of the world, or sits in her hall Fensal, with her handmaids, and spins golden thread with which to reward the diligence of men. In later traditions she is sometimes represented as a cunning housewife gaining all her ends by craft; but in the old legends she is uniformly represented under the names of Holda and Berchta, as the benefactress of mankind. She furthers agriculture, law and order, apportions the fields, consecrates the land-marks, keeps and takes care of the souls of unborn children in her lovely gardens under the streams and lakes, and takes back there the souls of those who die young, that their mothers may cease to weep. As Holda or Dame Gode, she appears as a mighty huntress, devoted to the noble pursuit of the chase. The maidens of the northern Freya are called Siöfna, the lady of sighs; Lofna, whose work it is to bring lovers together in spite of every obstacle; and the wise Wara, who listens to the desire of each human heart, and avenges every breach of faith.

Thor or Thunar, whose turn it now is to be described, is the ideal of the German peasant, as untiring at work as in eating and drinking; open-hearted, therefore often deceived, but when made

FRIGGA, ENGAGED IN HUNTING.

aware of the deception that has been practised on him, terrible in his wrath, and overthrowing his opponent with fierce and mighty blows. He receives Miölnir, the storm-hammer, from the dwarfs who made it for him : he conquers Alwis, the all-wise, in a battle of words. The giant Hrungnir pays for his temerity in challenging him to fight, with a broken head. When deceived by Utgard-Loki's magic, it is only want of opportunity, not of power, that prevents him taking vengeance. When he goes to the ice-giant Hymir to get the cauldron for brewing the beer for the feasts of the gods, he appears in all the fulness of his god-like power. Enveloped in Freya's bridal raiment, he gets back the stolen hammer from the mountain-giant Thrym, destroys the whole race of giants in Thrymheim, and makes the place over to his hard-working peasantry to till. He does the same at Geirödsgard after having overthrown the wily Geiröd. Although not to be withstood in his anger, he is yet mild and gracious when with his hammer he is fixing the landmarks, sanctifying the marriage bond, or consecrating the funeral-pile. Then he is the god who blesses law and order and every pious custom. For this reason he was deeply reverenced in all German and Scandinavian lands, and it is only the later skalds, as is seen in the Harbard lay, that make his glory less than that of the hero-god Odin.

Tyr, Tius, or Zio.—And now, tall and slender as a pine, brave Tyr comes forward. He has only one hand ; for when the terrible Fenris-Wolf grew so powerful that he even threatened the gods themselves in Asgard, Tyr ventured to chain him up with bonds that could not be unloosed, and in so doing lost his hand. He bears a sword as his proper badge, for he is the god of war. The German people held him in high honour under the name of Tius or Zio.

Heru, Cheru or Saxnot.—Another naked sword flashes on the wooded heights in the land of the Cherusci ; it is the weapon of the sword-god Heru, Cheru or Saxnot, who some think is no other than Tyr. Of this weapon Saga tells us that it causes the destruction of its possessor, should he be unworthy of owning it ; but that in the hand of a hero it brings victory and sovereignty.

Heimdal or Riger.—The third sword-god is known as Heimdal or Riger ; he always appears with his sword girded to his side, and is the watchman stationed at the Bridge Bifröst to protect Asgard. He lives on his heavenly hill near the bridge, and drinks sweet mead all day. The faintest sounds are heard by him, and his piercing gaze penetrates even rocks and forests to the farthest distance. Then again he goes out into the world of men, and makes laws and ordinances. He blesses the human race, and keeps clear and visible the line of demarcation between the different classes.

Bragi and Iduna.—Heimdal is born of nine mothers, the wave-maidens, and Bragi also, the god of poetry, rises upon the waves from the depths of the sea. Nature receives him with rejoicing, and the blooming Iduna marries the divine bard. She accompanies him to Asgard, where she gives the gods every morning the apples of eternal youth.

The Wanes, Niörder, Freyer, Freya.—The Wanes are probably a race of gods who were worshipped by the earlier inhabitants of Germany and Scandinavia. Their war with the gods points back to the battles fought between these people and the invading Germanic races. At the conclusion of peace, the Prince of men, Niörder, his son bright Freyer, and his daughter Freya, are given as hostages to the gods, who on their side give up Mimir and Hönir to the Wanes. These Wanes rise to high honour and receive wide-spread adoration.

Fate, Norns, Hel, Walkyries.—Orlog, Fate, a Power impossible to avoid or gainsay, rules over gods and men ; it is impersonal, and bestows its gifts blindly. Out of the dense darkness surrounding it on every side, it also comes forth in visible shape as Regin, and guides and rules all things, and sometimes in the form of the gods, determines the life and actions of mortals. The Norns come out of the unknown distance enveloped in a dark veil, to the Ash Yggdrasil. They sprinkle it daily with water from the Fountain of Urd, that it may not wither, but remain green and fresh and strong. Urd, the eldest of the three sisters, gazes thoughtfully into the Past, Werdandi into the Present, and Skuld into the Future, which is either rich in hope or dark with tears. Thus they make known the decrees of Orlog, or Fate; for out of the past and present the events and actions of the future are born. Dark inscrutable Hel holds sway deep down in Helheim and Nifelheim. According to most ancient tradition she was once the earth-mother who watches over life and growth, and who finally calls the weary pilgrim home to her through the land of death.

In the poems of the skalds she becomes the dark, terrible Queen of the Realm of Shades, who brought death into the world. She has, however, no power over the course of battles where brave men struggle for the honour of victory. There Odin's Wish-maidens, the Walkyries, rule and determine the fate of the combatants. Armed with helmet and shield, they ride on white cloud horses to choose their warriors as the Father of the gods has commanded them. They consecrate the fallen heroes with the kiss of death, and bear them away to Walhalla to the feast of the Einheriar.

Ögir and his companions.—Ögir or Hler moves about on the stormy seas accompanied by his wife Ran. Ögir is of the race of giants, but lives in friendly alliance with the gods. His comrades are the Mumel-king, the wonderful player, and the nixies, necks, and water-sprites.

Loki, the father of terrible Hel, the Fenris-Wolf and Midgard-Snake; Loki, the crafty god who is ever devising evil, now steals forward that we may observe his corrupt practices and his real

character. In primeval times he was Odin's brother by blood, the
god of life-giving warmth, and in particular of the indispensable
household fire.   As a destructive conflagration arises from a hidden
spark which gradually increases in strength and volume, until at
last it bursts out furiously and consumes the house and all that it
contains, thus, as we shall show later on, the conception of Loki
was developed in the minds of these old races, until he was at last
held to be the corrupter of the gods, the principle of evil.

The other Gods.—As regards the other gods, the silent Widar,
son of Odin, first appears, armed with a sword and wearing iron
shoes.   Joyfully he hears the prophecy of the Norns, that he should
on a future day avenge his father by killing the destroying wolf,
and that he would afterwards live for ever in blissful peace in the
renewed world.   Then comes Hermodur, the swift messenger of
the gods, who fulfils his office at a sign from Odin.   Another
avenger, the blooming Wali, is received with acclamation when
he enters the halls of Odin, for he is the son of Odin and the
northern Rinda, is chosen to avenge bright Baldur the well-beloved, and to give the deadly blow which shall send dark Hödur
down to the realms of Hel.   So the story brings us to Baldur, the
giver of all good, and to Hödur, who rules over the darkness.   The
myth tells us how both fought for the sake of the lovely Nanna,
and how the former received his death wound by magic art.   His
son Forseti, who resembles his father in holiness and righteousness,
is the upholder of eternal law.   The myth shows him to us seated
on a throne teaching the Northern Frisians the benefits of law,
and surrounded by his twelve judges, all of whom are somewhat
like him both in face and form.

The Golden Age.—From this brief glance at the individual
gods we pass on to the description of the events which concern
these divinities as a whole, and which lead up to the epic poems in
which they figure.   The golden age, the time of innocence, is next

to be described, when the lust for gold was as yet unknown, when the gods played with golden disks, and no passion disturbed the rapture of mere existence. All this lasts till Gullweig (Gold-ore), the bewitching enchantress, comes, who, thrice cast into the fire, arises each time more beautiful than before, and fills the souls of gods and men with unappeasable longing. Then the Norns, the Past, Present and Future, enter into being, and the blessed peace of childhood's dreams passes away, and sin comes into existence with all its evil consequences.

Sin.—The poems of the skalds give another account of the way in which sin makes its first appearance. The gods wish to have a strong wall of fortification round their Asgard, to pro-tect it against the assaults of the Jotuns, the giants. Acting on Loki's advice, they swear by a holy oath to give the sun and moon, and even Freya herself, the goddess of grace and beauty, to an unknown builder, on condition that he finishes the wall in the course of one winter. The master-builder turns out to be a Hrimthurse (Frost-giant), who, with the help of his horse, seems about to finish the high wall of ice, the sides of which are as smooth as polished steel, within the allotted time. If the bar-gain were to hold good, darkness would envelop the world, and sweetness and love would disappear from life; so the gods com-mand Loki, as he values his head, to tell them what to do. He outwits the giant by means of treachery and magic, and Thor pays the master-builder in blows of his hammer. Thus the gods break their oath, and inexpiable guilt rests upon them.

Iduna's departure.—Evil portents precede the coming horrors. Iduna, the distributor of the apples of immortal youth, sinks from her bright home amid the boughs of the Ash Yggdrasil, into the gloomy depths below. She can only weep when the messengers ask her the meaning of her leaving them. Bragi remains with her, for with youth, games and song also pass away.

Baldur's death.—The day of judgment approaches, and new
signs bear witness of its coming. Baldur, the holy one, who alone
is without sin, has terrible dreams. Hel appears to him in his
sleep, and signs to him to come to her. Odin rides through the
dark valleys which lead to the realm of shades, that he may
enquire of the dead what the future will bring forth. His incantations call the long deceased Wala out of her grave, and she foretells
what he has already feared, Baldur's death. Whereupon Frigga,
who is much troubled in spirit, entreats all creatures and all lifeless
things to swear that they will not injure the Well-beloved. But she
overlooks one, the weak mistletoe-bough. Crafty Loki discovers
this omission. When the gods in boisterous play throw their
weapons at Baldur, all of which turn aside from striking his holy
body, Loki gives blind Hödur the fatal bough, which he has made
into a dart. He guides the direction of the blow, and the murder
is committed—Baldur lies stabbed to the heart on the bloodstained
sward. Peace and joy, righteousness and holiness disappear with
him. For this reason the gods and men, and even the dwarfs who
fear the light, the elves in their caverns, and the malicious race
of giants weep for him. They all assemble round his funeral pile.
Two corpses are stretched on the litter; for Nanna, Baldur's beautiful bride, has died of a broken heart. When the sunny-hearted
god of light dies, the flowers must also wither. At Odin's command Hermodur rides along the road leading to Hel's dominions,
to entreat the terrible goddess to permit the return of the Well-
beloved. He finds Baldur and Nanna seated at a table on which
are placed cups of mead, but they leave the foaming draught untouched; they sit there as silent and sad as the other flitting
shades, which glide past them like misty phantoms. The dreadful
queen of the realm of the dead is seated on her throne grave and
silent. This is her reply to Hermodur's message: " If every creature weeps for the Beloved he shall return to the upper world.

otherwise he must remain in his place." The messenger of the gods brings back this answer. Every creature weeps for her son at Frigga's entreaty; but one giantess alone, dwelling in an obscure cleft in a rock, refrains from weeping, and so Baldur remains in Hel's possession. But vengeance has yet to be executed on the god who lives in darkness, and that duty is fulfilled by Wali, who kills strong Hödur with his darts. Wali is the god of spring, who destroys dark gloomy winter; he is the risen Baldur.

Ögir's banquet.—The northern poems, apparently to break the course of these tragic events, now lead us to Ögir's palace, where the gods are assembled to hold a joyous feast after a long period of mourning. The hall is brilliantly lighted by the golden radiance of the treasures of the deep, and the tankards are full of foaming beer or mead; but the bard no longer sings to the music of the harp. Instead of that, Loki forces his way into the assembly; he does not now hide his wickedness under the cloak of hypocrisy, but openly boasts of what he has done. As the evil-doer amongst men does not become a villain or a hardened criminal all at once, but gradually ascends the ladder of wickedness step by step until he reaches the summit, so it is with Loki; at first his actions are beneficial and good, then he begins to give bad advice; after that he plots against the general peace, steals a costly treasure, and pitilessly works to bring about murder. At last he shows his diabolical nature without disguise, when, throwing aside the veil of hypocrisy, he hurls invectives at the gods, and openly acknowledges his horrible deeds of wickedness. The appearance of Thor forces him to take flight, and he barely escapes the dread hammer of the god.

Loki in chains.—The murderer of Baldur, the blasphemer of the gods, cannot remain unpunished. In vain he conceals himself in a solitary house on a distant mountain, in vain he takes the form of a salmon and hides himself under a waterfall, for the avengers catch him in a peculiar net which he had formerly invented for the destruction of others. They bind him to the sharp ledge of a rock with the sinews of his son, which are changed into iron chains. A snake drops poison upon his face, making him yell with pain, and the earth quakes with his convulsive tremblings. His faithful wife Sigyn catches the poison in a cup ; but still it drops upon him whenever the vessel is full.

Ragnarök.—The destroyer lies in chains on the sharp ledge of rock ; but he is not bound for ever. When the salutary bonds of law are broken, when discipline and morality, uprightness and the rear of God vanish, destruction comes upon states and nations. This is what is to happen at the time of which the legend now tells us. Nothing good or holy is respected. Falsehood, perjury, fratricidal wars, earthquakes, Fimbul-Winter (such severe winter as was never known before), are to be the signs that the end of the world is near. The sun and moon will be extinguished by their pursuers, the stars fall from the heavens, Yggdrasil will tremble, all chains be broken, and Loki and his dread sons be freed. Then the fiery sons of Muspel with dark Surtur at their head come from the South, and the giants from the East ; the last battle shall be fought on the field of Wigrid. There the enemy's forces are drawn up in battle array, and thither Odin goes to meet them with his host of gods, and his band of Einheriar. And now the mountains fall down, the abyss yawns showing the very realms of Hel, the heavens split open and are lost in chaos, the chief warriors, the strong, are all slain in that deadly fight. Surtur, terrible to look upon, raises himself to the very sky ; he flings his fiery darts upon the earth, and the universe is all burnt up. Our forefathers' conceptions as to the last battle, the single combats of the strong, the burning of the world, are all to be learnt from ancient traditions, as we find them described in the poems of the skalds.

The Renewal of the World.—The myth compensates for the

tragic end of the divine drama by concluding with a description of the renewal of the world. The earth rises green and blooming out of its ruin, as soon as it has been thoroughly purged from sin, refined and restored by fire. The gods assemble on the plains of Ida, the gods Widar and Wali are there, with Magni and Modi, the sons of Thor, who bring with them their father's Miölnir, a weapon no longer used for striking, but only for consecrating what is right and holy. They are joined by Baldur and Hödur, who

ANCIENT HINDU IDEA OF THE WORLD.
From the drawing of a Brahmin.

are now reconciled, and united in brotherly love. Human beings are also to be found there, Lif and Lifthrasir, who, hidden in Hoddmimir's wood, dreamed the dreams of childhood, while the horrors of the last battle were taking place, and who, being pure and innocent and free from sinful desires, are permitted to enter the world where peace now reigns.

We have thought it requisite, for the better understanding of our

C

history, to throw a cursory glance over the whole of the great drama, which describes to us the creation, prime, fall, destruction, and restoration of the world and the gods. The separate parts of the drama are not always connected with one another; they have grown up gradually in the course of centuries, and therefore are not calculated to fit into each other. Sometimes, indeed, they are in complete opposition to each other; yet in spite of this, one fundamental idea runs through all myths: we find in all that sin causes universal destruction, and that the world, purified by fire, rises again more beautiful and glorious than before. We have classified the myths as much as possible in accordance with this leading idea, and have also added their interpretations.

A good many parts of the Edda have, most likely, arisen in the land of the Cherusci, in Osning or Asening, and have been founded on songs in honour of the gods and heroes worshipped there. Moreover, it is an undoubted fact that the Northern skalds translated those songs, changing partially their form, and incorporating them with their own poems, so that the whole gained a northern colouring.

LAY OF THE NORSE GODS AND HEROES.

Step out of the misty veil
Which darkly winds round thee;
Step out of the olden days,
Thou great Divinity!
Across thy mental vision
Passes the godly host,
That Bragi's melodies
Made Asgard's proudest boast.

AFTER PROF. ENGELHARD'S STATUE.

(*See accompanying verses.*)

There rise the sounds of music
From harp strings sweet and clear,
Wonderfully enchanting
To the receiving ear.
Thou wast it, thou hast carried
Sagas of northern fame,
Did'st boldly strike the harp strings
Of old skalds ; just the same
Thou spann'st the bridge of Bifröst,
The pathway of the gods ;—
O name the mighty heroes,
Draw pictures of the gods !

Let the reader now follow us into the world of Germanic gods, giants, dwarfs, and heroes. These fairy tales are not senseless stories written for the amusement of the idle ; they embody the profound religion of our forefathers, which excited them to brave deeds, inspired them with strength and courage enough to shatter the Roman Empire, and to set up a new order of things in its stead. But when four hundred years after their dreadful battles against Germanicus, the Teutons victoriously entered their new country, the old faith had already faded, and they exchanged without difficulty their hero-god for St. Martin or the archangel Michael, and their Thunar for St. Peter or St. Oswald. The Saxons alone, in whose land the much revered holy places were to be found, clung to their gods, and when they were afterwards conquered by Charles the Great, some of them fled the country, carried their old religion to their northern brothers, and preserved it, until, at the time of the Wiking wars, it lost its glory in Scandinavia, and fell before the preaching of the Cross

PART FIRST.

LEGENDS AND MYTHS.

IN the beginning was a great abyss; neither day nor night existed; the abyss was Ginnungagap, the yawning gulf, without beginning, without end. Allfather, the Uncreated, the Unseen, dwelt in the depth of the abyss and willed, and what he willed came into being. Towards the north, in immeasurable space where dwell darkness and icy cold, arose Nifelheim (the Home of the Mists), and to the south was Muspelheim (the Home of Brightness), fiery, glowing with intense heat. The spring Hwergelmir (the seething cauldron) sprang into life in Nifelheim, and out of it flowed twelve and more infernal streams (Eliwagar) with their ice-cold waters. The dreadful cold soon froze the waters, and blocks of ice rolled over and under each other through the boundless gulf towards the south and Muspelheim. In the air above, the storms roared from Nifelheim, rooting up the icebergs; while from the Home of Brightness rays of beneficent heat poured forth over Ginnungagap, and when the great blocks of ice began to melt under the influence of this warmth, and drops of water to form and run down their sides, then it was that life first showed itself, and there arose a monster, the giant Ymir, or Örgelmir (seething clay), terrible to look upon. From him are descended the Hrimthurses or Frost-giants.

The warm rays awakened more life in the waters. The cow Audumla, the nourisher, came into being ; from her flowed four streams of milk which fed the dreadful Ymir and his children, the Hrimthurses. But she had nothing to graze on except the salt of the ice-rocks, which she licked. On the first day after she had licked the rock, a head of hair was visible ; on the second day, the whole head ; and on the third, the rest of the body, beautiful and glorious of limb. This was now Buri (the Producer), who had a son named Bör (born), and Bör married Bestla, daughter of the Hrimthurses, by whom he had three sons, Odin (spirit), Wili (will) and We (holy).

After this, war was made on the violent Ymir, and the sons of Bör slew him, and flung his great body into Ginnungagap, which was filled with it. But the blood of the monster flowed out covering all things, so that there was a great flood (Deluge) in which the Hrimthurses were drowned. One of them alone, the wise Bergelmir, saved himself and his wife from destruction by taking refuge in a cunningly made boat, and he became the father of the race of giants. This is the northern version of the story of Noah.

Space was now void and drear, as we learn from an ancient German lay :—

> " I regarded among men as the greatest of wonders,
>   That the earth was not, nor yet the firmament,
>   Nor was there yet a tree, nor mountain, nor even sunshine,
>   Nor moon so radiant, nor ever a mighty sea."

The new rulers, who called themselves Ases, *i.e.*, pillars and supports of the world, did not like this state of things at all. So they began to create as Allfather willed that they should. They made the earth of Ymir's body, the sea of his sweat, the hills of his bones, and the trees of his curly hair. Of his skull they made the firmament, and of his brain the clouds which float below. Then, out of the giant's eyebrows the gods formed Midgard (Middle-garden), the dwelling-place of the children of men, who as yet unborn slept in the lap of time.

Darkness reigned throughout space ; only a few fiery sparks from Muspelheim wandered aimlessly through the air ; the sun did not know her place, nor the moon his* course, nor did the stars know where they were to stand. But the gods collected the sparks,

DAY.

made them into stars and fastened them in the firmament. They created the chariot of the sun, harnessed to it the horse Arwaker (Early-waker), which was driven by the maiden Sol; she was rapidly followed by the shining moon drawn by the horse Alswider (All-swift), bridled and managed by the beautiful boy Mani. Mother Night talked lovingly to Mani as she preceded him on her dark horse Hrimfaxi (Frost-mane), whilst her son Day followed her with his bright Skinfaxi (Shining-mane).

* In German the sun is feminine, the moon masculine.

Creatures of all sorts crept like maggots in and out of Ymir's body and bones. The gods therefore consulted together as to what was best to be done, and they thought that their wisest course would be to change these creatures into a useful people. So they at once changed them into Dwarfs and Trolls, who were gifted with a wonderful knowledge of minerals and stones of all kinds, and an extraordinary power of working in metals. One class of dwarfs was of dark complexion, cunning and treacherous; the other was fair, good and useful to gods and men. Three mighty gods once left the place where the Thing or council was

NIGHT.

held; they were Odin, Hönir or Hahnir (the Bright One) and Lodur. While wandering over the face of the earth, which was green with grass and with the juicy leek, they found two human forms lying near the shore, Ask (the ash), and Embla (the alder), both of whom were without power or sense, motionless, colourless. Odin gave them souls; Hönir, motion and the senses; and Lodur, blood and blooming complexions. From these two are descended all the numerous races of men.

Allfather dwelt in the deep and willed, and what he willed came to pass. Then the ash Yggdrasil grew up, the tree of the universe, of time and of life. The boughs stretched out into heaven ; its highest point, Lärad (peace-giver) overshadowed Walhalla, the hall of the heroes. Its three roots reached down to dark Hel, to Jotunheim the land of the Hrimthurses, and to Midgard the dwelling-place of the children of men. The World-tree was ever-green, for the fateful Norns sprinkled it daily with the water of life from the fountain of Urd which flowed in Midgard. But the goat Heidrun, from whom was obtained the mead that nourished the heroes, and the stag Eikthyrnir browsed upon the leaf-buds, and upon the bark of the tree, while the roots down below are gnawed by the dragon Nidhögg and innummerable worms : still the ash could not wither until the Last Battle should be fought, where life, time and the world were all to pass away. So the eagle sang its song of Creation and Destruction on the highest branch of the tree.

This is what a skald, a Northern bard, related to the warriors who were resting from the fatigue of fighting, by tables of mead. He and his comrades, intoxicated with the divine mead of enthusiasm, used to tell these stories to the listening people. The myths were founded on the belief of the Norse people regarding the creation of the world, gods and men, and as such we find them preserved in the Songs of the Edda. At the same time the catastrophe is hinted at by which, in the opinion of these races, the great world-drama was to end. It is true that many unlovely and even coarse ideas are to be found mixed up with the rest, and that they cannot be compared with the beautiful fancies of Hellenic poetry ; but the drama as a whole is grand and philosophical, and had its birth in that heroic spirit which forced the Teutons and Northern Wikings out into their battles of life or death. We have also the idea of Allfather, the unquestionable original cause of all things. though he is scarcely more than mentioned in the poems. This idea came more prominently forward in later times, but could not grow

THE ASH YGGDRASIL.

to its full proportions, because the preaching of the Gospel soon afterwards did away with the old faith. Whilst struggling against the horrors of a northern climate and sending out armies into distant land, the Teutons fixed their eyes on certain aspects of nature, and could not rise to distinct conceptions of the Eternal. Still this idea lay originally at the foundation of the Northern religion, and the kindred Aryan race in India developed and exhibited it in a wonderful and poetical manner.

Neither in the one case nor in the other, did the myths arise complete and perfect in the minds of these kindred people in the form in which we read them in the ancient documents. They needed a long time, a long period of development, before they appeared as regular myths or mythical tales. We must try to make clear to ourselves the process of the formation and development of the myth. Nations, like individuals, have their childhood, youth, prime and old age. In their childhood they cannot look upon the inexplicable facts and manifestations of the forces of nature, and on those of their own soul, otherwise than under certain forms. Nature, on which they feel themselves dependent, seems to them a Personality possessed of thought, will and perception. Nature is the Divinity they worship; she is the Self-existent Power of the Indian Aryans, the Eros of the Hellenes in their earliest home by the Acherusian Lake, and the Allfather who dwelt less clearly in the mind of the Germanic races. Amongst the Greeks the first departure from their earliest religious conceptions was the deification of Gaia, the all-nourishing earth; amongst the Hindus and Teutons, it was that of the shining firmament with its stars, its moon, its life-giving sun and its clouds with their refreshing rains.

The vague notion of a deity who created and ruled over all things had its rise in the impression made upon the human mind by the unity of nature, but was soon overcome by that produced by certain particular aspects of nature. The sun, moon and stars, clouds and mists, storms and tempests, appeared to be higher powers, and took distinct forms in the imagination of man. The sun was regarded now as a fiery bird which flew across the sky, now as a horse and now as a chariot and horses; the clouds were cows from whose udders the fruitful rain poured down, or nursing mothers, or heavenly streams and lakes; the storm-wind appeared as a gigantic eagle that stirred the air by the flapping of his great wings. As the phenomena of nature seemed to resemble animals either in outward form or in action, they were represented under the figure of animals. The beast which does not think, and which yet acts in accordance with some incomprehensible impulse, appears to be something extraordinary, something divine.

After riper consideration, it was discovered that man alone was gifted with the higher mental powers. It was therefore acknowledged that the figure of an animal was an improper representation of a divine being. Thus in inverted relation to that described in Holy Writ, when "God created man in His own image, in the image of God created He him," men now made the gods in their own likeness, but at the same time regarded them as greater, more beautiful and more ideal than themselves.

The monotheistic idea of Allfather, which formed the basis of the Germanic religion, soon gave place to that of a trilogy, consisting at first of Odin, Wili and We, and afterwards of Odin, Hönir and Lodur. From these proceed the twelve gods of heaven, and they again are associated with many other divinities.

Polytheism has its origin in a variety of causes. The primary reason for it is to be found in the numerous qualities attributed to each one god, and also in his varying spheres of action. Hence the many additional names bestowed upon him. In course of time his identity with nature is forgotten, and people grow accustomed to accept his attributes as so many separate personalities. Thus, for instance, the powerful storm-god Wodan, the Northern Odin, was regarded as the highest god, the king of heaven. He it was who inspired both warlike and poetical enthusiasm. But still, the dispossessed king of heaven, Tyr, was worshipped as the god of war, while the art of poetry was placed under the protection of the divine Bragi, who was unknown in earlier times. Freya, the goddess of beauty and love, was essentially the same as the goddess of Earth, yet the German Nerthus and the Northern Jörd and Rinda were honoured as such ; from Freya was also derived Frigg, the queen of heaven, who was raised to the position of Odin's lawful wife. Another cause of the increase of the number of divinities is attributable to the vast extent of country over which the great Germanic race was spread, viz., over Germany, Scandinavia, and far away to the east amongst the Russian steppes. The numerous tribes into which the race was divided was another circumstance in favour of polytheism. These tribes preserved their language and their faith as a whole, but each had its own distinctive peculiarities and its own particular tribal god. They were sometimes communicated to other tribes, and in times of war the conquerors either dethroned the gods of the vanquished or else accepted them in addition to their own.

The divine kingdom as described in the legends of the gods and heroes.—After the gods, the giants and the dwarfs had become personalities capable of free action ; they were supposed to have stood in human relation to each other. They were given family ties and were finally brought under the laws of a divine kingdom. As people had now forgotten that the origin of the gods was to be found in the phenomena of nature, other motives for their fate and actions had to be sought, and thus the myth was added to, was made of wider significance, and its former meaning completely altered.

During the centuries that were necessary to bring about this

development, there had been many changes in the fortunes of the
Germanic tribes. They had destroyed the Roman empire, and
had made their dwelling amongst its ruins. After that the proud
victors bent their heads beneath the Cross, and accepted the
Christian faith. Then the teaching of the Cross gradually made
its way into Germany, the home of these warlike tribes; the
messengers who brought it endeavoured to root out all relics of
heathenism, and when preaching was of no avail, the power of the
already converted ruler was brought into play. Thus was the old
religion expunged from Germany proper. Still remnants of it are
to be found in popular customs and traditions, and in a few
fragmentary writings which suffice to show us the connection
between the religion of our fathers and that preserved in the
northern mythology.

It was different in the north, in Scandinavia. The preachers of
the Gospel did not make their way there until much later. In that
land the warlike chieftains dwelt in their towers and castles
surrounded by their retainers, drinking sweet mead and beer, or
the foreign wine they had brought home from their campaigns.
There the victorious warriors delighted to tell of their adventurous
voyages and Wiking raids, of battles with ice-giants, with winds
and waves, and with the men of the south. There the skalds
sang their lays in honour of the gods and heroes, and formed the
myths into an artistic whole, a world-drama, which a happy chance
has preserved to us. How this was done we shall now proceed to
show.

In the tenth century Harald Harfager (fair hair) was acknowledged King of the whole realm of Norway. Many of the
Jarls and Princes, who had formerly been independent rulers, were
too proud to bear the yoke of the conqueror, and set out in search
of other homes. The brave Rollo and his followers conquered
Normandy and Brittany in France, others of the emigrants settled

in the Shetland and Faroe islands, while others again under Ingulf
and Hörleif landed on the inhospitable coasts of Iceland, and
cultivated and peopled the island as far as its severe climate would
permit. These people carried with them from their native land the
old songs of the skalds, which the fathers sang to their sons, and
the sons again to their sons, passing them on to each new generation as a most precious heritage. It is true that Christianity was
introduced into Iceland towards the end of the tenth century, but
before that time the people had preserved the songs of their forefathers, first by means of very imperfect runes, and then by the
use of letters which had been brought to them from other lands,
besides which the Christian priests, who were mostly Icelanders,
were far from wishing to destroy the old tales. Many of them went
so far as to listen to the songs of the people and afterwards write ·
them down, and thus these treasures were saved from oblivion both
in Iceland and in the Faroe islands. It is believed that the learned
Icelander, Sæmund the Wise (A.D. 1056–1133), compiled the Elder
Edda, the first collection of these old songs, partly from oral tradition and partly from imperfect runic writings which had been copied
in Latin characters. This collection, which is called Sæmund's
Edda after its supposed compiler, contains first in the Wöluspa
(Song of Wala) the mythical account given by the northern imagination of the creation of the world, of giants, of gods, of dwarfs, and
of men ; then there is a description of the Last Battle and of the
destruction and renewal of the world ; after that come songs about
the adventures and journeys of the individual gods, and lastly
others are given in honour of the Heroes, especially the Niflungs,
Sigurd the slayer of the dragon Fafnir, and so on. The Younger
Edda, a collection of the same kind, is supposed to have been
compiled by Bishop Snorri Sturlason (A.D. 1178–1241), and for
that reason generally goes by the name of the Snorra-Edda. It is
for the most part written in prose, and serves as a commentary on

the Elder Edda, but was originally meant more particularly for the
instruction of the Icelandic skalds.

The Runic language and characters.—The word *rûna* really
means "secret"; runes are therefore "mysterious signs requiring
an interpretation." The shape of the letters leads to the supposi-
tion that they were formed in imitation of the Phœnician alphabet.
It is clear that the runes were, from various causes, regarded even
in Germany proper as full of mystery and endowed with supernatural power.

After Ulphilas made a new alphabet for the Goths in the fourth
century by ingeniously uniting the form of the Greek letters to
that of a runic alphabet consisting of twenty-five letters which
was nearly related to that of the Anglo-Saxons; the runes
gradually died out more and more, and as Christianity spread, the
Roman alphabet was introduced in place of the old Germanic
letters.

The runes appear to have served less as a mode of writing than
as a help to the memory; they were principally used to note down
a train of thought, to preserve wise sayings and prophecies, and
the remembrance of particular deeds and memorable occurrences.
Tacitus informs us that it was also customary to cut beech twigs
into small pieces and then throw them on a cloth which had been
previously spread out for the purpose, and afterwards to read future
events by means of the signs accidentally formed by the bits of
wood as they lay on the cloth.

The heroic lays of the old time have died out, and the runes
have with few exceptions been rooted out of our fatherland by
priestly zeal which looked upon them as magical. Our knowledge
of the full-toned, powerful language of our ancestors is therefore
very imperfect. But we know that it belonged to the great Aryan
branch, and was thus related to the noblest of the Aryan languages, the Sanscrit or holy tongue, and was rich in inflexions.

In the Chinese and Indo-Chinese languages the ancient poverty of expression is still to be found, and even at the present day we find in them monosyllabic roots placed next to each other with hardly a connecting link; in the Turanian language of Central Asia the people have endeavoured to express the association of their ideas by the use of suffixes, but these suffixes are in themselves complete words, and thus the combination is as distinctly visible as the separate strokes of the brush in a bad painting. The language of the Teutonic race had already got beyond that point before the different tribes set out on their wanderings in search of a new home. The added words had fused with the others, and were capable of expressing an unbroken current of thought. The language had been developed by means of the Sagas and songs which had been handed down amongst the people from generation to generation.

A NORTHERN LANDSCAPE.

PART SECOND.

THE GODS, THEIR WORLDS AND DEEDS.

THE NORNS.

THE three fatal sisters played a prominent part in many German tales. They used to watch over springs of water, and to appear by the cradle of many a royal infant to give it presents. On such occasions two of them were generally friendly to the child, while the third prophesied evil concerning it. Sometimes the Norns were supposed to be one, and then they were called

Urd ; but they were oftener looked upon as many, especially as the twelve Urds. In the pretty story of the "Sleeping Beauty" thirteen fairies appear. The king invited twelve of them to the birthday feast given in honour of his little daughter. Eleven had endowed the child with intelligence, beauty, wealth, and other good gifts, when suddenly a thirteenth fairy entered unbidden and ordained that the princess should die early of the prick of a spindle. The twelfth now came forward and took some of the bitterness out of the terrible prophecy by saying that the girl should not die, but should fall into a sleep of a hundred years' duration, out of which she should at last awake when the right hour for setting her free should strike. This hour came when a young hero forced his way through the thorn hedge that surrounded her, and awoke the sleeper with a kiss of love.

Urd or Wurd is also connected with Hel, the goddess of death : for the Past, being dead, falls into the nether world. Hel herself appears in the story as the Norn who span the irrefragable thread of fate, and in the German version of the tale in which the fatal sisters appear, she was the bad fairy whose name, Held, betrays her identity with the goddess.

The origin of the Norns is wrapped in mystery ; while the dwarfs, who are at times somewhat difficult to distinguish from the elves, were, as we have seen, created by the gods.

ELVES.

DWARFS AND ELVES.

Three kinds of dwarfs existed in northern mythology, Modsognir's folk, Durin's band, and Dwalin's confederacy of Lofar's race. Lofar is perhaps the same as Loki, the fire-god, for all the dwarfs needed his help in their subterranean labours. In the old German poems we often find descriptions of dwarf-kings, who ruled over underground realms, and the Norse nations regarded Modsognir's and Durin's people as especially great and powerful, more, however, from their miraculous strength and knowledge of magic than from their having rule over any definite territory. The ideas respecting these deformed and goblin-like creatures, some writers state, are connected with the appearance of the Phœnicians in the North. Wherever these roving merchants went, they always endeavoured to get at the raw products of the countries they visited. They fished for the purple mussel on the shores of Greece and Asia Minor ; they dug for gold in the rich auriferous veins they found in Lemnos, where a volcanic mountain was looked upon as the forge of Hephæstos, and also in the island of Thasos, and in the Pangean mountains. They mined for silver in Spain, in which country old shafts and passages, mining implements and even vaulted underground chapels have been discovered. In Ireland they dug for silver, in England for the much esteemed tin-ore, and in the North also, they undoubtedly worked in the mines, and had furnaces and smithies above ground for smelting and forging the minerals they obtained. It was very natural that a barbarous people should imagine the existence of the Kobolds, when they heard the noise of working and hammering, and saw the sooty figures of what seemed to be a short, weakly race emerging from the earth. They regarded the strangers as mighty and powerful, because their minds were deeply impressed by their magical surroundings, and by the excellent weapons, beautiful ornaments, and delicately fashioned works of art they made in their flaming furnaces. The shrewd craftsmen must often have brought disaster upon the simple-minded barbarians by their deceit and cunning, and the dwarfs were therefore considered false and treacherous, and every one was warned against their malice.

These features, however, might with equal probability apply to the former inhabitants of the country who had been dispossessed by the Germanic invaders, perhaps even better than to the Phœnicians. These people were of a much weaker race than their conquerors ; they took refuge in lake-dwellings or in subterranean caverns, hid in the mines they themselves had made, forged utensils of all sorts, and often over-reached their invaders by the sharpness of their wits.

Poetry created out of these dwellers in holes and caves of the rock those fantastic beings called Dwarfs and Black-Elves, because they were black and grimy, and because they rummaged in the dark places of the earth, did smith's work, were learned in the black art, and treacherous. The gloomy world in which they lived was called the Home of the Black-Elves.

In Germany they were known under the same name, but slightly altered in form. Their ruler in the middle ages was King Goldemar, whose brother Alberich or Elberich, and the sly, thievish Elbegast, were even more celebrated in poetry than he. In England, these are represented by the light airy elves, who danced their rounds on the hill-sides and in the valleys, but who love best to haunt lonely green woodlands and groves, and here King Oberon and Queen Titania had their invisible palaces and gardens, to which men sometimes found the way, and of which they related the wonders to believing multitudes after their return. Whoever has a touch of poetry in his soul, and is in the habit of wandering through the woods in the still summer evening, can even now-a-days see the mist-like forms of the little people dancing merrily in the openings of the wood or by the banks of the murmuring brook.

Equally celebrated in tales and legends is Number Nip, the mighty king of the Riesengebirge, of whose power many strange tales were told; until at last modern enlightenment forced him to retreat into his underground realm.

The Light-Elves were different from the Black-Elves. They lived in the Home of the Light-Elves, were fair and good, and somewhat resembled the elves, but were not so airy or ethereal as the spirits of the later fairy-world. There are no myths about these kindly beings, which is a clear proof that the difference between the Black and Light-Elves was originally unknown.

The elves were popularly believed to be spirit-like beings, who were deeply versed in magic lore, and who had charge of the growth of plants. Some of them lived under the earth and others in the water; they often entered into friendly alliance with mortals, and demanded their help in many of their difficulties, handsomely rewarding all who assisted them. They were not always ugly to look upon ; indeed, their beauty was sometimes extraordinary, and whenever they showed themselves amongst men, they used to wear splendid ornaments of gold and precious stones. If ever any one of mortal birth approached them, while they were dancing their rounds at midnight in the light of the full moon, they would draw him within their circle, and he never returned again to his people. The dwarfs and elves possessed rings by means of which they discovered and gained for themselves the treasures of the earth ; they gave their friends magic rings which brought good-luck to the owner as long as they were carefully preserved; but the loss of them was attended with unspeakable misery.

A Polish count once received a ring of this kind from a tiny mannikin, whom he had allowed to celebrate his marriage festivities in the state rooms of his castle. With this jewel on his finger he was lucky in all his undertakings; his estates prospered ; his wealth became enormous. His son enjoyed the same good fortune, and his grandson also, who both inherited the talisman in turn. The last heir gained a prince's coronet and fought with distinction in the Polish army. He accidentally lost the ring while at play, and could never recover it, although he offered thousands of sovereigns for its restoration. From that moment his luck forsook him: locusts devoured his harvest ; earthquakes destroyed his castles. It even seemed as if the disasters of his native land were connected with his, for the Russians now made good their entrance into the country, and when Suwarrow stormed Praga, the unhappy prince received a sabre-cut over one of his eyes. When somewhat recovered, but quite disfigured by his wound and almost in as wretched plight as a beggar, he reached his ancestral castle, and there he was crushed to death under the falling building on the very first night. Exactly a hundred years had elapsed since that fateful hour in which his ancestor had placed his halls at the disposal of the underground spirit!

Besides these rings, the dwarfs and wights, like the elves, had other valuable possessions, such as hoods of darkness, by means of which the mannikins became invisible, and girdles that made the wearer supremely beautiful.

This was the reason why so many noble knights were over-mastered by love for beautiful elf-women ; but the marriages which were thus contracted had always a sad ending, because the natures of husband and wife were too dissimilar, and because there can be no real bond between men and spirits. For the elves were also regarded as the souls of the dead, and it was therefore impossible that any alliance formed by them with the living could be happy.

GIANTS.

To the traveller passing through some desolate valley in the dusk or in a fog, the rocks jutting out from amongst the woods or ravines at his side seem to take strange, fantastic shapes. Not less spectral than these is the uncertain outline of the mountain tops, and especially of the bare granite or basaltic horns of rock which are scattered in great number over the face of the earth. In the old time, when man was more susceptible to impressions made by the ·life and working of nature, when he peopled the wilderness with the creatures of his own fancy, those dead stones appeared to him as living beings, moving about busily in the grey mist, endowed in the dusk or moonlight with magic powers and approaching him as giants and monsters, but which were once more turned into stone as soon as they were touched by the first rays of the morning light.

These figures grew far more monstrous, far more weird in the great Alpine ranges and in Scandinavia. There the peaks, the ridges, and the ravines are covered with eternal ice and snow; there the swollen, destructive mountain-torrents, growing glaciers, falling rocks and thundering avalanches, were regarded as the work of the infernal powers, the rime and frost-giants of northern legends. These evil beings are also to be found in the lower ranges of mountains. The Riesengebirge owe their name to them, while the Harz mountains were haunted by the Harz spirit and other demons.

Nearly related to these were the spirits of the storms and tempests, who came out of their dwellings in the clefts of the hills, massed up the storm-clouds, and spread destruction over the fields. The raging sea also was sometimes regarded as a giant, sometimes as a huge snake which encircled Midgard. As a snake they likewise personified those waters, which, breaking down the artificial breast-work man had built for their restraint, dashed and roared over the fruitful plains, engulfing towns, villages and their inhabitants in their course. The giant Logi (Flame), with his children and kindred, finally made themselves known as the authors of every great conflagration, when they might be seen in the midst of the flames, their heads crowned with chaplets of fire. These demons were all enemies of man, they strove to hinder his work and to destroy what he had made.

> For the elements are hostile
> To the work of human hand —*Schiller*

Men therefore sought to propitiate them in ancient times by offering them sacrifices, and consecrating altars and holy places to them, until the moral powers, the gods, rose and fought against them and their worship, but did not succeed in rooting them out of the minds of the people. In the Greek myth, the rude destructive powers of nature, which were personified in the Titans and Giants, were completely overcome and abandoned ; but in the

ROCKS IN THE RIESENGEBIRGE.

North, where these forces are more wild and terrible, the struggle lasted until the Fire-giant Surtur, together with the sons of Muspel, set out for the Last Battle to destroy gods, men and worlds, and make place for a better order of things.

The legends of the giants and dragons were developed gradually, like all myths. At first natural objects were looked upon as identical with these strange beings, then the rocks and chasms became their dwelling-places, and finally they were regarded as distinct personalities, and had their own kingdom of Jotunheim. They showed themselves now in this place, now in that, and met gods and heroes in peace and in war. Perhaps they were not originally held to be wicked and altogether hostile, for springs and brooks flowed out of the earth for the refreshment of man and beast. They watered the fields so that they bore rich harvests; storms purified the air; the sea was an open roadway for ships, and the household fire, or the spirit which dwelt in it, was the

THE SLEEPING GIANT.

most cheering companion of the Northman during his long winter evenings. But the thinking, ordering gods took their place, and then they only appeared as the wild unbridled forces of nature, against which man had to strive with the help of the heavenly powers.

In the North the giants were called Jotuns, signifying the voracious ones, and perhaps connected with the name of a German tribe, the Jüten, that chased the aborigines out of Jutland. They were also called Thurses, *i.e.* the thirsty, the great drinkers. In Germany the giants were named Hünen, after their old enemies, the Huns. In Westphalia the gigantic grave-mounds and sacrificial places belonging to heathen times, that are to be found by the Weser and Elbe, are designated Huns' beds; and in the same way we recognise the Huns' rings. These are circular stone-walls, intended to enclose holy objects and consecrated spots of ground, in like manner as the dwellings of the gods are described in the Edda as surrounded by a fence or hedge.

Here in conclusion let us relate a myth made up of two kindred stories put together. We can still recognise the natural phenomena in the names.

From the first giant, Ymir, were descended three mighty sons: Kari (air, storm), Hler (sea), and Logi (fire). Kari was the father of a numerous race, and his most powerful descendant, Frosti, ruled over a great empire in the far north. Now Frosti often made raids and incursions into neighbouring states, and on one occasion he went to Finland, where King Snär (snow) reigned. There he saw the king's daughter, fair Miöll (shining snow), and at once fell in love with her. But the haughty monarch refused him the hand of the maiden. He therefore sent a message to her secretly to tell her: " Frosti loves thee, and will share his throne with thee." To which she replied : " I love him also, and will await his coming by the sea-shore." Frosti appeared at the appointed time and took his bride in his strong arms. Meanwhile the plot had been discovered ; Snär's fighting men lay in ambush to attack the lovers, and shot innumerable arrows at the bold warrior. But Frosti laughed at them all ; the arrows fell from his silver armour like blunted needles, his storm horse broke through the ranks of the enemy and bore the lovers safely over the sea and over mountains and valleys to their Northern realm.

WORLDS AND HEAVENLY PALACES.

" Nine homes I know, and branches nine,
    Growing from out the stalwart tree
    Down in the deep abyss."

This is the saying of Wala the prophetess, who sang of the creation, of the gods, and of the destruction of the world. She describes the Ash Yggdrasil as if the homes or worlds grew out of it like branches. Still the nine worlds are never enumerated in succession or in their full number, but are only to be distinguished by their characteristics.

In the centre of the universe the gods placed Midgard, the dwelling-place of man, and poured the sea all round it like a snake. They fortified it against the assaults of the sea and the inroads of the giants, by building a wall for its defence. The giants lived far away by the sea-shore in Jotunheim or Utgard, the giants' world. Above the earth was Wanaheim, the home of the wise shining Wanes, whom we shall describe further on. The Home of the Black-Elves was to be found under the earth, perhaps in those gloomy vales that led to the river which separated the realm of the dead from that of the living. This kingdom of the dead, Helheim, surrounded the Northern Mistworld, Nifelheim.

To the south was Muspelheim, where Surtur ruled with his flaming sword, and where the sons of Muspel lived. Over Midgard in the sunny æther was the Home of the Light-Elves, the friends of gods and men. Over the earth also, but higher than the Home of the Light-Elves, the gods founded their strong kingdom of Asgard, which shone with gold and precious stones, and where eternal spring reigned. The broad river Ifing divided the home of the gods from that of the Jotuns, but was not sufficient protection against the incursions of the giants, who were learned in magic.

The gods built themselves castles in Asgard, and halls that shone with gold. It is recorded that there were twelve such heavenly palaces, but the poems differ from each other in describing them.

High above Asgard was Hlidskialf (swaying gate), the throne of Odin, whence the all-ruling Father looked down upon the worlds and watched the doings of men, elves and giants. The palaces of the Ases were: Bilskirnir, the dwelling of Thor, 540 stories high and situated in his province of Thrudheim ; Ydalir (yew-vale), where Uller, the brave bowman, lived ; Walaskialf, the silver halls of Wali ; Sökwabek, the dwelling of Saga (goddess of history), of which the Edda tells us : " Cool waters always flow over it, and in it Odin and Saga drink day after day out of golden beakers." In this palace the holy goddess Saga lived, and sang of the deeds of gods and heroes. She sang to the sound of the murmuring waters, until the flames of Surtur destroyed the nine homes and all the holy places. Then she rose and joined the faithful, who had escaped fire and sword, and fled with them to the North, to the inhabitants of Scandinavia. To these she sang in another tongue of the deeds of the Germanic heroes. But her songs did not pass away without leaving a trace behind ; some of them are probably preserved in the Edda, and remain a treasure of poetry which can never be lost.

The fifth palace was called Gladsheim (shining-home) ; it belonged to the Father of the gods, and contained Walhalla, the hall of the blessed heroes, with its 500 doors. The whole shining building was enclosed within the grove Glasir of golden foliage. Thrymheim (thunder-home), where Skadi, daughter of the murdured giant Thiassi, lived, was originally supposed to be in Jotunheim, but the poems place it in Asgard.

Breidablick (wide out-look) was the dwelling of glorious Baldur, and in it no evil could be done. Heimdal, the watchman of the gods, lived in Himinbiörg (Heaven-hall), and there the blessed god drank sweet mead. Folkwang, the ninth castle, belonged to the mighty Freya. It was there that she brought her share of the fallen heroes from the field of battle. In Glitnir dwelt Forseti, the righteous, whose part it was to act as umpire, and smooth away all quarrels. Noatun was the castle of Niörder, the prince of men and protector of wealth and ships. Saga recognised as the twelfth heavenly palace Landwidi (broad-land), the dwelling of the silent Widar, son of Odin, who avenged his father's death in the Last Battle.

It is enough to say here regarding the mythological signification of these heavenly castles, that it is very probable that they were meant for the twelve constellations of the zodiac. For amongst these palaces none were allotted to the warrior god Tyr, nor do they count amongst their number Wingolf, the hall of the goddesses, or Fensal, the palace of Queen Frigga. According to this hypothesis the deities who possessed these twelve palaces were gods of the months. For instance, Uller, who lived at Ydalir, was the god of archery, and used to glide over the silvery ice-ways on skates. He ruled, in his quality of protector of the chase, when the sun passed over the constellation of Saggitarius in winter. Frey or Freya was called after him in the myth, and to him the gods gave, as a gift on his cutting his first tooth, the Home of the Light-Elves, which lies in the sun and is not to be found amongst the dwellings of Asgard.

The sun-god was also reborn at the time of the winter solstice, as Day was in the North. The Yule-feast was therefore celebrated in honour of the growing light with banquets and wine; Frey's boar was then sacrificed, and the drinking-horn was passed down the rows of guests. Wali's palace was, the story tells, covered with silver. By this the constellation of Aquarius was meant; when the sun passes over that part of the heavens where this

E

constellation rules, it is a splendid sight in the far North to see the silvery sheen of the snow that covers the mountains and valleys. We refrain from further discussion of this theme, for these are only hypotheses, and myths of deeper meaning are awaiting us.

SURTUR WITH HIS FLAMING SWORD.

PART THIRD.

OPPONENTS OF THE GODS.

THE holy gods dwelt peacefully in their golden palaces and rejoiced in their power. The Walkyries, choosers of the dead, messengers of Odin, rode about in splendid armour on their white horses. They bore the hero-spirits they had taken from bloody battle-fields back with them to Asgard. On reaching the grove Glasir, they dismounted from their horses, and led the heroes under the shade of its golden foliage to Walhalla. There

the mists of death passed from the eyes of the warriors ; they
recognised the hall intended for them on seeing Odin's coat of
arms, the wolf and the eagle. They saw the roof made of the
shafts of spears covered with shields, and the seats spread with
soft chain-mail. Weapons flashed as they entered, and foaming
goblets were emptied in their honour by the great band of heroes,
who had reached the halls of blessedness before them. And they
drank of the sweet mead provided for them by the goat Heidrun,
and feasted on the roasted flesh of the boar Sährimnir, which was
restored to life every evening, that it might again furnish a repast
for the heroes on the following day.

The ruling gods sat on twelve thrones, and highest amongst
them was Odin in all his glory, his spear Gungnir in his right
hand, and his golden helmet on his head. He was not now
terrible to look upon, as when he led armies on to battle or when
he hurled the death-spear over their ranks ; a gentle smile lighted
up his face, for he rejoiced in the arrival of the noble warriors.
Two pet wolves played at his feet and fawned upon him, when
he threw them the food provided for himself at the board. For
he needed no food to eat ; for him it was sufficient to drink of
the blood-red wine, which refreshed and strengthened his mind.
Then great Odin rose from the board, walked through the hall,
and went to his throne Hlidskialf, all Asgard trembling beneath
his tread. He seated himself, and gazed thoughtfully over the
worlds. Far away in the distance gleamed Muspelheim, where
dark Surtur, flame-girdled, and holding his fiery sword in his
hand, watched his opportunity as yet in vain ; in Midgard were
the mortal men ; in the depths below, the Dwarfs toiled and
laboured. The mighty god's two ravens, Hugin (thought) and
Munin (memory), flew quickly up to him ; they perched one on
his right shoulder and the other on his left, and whispered in his
ears the secrets they had heard during their flight through the

worlds. Anxiously the monarch turned his gaze towards Jotunheim, for things were going on there which threatened the general
peace.

LOKI AND HIS KINDRED.

In the grey twilight enveloping the giants' world, the king
recognised his old comrade Loki, with whom he had sworn
brotherhood at the beginning of time. Loki had set up house
in Jotunheim and had married the dreadful giantess Angurboda
(bringer of anguish). They had three children, all horrible
monsters : the Wolf Fenris, the Snake Jörmungander, and terrible
Hel, at the sight of whom all living creatures stiffened in death.
One side of her face was of corpse-like pallor, and the other was
dark as the grave. The young wolf was not less appalling to
look upon, when he opened wide his blood-red jaws to devour the
food his father offered him ; nor the snake which wound itself
round Angurboda as though desirous of crushing her to death in
its coils.

Allfather turned away from the horrible sight with a shudder
of disgust, and saw his bright son Hermodur standing before him.
Pointing down at Jotunheim, he desired him to bear his commands to the gods, that they should at once go and bring him the
brood of giants. In obedience to the king's orders, the powerful
gods at once arose, and with brave Tyr at their head, crossed the
bridge Bifröst and the river Ifing, and so reached the inhospitable
land of the Hrimthurses.

Loki was beautiful like all the gods, but his heart was full of
guile. They found him in the court-yard of his castle. He went
on playing with his monstrous progeny, and took no notice of the
messengers, until they approached quite close to him, and made
known the commands of Odin. He would have refused to obey,
but strong Tyr shook his fist threateningly, upon which he gave

way, and followed them to Asgard, accompanied by his children. He was immediately brought before the king's throne. Terrible Hel grew visibly more gigantic, lightnings flashed from her deep-set eyes, and she stretched out her arms as though she wished to destroy the great Father. At the same moment Jörmungander reared her head in the air, till she resembled a twisted column, gnashed her jaws and emitted a venomous foam, before which the very gods shrank back. But the king seized both monsters in his powerful arms, and flung them far out of Asgard into immeasurable space.

Hel sank nine days' journey past the bogs, morasses, and rocks of ice in Nifelheim, past the river Giöll and down into the kingdom of Helheim, which was allotted to her, and where she henceforth ruled over the dead. But the Snake fell into the ocean that flows round Midgard. Hidden in its depths, and unseen by gods and men, she was to grow, until, after having twisted herself into innumerable coils, her ugly head should touch the tip of her tail. Then, at last, when the twilight of the gods (the judgment of the gods) should come to pass, she was again to rise, and help to bring about the destruction of the worlds. When the Wolf saw his playfellows flung out of Asgard, he began to howl so loud, that his voice was heard over in Jotunheim. Yet he did not venture to resist, and great Tyr bore him away from before the face of the angry Father, away from the heavenly towers, to where the hills of Asgard slope towards Midgard; there he brought him food every day

Odin still remained on Hlidskialf, thinking of all, caring for all. The gods stood silently around him ; but Loki slipped out of the circle unnoticed, and went out to plan more mischief. Then the king pointed towards the south, where the sons of Muspel were moving about in the fiery heat like flashes of lightning, and where the dark giant Surtur was pointing his flaming sword up at the heavenly palaces. "Gird on your armour," said Allfather, "keep your swords drawn, ye faithful ones, for the day approaches when the heavens shall fall and the Destroyer shall come up from the South across Bifröst with his fiery hosts. The spirit of prophecy has come upon me, and I foresee that the monsters, whose power we have broken for the present, will one day join the Destroyer and fight against us. Up, brave ones! Watch lest any sin defile the purity of the holy towers, for thus only can we ward off the hour of our destruction."

Having said this, great Odin went on before his loyal subjects to Walhalla.

Meanwhile the wicked race of giants remained hostile to the gods. They brooded over schemes for avenging the murder of their ancestor, Ymir. The warlike Hrungnir awaited his opportunity in Jotunheim; Thrym, who was hard as his native rocks, Thiassi and Geiröd, who dwelt in proud castles, and other giants besides, were all armed for the fight, and often made onslaughts upon the hated gods. But Heimdal watched over the safety of Asgard, and strong Thor was always ready to go out and fight the monsters.

This myth reveals to us in its deeper meaning, the ideas of these northern races respecting the struggle between good and evil in the world, the eternal warfare waged by the kingdom of light against the kingdom of darkness, by the mild beneficent powers of nature against those that are hurtful and destructive. The terrors of the long dark winter, or the dreadful snow-storms, of the wild mountain ranges with their glaciers, and of the tempestuous ocean, appeared in the imagination of the people to take the form of pernicious monsters intended to bring about the destruction of the world. Thus Hel, the secret, healing goddess, who was originally the all-nourishing Mother Earth, became the goddess of death, a hideous monster the very sight of whom caused death ;

the stormy sea, which according to the northern idea encircled the round earth, was transformed to the Midgard-Snake ; the universal destruction which was to come at the end of days was typified in the all-devourer, the Fenris-Wolf, who was to devour the Father of the world himself. It is striking, that Loki, who in earlier times was looked upon as a beneficent being, as the god of fire, of the warming domestic hearth, is accounted one of the powers of evil in the foregoing legend, and that he grows even more diabolical in the later poems, in spite of the fact that fire is absolutely indispensable to the North-man.

The first divine trilogy given us was that of the sons of Bör, *i.e.* Odin, Wili and We ; and these correspond to the elements, air, water and fire. The last of the three gave the newly created human beings blood and blooming complexion ; he was therefore a beneficent god. Nevertheless he was also represented as a giant in the trilogy Kari, Ögir, and Logi, another form of air, sea and fire. That he belonged to the race of giants is proved from further evidence, by which it appears that his father was the giant Farbauti (oarsman), and his mother the giantess Laufey (leafy isle), the former of whom was perhaps the giant who saved himself from the flood in a boat, and the latter, the island to which he rowed.

At the beginning Loki was a helpful and a great god, as the pretty Faroe-island song of the Peasant and the Giant shows. He was not regarded as the principle of evil, until he had been completely separated from the element to which he belonged, and had been developed into an independent personality. The idea of the destructive power of fire was equally connected with the giant Muspel, but he never showed himself as an active agent of harm. His sons, the flames, alone threatened evil in Glow-heim or Muspel-heim, and finally mustered in great force for the Last Battle on the field of Wigrid. Their leader, however, was not Muspel, but dark Surtur (black smoke), out of which flashed a tongue of flame, like a shining sword.

That these ideas were common to all the Germanic races is shown by some Bavarian and Saxon manuscripts of the 8th and 9th centuries, which contain the mysterious word Muspel, as will be seen from the following translations : " Muspel's (world-fire's) power passes over man." " Muspel creeps in stealthily and suddenly, like a thief in the darkness of night." " Then will a friend be of no profit to his friend because of Muspel, for even the broad ocean will be burnt up," viz. at the Last Day.

This struggle was an eternal one ; it went on and on without being decided. But if the Aryans believed Ormuzd to be pure and spotless, the gods certainly were not so ; they were neither sinless nor immortal. Like the Grecian Herakles, they fought against harmful monsters ; they were victorious over them to a certain extent, but not entirely ; they sinned, and at last, like the Greek hero who burnt himself to death, they passed away in the universal fire that burnt up the world. These conceptions are peculiar to the Germanic races; it is possible, however, that they brought the seeds of their grand poems from the common home of the Aryans, then developed and polished them in their own peculiar way, when settled in the land they had colonized, and when surrounded by the influences of a climate and country favourable in some points and disadvantageous in others.

PART FOURTH.

KING GYLPHI AND THE ASES.

I. GEFION.

ONCE upon a time when, as tradition informs us, Swithiod (Sweden) still lay hidden under the sea, yawning chasms suddenly opened in the depths below, and swallowed up the waters until the land appeared. As soon as it was dry, the fowls of heaven brought there the seeds of all kinds of trees, grass and herbs. Then the face of the country grew green, and flowers sprang up and adorned it, so that it was brilliant to look upon, as the carpet in a king's banqueting hall. Animals of all sorts were there also, some of which were useful and serviceable to man, while others dwelt shyly hidden away in remote places; and besides these there were wild beasts, such as bears, lynxes, and grim voracious wolves.

Men afterwards settled down in Sweden, tilled the land and began to trade; they spread themselves out over the country as they grew more numerous, and built villages, towns, and proud castles for the nobles. They were a warlike race. They fought against the wild beasts that lived in the forests, and against the marauding Jotuns and Trolls of the mountains. They were a free people and chose out the bravest of their heroes to be their leaders, Jarls and Princes, who protected the country from the inroads of any enemies who might venture to disturb the diligent husband-men in their toil.   The mightiest of the Jarls was called King, and lived in the town of Sigthuna.

Now King Gylphi once ruled over this people, who were greater in power, righteousness and wisdom than any of the other nations that dwelt in Midgard.   Neither hostile armies nor robbers dared to cross the borders of the kingdom, and it was said that even the wild beasts refrained from harming any of the people, so much did they hold their chief in awe.   Thus Gylphi ruled in undisturbed peace, and had abundant leisure to indulge his thirst after the highest knowledge and wisdom.   He knew about the stars in the heavens; he visited the dwarfs in the interior of the earth, from whom he learned how to discover veins of gold and how to work metals into household utensils, weapons and shining orna-ments.   Moreover, he understood the art of using magic runes, by means of which he was able to get rid of snakes, to conjure up the spirits of the dead from their graves, and to change his form so as to escape recognition.   He often feasted with his warriors, and together they drank mead and foaming ale.   During these entertainments, skalds were always present to delight him and his heroes by the melody of their harps, and by their songs; for he loved music above all things, and would rather have gone without food than it.

The king once thrust his frothing cup from him impatiently, for the skalds who used to make his feasts pleasant to him had not come.   Suddenly the sound of harp-playing was heard without; so sweet that all hearts were filled with longing, and the chords vibrated as powerfully as if twelve skalds had assembled to tune their strings.   The door opened, and a tall female figure entered the hall; she was gentle and beautiful to look upon, and like a goddess in her bearing.   Approaching the king she touched the harp-strings, and sang:

In gruesome grave no knowledge grows ;
Yet the king shall ken what things must come.
High up to Heaven I raise my hymn,
And louder and louder I let it sound.

My wistful eyes watch Walkyries
Wafting the warriors by weirdly kiss,
From blood-stained field to blessèd rest,
Where night and death are never known.

And I see here in the lofty hall
The hosts of heroes who with their lord
Shall wander to Walhall, the battle won,
And meet the maidens' melodious hail.

They soar in silence on wingèd steeds,
Alighting on grave-grounds, green with pines,
And singing lays of the light and love
That e'er abide in Odin's Home.

Gloomy and sad the song began, like a voice from the grave ; but the music grew deeper and fuller as it went on to praise the fate of glorious warriors, and then again it sank soft and low as the whisper of the wind on a warm spring day, which tells of nature's resurrection.

Once more the figure repeated : "That e'er abide in Odin's Home," and as she did so, the notes of her harp were so sweet and thrilling, that the hearts of all the heroes present were filled with rapture, and they thought they saw the warrior-maidens who were to bear them to Walhalla.

Deep silence reigned in the hall ; but as soon as the intoxication of the sounds, which had held their senses in thraldom, gradually passed off, the king rose from his seat, and said : "Speak, fair maiden, tell me thy name, and what guerdon thou askest for the song with which thou hast delighted us. Be it even to the half of Swithiod, it shall be thine, and this I swear by my kingly word."

"Gefion, the Giver," she replied, "is what I was called by Ases and Jotuns, when I was young. If thou, indeed, desirest to reward me, I shall only ask thee to give me as much land as I can plough round with my four bulls in a day and a night."

Gylphi was surprised that the maiden did not ask for a larger gift, and at once granted her request. She took her departure, and soon afterwards returned, bringing with her four bulls, the like of which had never been seen in Swithiod before, so huge and well-formed were they. They were, in sooth, like moving mountains, and their white foreheads shone with the lustre of the full moon. They were harnessed to a plough with a hundred shares, which cut down into the lowest depths of the earth, and tore the soil away from its foundations. The bulls walked on dragging the ploughed land with them; they waded into the sea with it, and Gefion, who drove them, grew before the eyes of the astonished king and people until she was so tall that the great waves, high as they were, reached only to her waist, and seemed to be but sporting with her knees. She went on without stopping day and night, and then at length the land she had taken away with her rested in a shallow place. She fastened it down firmly there, and called it Zealand (sea-land). Having done this, she stepped upon it followed by the four bulls, which at once raised themselves up, and touched by her magic spells were changed into four strong youths, for they were her sons by a giant. The beautiful island soon flourished under her care. Wooded hills, green pastures and rich corn-fields provided the numerous population of Zealand not only with food, but also with all the pleasures and comforts of life. Hledra, a splendid royal residence, was next built, and there Gefion lived, and exercised undisputed sway over her subjects. She married a man named Skiöld, and became the mother of a long line of renowned kings.

GYLPHI BEHOLDING ASGARD.

2. GYLPHI IN ASGARD.

Now Gylphi heard of all these events in his town of Sigthuna, and he was filled with wonder how such things could be. He saw Lake Löger (now Maelar), which had taken the place of the land the bulls had dragged away with their plough. He heard from travellers that the promontories of Zealand running out into the sea had the same form as the bays of Lake Maelar in his own country. He knew that Gefion was of the race of the Ases, and he puzzled day and night over how they had come to be so power-ful. He enquired of the skalds and wise men of his kingdom, he consulted his runic signs; but he gained no information from any of these regarding that which he wished to find out. As his longing after wisdom gave him no rest, he determined to set off on a journey in search of the land where the mighty Ases lived, even though the attempt to find it might cost him his life. His heart was set on making his way into Asgard that he might learn from its inhabitants of the creation and the end of the world, of the Ases' power and their mode of government, and of the fate of mankind, that he might afterwards make all these things known to mortal men.

King Gylphi was learned in magic. He took the unpretentious form of a common traveller, and called himself Gangleri (weary wanderer). He walked on a long way through Midgard, until he at length reached a palace, the height and circumference of which he could not measure. When he entered the doorway, he saw a vast hall before him, whose length his eye could not pierce. He perceived other mansions to the right hand and to the left, each of which was crowned with turrets that shone like gold in the sunlight. There was a tree there also, whose top rose to the immeasurable skies, and whose branches seemed to spread out over the whole world.

A man, playing with seven knives, was standing at the entrance of the palace. He threw them up into the air and caught them again so that they seemed to form a shining circle. He asked the traveller what he wanted; Gylphi answered that his name was Gangleri, that he wished to have a night's lodging and to be admitted to the presence of the lord of the palace.

"He is our king," replied the door-keeper; "follow me, and thou shalt see his face."

Having said this, he preceded the traveller up the hall.

There they saw many noble warriors assembled, who were amusing themselves, wassailing, playing and wrestling. Three men of venerable aspect were seated on thrones, one of which was higher than the other two, watching the games.

"The first of these chieftains is Har (High)," said the guide, "the other is Jafenhar (Equally high), and the last is Thridi (the Third)."

While he was still speaking, Har turned to the new-comer, and said : "Dost thou need food, stranger ; if so, thou wilt find abundant store in Har's hospitable hall. Sit down, and share our meal."

Gangleri replied : "Higher than food and foaming beakers do I prize wisdom, which lifts the mind above earthly things. So I would fain find a wise man, who can answer my questions."

"Ask," said the chieftain, "and thou shalt be answered. But beware thy head, for it is forfeited if thou provest thyself unwise."

Gangleri drew nearer to the thrones, and began : "Who is the highest and the oldest of the gods, and what are his works and deeds that are most worthy of man's admiration ?"

Har answered : "Allfather is his name in our tongue, but all the nations of the earth give him a different name, each in their own way. He is the highest and mightiest at all times, and rules over all things, the smallest as well as the greatest."

Jafenhar went on : "He created heaven and earth, the sea and the air, and everything that lives and moves therein. He alone is the greatest Ruler."

"The greatest and most glorious of his works," said Thridi, "was the creation of man, whose spirit, given by him, will live on, and will not die even when the body containing it is turned to dust. The good will live with him for ever in the place that is called Gimil, or Wingolf. The wicked shall also live, but they will descend to Hel, or even to Nifelhel deep down below in the ninth world."

After that, Gangleri asked many more questions regarding the creation and the end of the world, about the gods and their works, and about all the riddles of life, and he received answers and explanations.

But when he still went on enquiring further, the great hall suddenly burst with a terrible, loud crash, and in another moment everything had vanished. Gylphi found himself alone on a wide, desolate plain, where neither palace, tree nor shrub were to be seen. He set out at once on his homeward journey, and at last reached his own realm. There he related what he had seen and heard, and wise skalds sang of the marvellous things he had told them, and so knowledge grew and spread from land to land and from generation to generation, and did not die out of the memory of the people.

We see from this, what idea the Northern people had formed of the way in which the divine revelation was made. The conception of Allfather and his works appears to us to be the most remarkable part of this story, and fully confirms what we have before said on this subject.

PART FIFTH.

ODIN, FATHER OF THE GODS AND OF THE ASES.

THE prophetess Wöla sat before the entrance of her cave, and thought over the fate of the world. Her prophetic power enabled her to pierce bounds that are impenetrable to the human eye. She saw what was going on near her, what was taking place at a distance. She watched the labours and battles, the patient endurance and the victories of nations and heroes. She saw how Allfather ruled the world, how he kept the giants in submission, how he flung the spear of death over the armies, and afterwards sent his Walkyries to bring to his hall those heroes who had fallen victoriously. Let us now turn our attention to what was revealed to her penetrating sight.

Mother Night was driving in her dark chariot on her accustomed course above Midgard, bringing peaceful slumber to all creatures. The bright boy, Mani (Moon), followed quickly in her steps, and the gloomy mountains were bathed in the light he shed around. Down below in the valley, the maiden, Selke, was wandering beside a stream, which playfully rippled and murmured at the feet of its mistress, and then flowed on quickly, and dashing over the stones that barred its course, flung itself into the depth below. But Selke saw nothing of all this; her eyes were fixed on the fountain from out of which the brook flowed, for there sat a woman wondrously beauteous of countenance, with long shining golden hair, looking down into the clear water in which her form was mirrored. After awhile she rose, and went higher up the steep side of the mountain to the place where grew the healing herbs that the goddess needed for the cure of wounds and sores.

While employed in this peaceful task, the rocky door leading into the interior of the mountain suddenly opened, and a monstrous giant came out from it. No sooner did the fiend sight the lovely maiden than he rushed towards her with a wild yell. She fled, while he pursued her, as higher and higher she climbed, until at length she reached the summit of a lofty rock, which hung over the edge of a great abyss. The hunt-cry from the distance now fell upon her ear, and the baying of hounds, and she knew who was coming to her assistance; but her pursuer drew nearer and nearer, and his icy talons almost grasped her neck; boldly she ventured the tremendous leap—the ground was reached in safety.

The mark of her foot is still to be seen on the rock, and the truth of this assertion can be verified by any one who chooses to go and look at the Maiden's Leap in the Selkethal (Harz Mountains).

The giant saw her take the fearful spring, and, surprised, he hesitated for a moment; but soon regaining courage, he rushed on and took the mighty leap after her. But, like a flash of lightning, and accompanied by loud peals of thunder, a shining spear came flying through the air, and the monster fell with a crash dead into the deep abyss.

The storm rose; it howled through the wood, and Wodan's raging host, the Wild Hunt, rushed past. The great god's nightly following was composed of armed men, armed women and children, hounds and ravens and eagles; and he, the King, preceded them all on horseback; together they stormed over the trembling fields and through the dark quaking forests. Ancient pines were broken down, rocks fell, and the mountains shook to their foundations, for the Father of Victory was on his way to a great battle.

The King had far to go, and his horse had lost a shoe, which forced him to halt for a time. Master Olaf, the smith of Heligoland, was still in his smithy at work in the midnight hour. A storm was howling round the house, and the sea was beating on the shore, when suddenly he heard a loud knocking at his gate.

"Open quick and shoe my horse; I have a long journey to make, and daybreak approaches."

Master Olaf opened the door cautiously, and saw a stately rider standing beside a giant horse. His armour, shield, and helmet were black, a broad sword was hanging at his side, his horse shook its mane, champing the bit and pawing the ground impatiently.

"Whither art thou going at this time of night, and in such haste?" asked the smith.

"I left Norderney yesterday. It is a clear night, and I have no time to lose, as I must be in Norway before daybreak."

"If thou hadst wings, I could believe thee," laughed the smith.

"My horse is swift as the wind. But see, a star pales here and there; so make thee haste, good smith."

Master Olaf tried on the shoe. It was too small, but, lo! it gradually grew and grew, until it had fastened itself round the hoof. The smith was awe-struck, but the rider mounted, and as he did so his sword rattled in its sheath.

"Good-night, Master Olaf," he cried. "Thou hast shod Odin's horse right well, and now I hasten to the battle."

The horse gallopped on over sea and land. A light shone round Odin's head and twelve eagles flew after him swiftly, but could not overtake him. He now began to sing in magic words of the stream of time, and the spirit that works in it, of birth, and of the passage to eternity. And all the time the storm-wind roared, and the waves dashed upon the shore, a harp-like accompaniment to the song. He who has ever heard that music straightway forgets his home and his cravings for the hearth. The sailor on the foaming water, the traveller in the valley and the shady grove, each feels it strangely stirring his soul, each longs to go out at once to Odin.

The warriors were gathered together in the green-wood, armed for the combat; the brave sons of King Eric of the bloody axe, who had lately fallen in battle, were there, and Hakon, too, his brother, the powerful king of Norway. All at once they heard sweet soft sounds in the air, like the sighing of the wind and the whisper of green leaves. Quickly the sounds grew louder, and the storm wind roared through the trees and over the assembled host. " Odin is coming," cried the warriors, " he is choosing his Einheriar." And then the Father of Battles came with his following ; he came in the storm that he might rule the combat. He halted high up above the armies in a grey sea of clouds. He called the Walkyries, Gondul and Skogul, before him, and bade them so to lead the chances of the fight, that the bravest should be victorious, and should then be received into the ranks of the Einheriar.

He flung his spear over the contending heroes, and immediately the blast of horns and loud war-cries were heard. A cloud of arrows hissed through the air ; javelins and heavy battle-axes broke through helmet and shield ; swords were crossed in single combat ; blood streamed from innumerable wounds, reddened the armour of the men-at-arms and trickled down upon the flowers that carpeted the crimson ground.

Foremost in the battle was King Hakon fighting with sword and spear. As he cut his way through the enemy's ranks over the fallen men, he heard the Walkyries talking beside him. They were in the midst of the strife, mounted on their white horses, holding their bright shields in front of them, and leaning upon their spears.

" The army of the gods is waxing great," said Gondul, " for the Ases are preparing to welcome Hakon with a goodly train of followers to the glorious home."

The King heard it, and asked: "Is it just that ye should reward me with death, instead of the victory for which I am striving with my might?"

Skogul answered: "We have decreed that thine enemies should give way before thee. Thou shalt win the battle, and then take thy part in the feast of the Einheriar. We will now ride on before thee, and announce that thou art coming to look upon the face of the Father of Victory himself."

When King Hakon ascended to Asgard from the field of glory, Hermodur, the swift, and Bragi, the divine singer, went out to meet him, and said: "Thou shalt have the peace of the Einheriar; receive therefore the draught prepared for the heroes of the Ases." Hereupon the king's helmet and coat of mail were taken off, but he retained his sword and spear, that he might enter the presence of the Father of Victory with his arms in his hands.

This was how the Northern skalds sang of the God of Battles, of the choosers of the dead, and of the fate of heroes. Is it then to be wondered at, that the princes and nobles of those races should have gone forth joyously on their bold Wiking raids, and that they should have esteemed a glorious death on the field of battle far better than to sink to inglorious rest at home? The German bards also sang after this fashion of their heroes; hence the struggle against Rome which lasted four hundred years, and the Germanic raids upon Britain, Gaul, Italy, Spain, and even upon far Africa. The War-god sang his storm-song in their ears; they heard the voices of the Walkyries through the din of the battle; they saw the gates of Walhalla open before them, and the Einheriar signing to them to approach. Therefore the day of battle was in their eyes either a feast of victory, or of entrance into the verdant home of the heroes.

In the foregoing tale, the events of which have been derived from German and Norse sagas and lays, we have seen the chief god of the North as leader of the Wild Hunt, conqueror of the earth-born giant, god of the storm and ruler of the battle ; but we must try to get a still deeper insight into his nature.

Wodan, Odin in the North, according to the oldest conceptions.—Wodan was the highest and holiest god of the Germanic races. His name is connected with the German word *Wuth*, and used to be both spelt and pronounced Wuotan, which word did not then mean rage or wrath, as *Wuth* does now, but came from the Old-German *watan*, impf. *wuot*, *i.e.*, to penetrate, to force one's way through anything, to conquer all opposition. The modern German *waten*, and the English *wade*, are derived from the old word, though considerably restricted in meaning. Wuotan was therefore the all-penetrating, all-conquering Spirit of Nature. The Longobards, by a letter-change, called him Gwodan ; the Franks, Godan or Gudan ; the Saxons, Wode ; and the Frisians, Woda. The Scandinavians called him Odin, from which the mythological name Odo was derived. He was known under the names of Muot (courage) and Wold by the South Germans. But everywhere he was regarded as the same great god, and was worshipped as such by the whole Germanic race.

When man had freed himself from the power of the impressions made upon him by nature as a whole, he began to have a more distinct consciousness of certain manifestations of the forces of nature, and after that to pay them divine honours. He then regarded the storm which tore through the forests with irresistible violence, which blew down the cottages of the peasants, and wrecked vessels out at sea, as the ruler of all things, as the god whose anger must be appeased by prayers and sacrifices. At first he was worshipped under the form of a horse or of an eagle, as these were types of strength and swiftness. But when the mastery of the human race over the animal world was better understood, the god was endowed with a human form. He was described in the legends and stories, now as a mighty traveller who studied and tried the dispositions of men, and now as an old man with bald head, or with thick hair and a beard which gained him in the North the name of Hrossharsgrani (horse-hair bearded). He had usually only one eye, for the heavens have but one sun, Wodan's eye. He wore a broad-brimmed hat pulled down low over his forehead, which represented the clouds that encircle the sun, and a blue mantle with golden spangles, *i.e.*, the starry heavens. These attributes again prove him to have been the Spirit of Nature. In the completely developed myth regarding him in the Edda, he was described as being of grand heroic form, with a golden helmet on his head, and wearing a shining breast-plate of chain-mail. His golden ring Draupnir was on his arm, and his spear Gungnir in his right hand. Thus attired, he advanced to attack the Fenris-Wolf, when the Twilight of the Gods was beginning to fall; thus attired, he sat on his throne Hlidskialf, wrapped in the folds of his mantle, and governed gods and men.

There are many tales and traditions about Wodan in his original form of storm-god. They are to be found in Germany, England, France, and Scandinavia, which shows how wide-spread the worship of him was. Chief amongst the stories referring to the old Teutonic god are those of the Wild Hunt, and of the Raging Host.

The Myths of the Wild Hunt and of the Raging Host.— These myths have their origin in the belief that the supreme One takes the souls of the dead to himself, carries them through the air with him, and makes them his followers on his journeys by night. As the Romans regarded Mercury as the leader of the dead, they thought that the Teutons also honoured him as the highest god. The soul was looked upon as aërial, because it was invisible like air. It was held that when a dying man had drawn his last breath, his soul passed out of him into the invisible element. Thus the Hebrews had the same word to express spirit and breath, and the old Caledonians, as Ossian's poems prove, heard the moans and loving words of their dead friends in the whisper of the breeze, in the soft murmur of the waves; they felt that the invisible was near them, when a solitary star sent down its rays to them through the dusk of the evening. The idea of a god has no place in these poems. The Teutons, on the contrary, believed that it was the god himself who bore the spirits of the dead up into his kingdom.

The traditions of the Wœnsjäger, the Wild Huntsman, Wuotan's or the Raging Host, have their origin in heathen times, as their names show, although they have undergone considerable modifications in many respects since then. They arose from the impression made upon the people by phenomena that they could not understand, and which they consequently supposed were caused by some divinity. Every noise sounds strange and mysterious on a quiet night. The solitary traveller passing through forests or over heaths or mountains, when the light of the moon and stars was obscured by drifting clouds, heard the voices of spirits in the hooting of owls, in the creaking of branches, and in the roaring, whistling, and howling of the tempest, and his excited imagination made him think that he saw forms, which became the more distinct the more his superstitious fancy was drawn upon. Forest rangers, solitary dwellers in remote places, especially charcoal-burners, who often spend long stretches of time without seeing a human being, tell strange stories even now-a-days. These tales are founded on the ancient beliefs of the race, are repeated by one man to another, and detached fragments of the old faith are still preserved by tradition.

In Pomerania, Mecklenburg, and Holstein, Wode is said to be out hunting whenever the stormy winds blow through the woods. In Western Hanover it is said to be the Woejäger, in Saterland the Woinjäger, and in other places, the Wild Huntsman that haunts the woods. He is supposed to ride on a white horse, to wear a broad-brimmed hat slouched over his forehead, and a wide cloak (the starry heavens) wrapped round his shoulders. This cloak has gained him the name of Hakel-bärend (Mantel-wearing) in West-phalia. Indeed, the story has even been transferred from the divine to the human.

It was said that Hans von Hakelberg, chief huntsman of the Duke of Brunswick, and an enthusiastic sportsman, liked hunting better than going to church, and used to devote his Sundays as well as week-days to this amusement, for which reason he was condemned to hunt for ever and ever with the storm. His grave is shown near the Klöpperkrug, an inn not far from Goslar, and a picture of both him and his hounds is carved on the headstone of the grave. His burial place is also pointed out in the Söllinger wood, near Uslar.

Wode seldom hunted alone. He was generally surrounded by a large pack of hounds, and accompanied by a number of hunts-men, who all rushed on driven by the storm, shouting and holloa-ing, in pursuit of a spectral boar or wild horse. He was also said to chase a spectral woman with snow-white breast, whom he could only catch once in seven years, and whom he bound across his saddle when he had at length succeeded in overtaking her. In Southern Germany it was a moss-woman or wood-maiden, a kind of dryad or wood-nymph, whom the Wild Huntsman pursued, and whom he bound to his horse in the same way as the other, when once he had caught her. Perhaps this story represents the autumnal wind blowing the leaves off the trees.

When the people heard the Wild Huntsman approaching them they threw themselves upon their face on the ground, as otherwise they would have been in danger of being carried off by the hunts-men. The story tells us that this was the fate of a ploughman who was caught up by them and taken away to a hot country where black men lived. He did not come home again until many years afterwards. Whoever joined in the holloa of the wild huntsmen was given a stag's leg which became a lump of gold; but whoever imitated the shout jeeringly had a horse's leg thrown to him, which gave out a pestiferous smell and stuck to the scoffer. A little dog was sometimes left on the hearth of a house through which the Wild Huntsman had gone. It immediately began to whine and howl miserably, so as to disturb the whole household. The people had then to get up and brew some beer in egg-shells, whereupon the creature would exclaim: "Although I am as old as the Bohemian Forest, I never saw such a thing in my life before." Then it would jump up, rush off and vanish. But if this charm was not applied, the people of the house were obliged to feed the creature well, and let it lie upon the hearth for a whole year, until Wode returned and took it away with him.

The Wild Hunt generally went on in the sacred season, between Christmas and Twelfth Night. When its shouts were particularly loud and distinct, it was said that it was to be a fruitful year. At the time of the summer solstice, and when day and night become of equal length, the Wild Hunt again passed in the wind and rain, for Wodan was also lord of the rain, and used to ride on his cloud-horse, so that plentiful rains might refresh the earth.

The traditions of the Raging Host much resemble those of the Wild Hunt. They are stories about the army of the dead under the leadership of Wodan. People thought they could distinguish men, women and children as the host passed them at night Those who had lately died were often seen in it, and sometimes the death of others was foretold by it.

"Walther von Milene!" cried out voices in that terrible army, and Walther, a celebrated warrior, was soon afterwards killed in battle. In this instance the story reminds us of Wish-father, the chooser of the dead, who called the Einheriar to his Walhalla ; and still more is this the case, when the Raging Host is described as rushing past like a troop of armed men, when knights and men-at-arms were seen in shining or even fiery armour, and mounted upon black horses, from whose nostrils shot forth sparks of flame. Then it was said that the war-cries of the combatants, the clash of arms and trampling of horses' feet, could be heard above the din of the storm.

Wodan has long since died out of the minds of the people, yet his character and actions are clearly shown in tradition, and his name also appears in proverbial sayings, charms, and invocations. Seventy years ago the Mecklenburg farmers, after the harvest was brought home, used to give their labourers Wodel-beer, a feast at which there was plenty to eat and drink. The people poured out some of the beer upon the harvest field, drank some themselves, and then danced round the last remaining sheaf of corn, swinging their hats and singing :

> "Wôld ! Wôld ! Wôld !
> hävenhüne weit wat schüt,
> jümm hei dal van häven süt.
> Vulle kruken un sangen hät hei,
> upen holte wässt manigerlei :
> hei is nig barn un wert nig old.
> Wôld ! Wôld ! Wôld !" *

> "Wold ! Wold ! Wold !
> The Heaven-Giant knows what happens here ;
> From Heaven downwards he does peer.
> He has full pitchers and cans.
> In the wood grows many a thing.
> He ne'er was child, and ne'er grows old,
> Wold ! Wold ! Wold !"

In Hesse and in Lippe-Schaumburg the harvesters stick a

---

* Grimm's "Teutonic Mythology," translated by J. S. Stallybrass, vol. i. p. 156. (London : Sonnenschein & Allen.)

bunch of flowers into the last sheaf, and beat their scythes together, exclaiming, Waul; in Steinhude they dance round a bon-
fire they have lighted on a hill-top, and shout, Waude. In many
parts of Bavaria they dance round a straw figure called Oanswald or
Oswald (Ase Wodan). But the people have now quite forgotten
the Ase and think only of St. Oswald. In these instances the
god appears in his highest form as the god of heaven, the giver of
good harvests. The Aargau riddle shows him as lord of the starry
heavens, who raises the dead up to his bright mansions above :—

> " Der Muot mit dem Breithuot
> Hat mehr Gäste, als der Wald Tannenäste."

> " Muot with the broad hat
> Has more guests than the wood has fir-twigs."

In England the Wild Hunt is called Herlething, from a mythical king Herla, who was once invited by a dwarf to attend his
marriage. He followed his entertainer into a mountain, and three
hundred years elapsed before he and his attendants returned to
the world. Amongst other parting gifts the dwarf gave him a
beautiful dog, which the head huntsman was desired to take before
him on his horse. At the same time every one was warned not to
dismount until the dog jumped down. Several of the king's followers disregarded this, and got down from their horses; but no
sooner did they touch the ground than they crumbled away to
dust. The dog is still sitting on the saddle bow, and the Wild
Hunt is still going on.

In the time of Henry II. it was said to have shown itself in a
meadow in full daylight. The blowing of the horns and shouts of
the hunters drew the people of the neighbourhood to the place.
They recognised some of their dead friends among the huntsmen,
but when they spoke to them, the whole train rose in the air, and
vanished in the river Wye.

In France, in Wales, and in Scotland, King Arthur is the leader of the Wild Hunt. In France, the Wild Hunt, or Raging Host, is called *Mesnie Hellequin*, the last word of which is evidently derived from Hel (kingdom of the dead), for the leader of the hunt is called the Hel-huntsman. According to other traditions, Charles the Great, Charlemagne, rides in front of the band, while strong Roland carries the banner. We recognise, moreover, the Raging Host (*l'armée furieuse*) under the name of *Chasse de Caïn* (Cain's Hunt), or *Chasse d'Hérode* (Hunt of Herodias, who caused the murder of John the Baptist). Perhaps, however, Hérode really means Hrodso (glory-bearer), one of the names by which Odin was known. Equally famous is *le grand veneur de Fontainebleau*, (the great Huntsman of Fontainebleau), whose shouts were heard beside the royal palace the day before Henry IV. was murdered by Ravaillac. The Raging Host also passed over the heavens twice, darkening the sun, before the Revolution broke out. The populace everywhere believes that its appearance is the foreshadowing of pestilence, or war, or of some other great misfortune.

THE SLEEPING HEROES.

The legend of the Wild Huntsman has, as we have seen from the foregoing, been applied to human beings, and circumstance and place have been added to the tale. There was not always an infernal element clinging to the appearance of the Hunt, for emperors, kings, and celebrated heroes were amongst the representatives of the Father of the Gods. In Lausitz, Dieterbernet— in Altenburg, Berndietrich, the great Ostrogothic king Theoderick of Bern (Verona) was supposed to rush through the air, and vanish in the mountains. In the same way, according to the Northern myth, the Summer Odin, who brought green leaves and flowers, and ripened the golden ears of corn, used to wander away through dark roads in Autumn, and then a false Odin came, and seating himself on the other's throne, sent snowstorms over the wintry earth.   Or, as another tale has it, the good god passed the period during which the imposter reigned, sunk in a deep enchanted sleep within a mountain.   But no sooner did Spring return, than he rose again in his power, drove the intruder from his throne, and once more scattered his blessings over gods and men.

These conceptions of Allfather, derived trom natural phenomena, were so deeply impressed in the mind and very being of the Teutonic race, that they personified them by applying to their early kings and heroes the attributes of Odin.   King Henry the Fowler, whose victories over the Slavs, Danes and Hungarians restored the power of the German empire, is supposed to be lying sunk in magic sleep in the Südemer hill near Goslar.   Amongst other sleeping heroes is Frederick Barbarossa, the story of whose death in the East is believed by no one, and who was and is still said to lie slumbering in Kyffhäuser.

There are a number of traditions about the ruins of Kyffhäuser and the great Hohenstaufe, who still lives in the memory of his people.   The high castle-hill rises sheer above the green fields away over in Thuringia.   On its western side, a tower is still in existence.   It stands eighty feet high, although with broken walls, and overlooks the wood and piles of stone below.   On solemn occasions the emperor is supposed to lead his processions thence, and afterwards to dine there with his followers.   According to the legend, the weary old emperor sleeps his " long sleep " in an underground chamber of the castle, with the companions of his travels, Christian of Mayence, Rainald of Cologne, Otto of Wittelsbach, the ancestor of the royal house of Bavaria, and many others besides. Barbarossa's beard has grown round and through the stone table, casks of good old wine, treasures of gold, silver and precious stones are lying about in heaps, and a magic radiance lights up the high vaulted hall ; that this is the case is proved by many fortunate eye-witnesses, who at different times have been permitted to enter the room.   One of these was a herdsman, who left his cattle browsing amongst the ruins, and went to gather flowers for his sweetheart.   He found a strange blue blossom, and no sooner had he put it in his nosegay than his eyes were opened, and he perceived an iron door that he had never seen before.   It opened at his touch ; he went down a flight of stairs and entered the lighted banqueting hall.   There he saw the heroes and their imperial leader sitting round the table, all sound asleep in their chairs.

Barbarossa was awakened by the noise.   "Are the ravens still flying round the battlements ? " he asked, looking up.

The herdsman said that they were, and the emperor went on : " Then I must sleep for another hundred years."

After that he invited the youth to help himself to as much as he liked of the treasures he saw before him, and not to forget the best.

The herdsman filled his pockets as he was told.   When he got out into the open air once more, the door shut behind him with a crash, and he could never find it again, for he had forgotten the best thing, the little blue flower.   So the emperor is still sleeping with his heroes in his favourite palace.   But the time will come when the empire is in greatest need of him, when the ravens will no longer fly round the battlements ; then he will arise in all his might, will break the magic bonds that hold him, and sword in hand fight a great and bloody battle against the enemies of his country upon the Walser Field or on the Rhine.   Then he will hang his shield on a withered pear-tree, which will immediately begin to sprout again, and blossom and bear fruit : the glorious old times of the German Empire will return, bringing with them unity and peace in their train.

THE HIGHER CONCEPTION OF WODAN (ODIN).

Wodan, the giver of victory. Ambri and Assi the Winilers, stood fully armed before the warlike Vandals. Their victory or servitude would be decided by the coming battle.

"Give us the victory, Father of Battles," prayed the princes of the Vandals, as they offered up sacrifices to Wodan. And the god answered: "To them will be given the victory who come first before me on the morning of the day of battle."

On the other hand Ibor and Ajo, dukes of the Winilers, went by the counsel of their wise woman, Mother Gambara, into the holy place of Freya, Wodan's wife, and entreated her to aid them.

"Well," said the Queen of Heaven, "let your women go out ere daybreak dressed in armour like the men, their hair combed down over their cheeks and chins, let them take up a position towards the east, and I will give ye a glorious victory."

The dukes did as she commanded.

As soon as the first rosy tints of dawn appeared in the sky, Freya wakened the great Ruler, and pointed eastwards towards the armed host.

"Ha!" said the god in astonishment, "what long-bearded warriors are these?"

"Thou hast named them," answered the queen, "so now do thou give them the victory." And thus the Winilers gained great glory, and were henceforth known by the name of Long Beards Longobards).

As in the Northern myths, the Longobards also held great Wodan to be the giver of victory. But above all other qualities, he was the god who blessed mankind, and brought joy and prosperity to his people.

In the heathen times many games and processions were held in

G

his honour, of which traces still remain in the customs and beliefs of the people. In many districts, for instance, the battle of the false Odin, who usurped the throne for the seven winter months, with the true Odin, who brought blessings and summer into the world, was celebrated by a mimic fight, succeeded by sacrifices and feasting. This lasted for centuries, and was continued until quite recent times in the festivals of the first of May.

A May Count or May King was chosen, and he was generally the best runner or rider, or the bravest in the parish. He was dressed in green and adorned with garlands of may and other flowers. He then hid himself in the wood; the village lads went out to seek him there, and when they had found him, they put him on horseback, and led him with shouts and songs of joy through the village. The May King was allowed to choose a queen to share his honours at the dance and at the feast.

In other places the most modest and diligent of the girls was chosen as Queen of May, and led into the village with the King, which was intended to commemorate the marriage of the Summer Odin with the Earth, whose youth was renewed by the genial Spring. It was at one time a regular practice to have a May-ride in Sweden, at which the May Count, decked in flowers and blossoms, had to fight against Winter, who was wrapped up in furs. May won the victory after a burlesque hand-to-hand engagement.

Odin, the good and beneficent god, was also called Oski, *i.e*, "wish" in Norse, a word that is related to the German *Wonne* (rapture) : he was the source of all joy and rapture.

ODIN AT GEIRÖD'S PALACE.

King Hraudung had two handsome sons, Geiröd and Agnar, the one ten and the other eight years old. The boys one day went out in a boat to fish. But the wind rose to a storm, and carried them far away from the mainland to a lonely islet, where the boat struck and broke in pieces. The boys managed to reach the shore in safety, and found there a cottager and his wife, who took compassion on them and gave them shelter. The woman took great care of the younger brother Agnar throughout the winter, while her husband taught Geiröd the use of arms and gave him much wise counsel. That winter the children both grew wonderfully tall and strong, and this was not surprising, for their guardians had been Odin and his wife Frigg. When spring returned, the boys received a good boat and a favourable wind from their protectors, so that they soon reached their native land. But Geiröd sprang on shore first, shoved the boat out to sea again, and cried, "Sail thou away, Agnar, into the evil spirits' power!" The great waves, as though in obedience to the cruel boy's behest, carried the boat and Agnar far away to other shores. Geiröd hastened joyfully up to the palace, where he found his father on his death-bed. He succeeded to the kingdom, and ruled over all his father's subjects and those he had gained for himself by force of arms and gold.

Odin and Frigg were once sitting on their thrones at Hlidskialf gazing down at the world of mortal men and at their works. "Seest thou," said the Ruler, "how Geiröd, my pupil, has gained royal honours for himself? Agnar has married a giantess in a foreign land, and now that he has returned home, is living in his brother's palace poor and despised." "Still Geiröd is only a base creature, who hoards gold and treats his guests cruelly instead of

showing them hospitality," replied the thoughtful goddess. Then
Allfather determined to prove his favourite, and to reward him
if all were well, but to punish him should he find that the accusa-
tion was just. He, therefore, in the guise of a traveller from a
far country, started for Geiröd's palace. A broad-brimmed hat,
drawn well down over his brows, shaded his face, and a blue cloak
was wrapped around his shoulders. But the King had been
warned by Frigg of a wicked enchanter, so he had the stranger
seized and brought before his judgment-seat.

To all the questions asked him, the prisoner would only reply
that his name was Grimnir, and disdained to give further information about himself. Whereupon the king got into a passion, and
commanded that the obstinate fellow should be chained to a chair
between two fires upon which fresh fuel was to be continually
thrown, so that the pain he suffered might induce him to speak
out.

The stranger remained there for eight nights, suffering bitter
agony, without having had a bite or a sup the whole time, and
now the flames were beginning to lick the seam of his mantle.
Secretly Agnar, the disinherited, gave him a full horn of beer,
which he emptied eagerly to the last drop. Then he began to
sing, at first low and softly, but afterwards louder and louder, so
that the halls of the castle echoed again, and crowds assembled
without to listen to the strain. He sang of the mansions of the
blessed gods, of the joys of Walhalla, of the Ash Yggdrasil, of those
that dwelt within it, and of its roots in the depths of the worlds.

The halls trembled, the strong walls shook as he sang of Odin's
deeds, and of him whom Odin's favour had raised on high, but
who was now delivered over to the sword because he had drunk
of the cup of madness. "Already," he said, "I see my favourite's
sword stained with his blood. Now thou seest Odin himself.
Arise if thou canst!" And Grimnir arose, the chains fell from his

hands, the flames played harmlessly about his garments; he stood there in all his Ase's strength, his head surrounded by rays of heavenly light. Geiröd had at first half drawn his sword in anger; but now, when he tried to descend from his throne in haste to

ODIN BETWEEN TWO FIRES IN GEIRÖD'S PALACE.

attempt to propitiate the god, it slipped quite out of its sheath, he tripped over it and fell upon it, so that its blade drank in his heart's blood. After his death, Agnar ruled over the kingdom, and by the favour of Odin his reign was long and glorious.

ODIN, THE DISCOVERER OF THE RUNES, AND GOD OF POETRY AND WISDOM.

Odin's power and wisdom and knowledge are described in the Edda and in many of the lays of the skalds. He went to Mimir, the wise Jotun, who sat by the fountain of primeval wisdom, drank daily of the water and increased his knowledge thereby. The Jotun refused to allow the god to drink of his fountain, unless he first pledged him one of his eyes. Allfather did as he requested him, in order that he might create all things out of the depth of knowledge, and from that day forward Mimir drank daily of the crystal stream out of Allfather's pledge. Other accounts make out that the water was drawn out of Heimdal's Giallarhorn. Both accounts are given in the Northern poems. The myth from which they came shows us the meaning that lay at their foundation.

Mimir, a word related to the Latin *memor, memini,* signifies *memory;* that it was known to the Germans is indicated by the similar sounds of the names of the Mümling, a stream in the Odenwald, and of Lake Mumel in the Black Forest, where the fairies lived. Mimir drew the highest knowledge from the fountain, because the world was born of water; hence, primeval wisdom was to be found in that mysterious element. The eye of the god of heaven is the sun, which enlightens and penetrates all things; his other eye is the moon, whose reflection gazes out of the deep, and which at last, when setting, sinks into the ocean. It also appears like the crescent-shaped horn with which the Jotun drew the draught of wisdom.

According to other poems, Mimir was killed, but his head, which still remained near the fountain, prophesied future events. Before the Twilight of the Gods came to pass, Odin used to whisper mysterious things with him about the Destruction and Renewal of the world.

At one time when the god was standing with his golden helmet on, by the side of the holy fountain on the high hill, and learning the runic signs from Mimir's head, he discovered the Hugruncs (spirit-runes). As we have already shown, these runes were not exactly used as formulæ for writing connected sentences. They were only the accented letters used in Northern and Old-German poems ; that is to say, they were letters of similar sound used for alliterative purposes. The following examples are some of those that remain to us from olden time : hearth and home ; wind and weather ; hand and heart. They were intended as a help to the memory when learning and singing the lays.

Odin gained power over all things by means of the runes, through which he was able to make all bend to his will, and to obtain authority over the forces of nature. He knew runic songs that were effectual in battle, in discord, and in time of anxiety. They blunted the weapons of an opponent, broke the chains of noble prisoners, stopped the deadly arrow in its flight, turned the arms of the enemy against themselves, and calmed the fury of angry heroes. When a bark was in danger on the stormy sea, the great god stilled the tempest and the angry waves by his song, and brought the ship safe to port. When he sang his magic strain, warriors hastened to his assistance and he returned unhurt out of the battle. At his command a man would arise from the dead even after he had been strangled. He knew a song that gave strength to the Ases, success to the elves, and even more wisdom to himself ; another that gave him the love of woman so that her heart was his for ever more. But his highest, holiest song was never sung to woman of mortal birth, but was kept for the Queen of Heaven alone, when he was sitting peacefully by her side.

THE DRAUGHT OF INSPIRATION. ODIN'S VISIT TO GUNLÖD. JOURNEY TO WAFTHRUDNIR.

Kwasir, a man whom the Ases and Wanes had created amongst them, and whom they had inspired with their own spirit, was loved by gods and men for his wisdom and goodness. He travelled through all lands, teaching and benefiting the people. Wherever he went he tamed down the wild passions of all men, and taught them better and purer manners and customs.

The evil race of Dwarfs alone, they that burrowed in the earth in search of treasures, cared nought for the love, although they envied the wisdom of Kwasir. Fjalar and Galar, brothers of this people, invited him one day to a feast, and then murdered him treacherously with many wounds. They caught his blood in three vessels, the kettle Odrörir (inspiration), and the bowls Son (expiation) and Boden (offering). They mixed rum-honey with it, and made it into mead, which gave all who drank of it the gift of song and of eloquence that won every heart.

As the wicked deed of the Dwarfs had brought them such good luck, they invited the rich giant Gilling and his wife to visit them, and took the former out fishing with them. Then they upset the boat in the surf under great over-hanging rocks, so that Gilling was drowned, while they, being good swimmers, righted the boat again, and rowed to land.

When the giantess heard the sad fate of her husband, she wept and moaned, and refused to be comforted. The Dwarfs offered to take her to the rock on which the body had been washed. But as she was leaving the house, Galar threw a mill-stone from above down upon her head, so that she also was killed. Now Suttung, son of the murdered giant's brother, heard of the evil deed, and set out to avenge it. He seized the Dwarfs and made ready to bind them to a solitary rock out in the sea, that they might die there of hunger. They begged for mercy, promising to give him the wonderful mead concocted out of Kwasir's blood, in atonement for what they had done. The giant accepted the expiation offered ιιim ; he took the three vessels containing the liquor to a hollow mountain that belonged to him, and set his daughter Gunlöd to keep guard over the magic drink.

Odin, the God of Spirit, was told of all these things by his ravins Hugin and Munin. He determined to get possession of the Draught of Inspiration at any cost to himself, that it might no longer be kept uselessly hidden away by the giant in the interior of the earth, but might refresh gods and heroes, so that wisdom and poetry might delight the world. He therefore, in the guise of a simple traveller, started for Jotunheim. He came to a field where nine uncouth fellows were mowing hay. He offered to sharpen their scythes for them, and make them cut as well as the best swords. The men were pleased with his offer, so he pulled a whet-stone out of his pocket, and whetted and sharpened the scythes. When he at last returned them to the mowers, they found that they could work much quicker and better than before, and each wanted to have the whet-stone for himself. So the traveller threw it amongst them, and they struggled and fought for it with their scythes, until at length they all lay dead on the ground.

The traveller went on his way till he came to the master of the estate, the Jotun Baugi, a brother of Suttung, who received him hospitably. In the evening the giant complained that his farm-servants were all killed, and that his splendid crop of hay could not be harvested. Then Bölwerker (Evil-doer), as the traveller called himself, offered to do nine men's work if his host would get him a draught of Suttung's mead.

" If thou wilt serve me faithfully," answered the Jotun, " I will try to fulfil thy desire; but I will not hide from thee that my brother is very chary of giving a drop of it away."

Bölwerker was satisfied with this promise, and worked as hard as the nine farm-servants for the whole summer.

When winter came, Bangi, true to his promise, drove to his brother's dwelling with the traveller, and asked for a draught of the mead. But Suttung declared that the vagabond should not have a single drop.

"We must now try what cunning will do," said Bölwerker; "for I must and shall taste that mead, and I know many enchantments that will help me to what I want. Here is the mountain in which the mead is hidden, and here is my good auger, Rati, which can easily make its way through the hardest wall of rock. Take it and bore a hole with it, no matter how small."

The Jotun bored as hard as he could. He soon thought that he had made a hole right through the rock, but Bölwerker blew into it and the dust came out into the open air. The second time they tried, it blew into the mountain, and Bölwerker, changing himself into a worm, wriggled through the hole so quickly that treacherous Bangi, who stabbed at him with the auger, could not reach him.

When he had got into the cave, the Ase stood before the blooming maiden Gunlöd, in all his divine beauty and wrapped in his starry mantle. She nodded her acquiescence when he asked her for shelter and for three draughts of the inspiring mead.

Three days he spent in the crystal mansion, and drank three draughts of the mead, in which he emptied Odrörir, Son and Boden He was intoxicated with love, with mead, and with poetry. Then he took the form of an eagle, and flew with rhythmical motion to the divine heights, even as the skald raises himself to the dwellings of the immortals on the wings of the song that is born of love, of wine, and inspiration. But Suttung heard the flap of the wings and knew who had robbed him of his mead. His eagle-dress was

ODIN'S VISIT TO GUNLÖD.

at hand, he therefore threw it round his great shoulders, and flew so quickly after the Ase that he almost came up with him. The gods watched the wild chase with anxiety. They got cups ready to receive the delicious beverage. When Odin with difficulty reached the safe precincts of holy Asgard, he poured the mead into the goblets prepared for it. Since that time Allfather has given the gods the Draught of Inspiration, nor has he denied drops of Odrörir to mortal men when they felt themselves impelled to sing to the harp of the deeds of the gods and of earthly heroes.

Odin possessed knowledge of all past, present, and future events, since he had drunk of the fountain of Mimir and of Odrörir. He therefore determined to attempt a contest with Wafthrudnir, the wisest of the Jotuns, in which the conquered was to lose his head.

In vain Frigg strove, in her fear, to dissuade him from the perilous undertaking; he set out boldly on his way and entered the giant's hall as a poor traveller called Gangrader.

Stopping on the threshold of the banqueting hall, he said, " My name is Gangrader, I have come a long way ; and now I ask thee to grant me hospitality and to let me strive with thee in wise talk."

Wafthrudnir answered him: "Why dost thou stand upon the threshold, instead of seating thyself in the room? Thou shalt never leave my hall unless thou hast the victory over me in wisdom. We must lay head against head on the chance ; come forward then and try thy luck."

He now proceeded to question his guest about the horses that carried Day and Night across the sky, the river that divided Asgard from Jotunheim, and the field where the Last Battle was to be fought. When Gangrader had shown his knowledge of all these things, the giant offered him a seat by his side, and in his turn answered his guest's questions as to the origin of earth and heaven, the creation of the gods, how Niörder had come to them from the wise Wanes, what the Einheriar did in Odin's halls, what was the origin of the Norns, who was to rule over the heritage of the Ases after the world had been burnt up, and what was to be the end of the Father of the gods.

After Wafthrudnir had answered all of these questions, Gangrader asked: "I discovered much. I sought to find out the meaning of many things, and questioned many creatures. What did Odin whisper in the ear of his son before he ascended the funeral pile ? "

Recognising the Father of the gods by this question, the conquered Jotun exclaimed: "Who can tell what thou didst whisper of old in the ear of thy son ? I have called down my fate upon my own head, when I dared to enter on a strife of knowledge with Odin. Allfather, thou wilt ever be the wisest."

The poet does not tell us whether the visitor demanded the head of the conquered Jotun. Nor does he mention the word that Odin whispered to his son before he went down to the realms of Hel; but the context leads us to suppose that it was the word Resurrection, the word which pointed to the higher, holier life, to which Baldur, the god of goodness, should be born again, when a new and purer world should have arisen from the ashes of the old, sin-laden world.

ODIN, FATHER OF THE ASES.
ODIN'S DECENDANTS.

From later poems Odin appears not only as Ruler of the world, and Father of all Divine beings, who gradually as time went on became more and more subordinate to him, but also as progenitor of kings and heroic races, such as the kings of the Anglo-Saxons and Franks, as well as of the rulers of Denmark, Norway, and Sweden.

According to the Edda, Odin had three sons, Wegdegg, the East Saxon; Beldegg (Baldur or Phol), the West Saxon (Westphalian); and Sigi, to whom Franconia was given; and three others, Skiöld, Säming, and Yngwi, who were made kings of Denmark, Norway, and Sweden. Other sagas show that Wals, Sigmund, and Sigurd, the hero of the Niflung Lay, were descended from Sigi, while Brand and Heingest or Hengist, Horsa and Swipdager were descended from Beldegg. The Anglo-Saxon genealogical tables make out that Voden (Wodan) and Frealaf (Freya) had seven sons, who were the founders of the Anglo-Saxon kingdom. Others, on the contrary, only show three sons here also, which makes them more in agreement with the northern genealogies.

According to the higher ideas regarding him, Odin was the father of gods and men; the latter were created by him, while the former were his direct or indirect descendants. His son by Jörd (the Earth) was strong Thor, father of Magni and Modi (Strength and Courage); by Frigg he had Baldur and Hödur; by Rinda, Wali, who afterwards became the avenger of Baldur; and by the nine mothers, the mysterious watchman Heimdal. Besides these, there were the poet-god Bragi; the divine messenger, Hermodur; the brave archer, Uller; and even the god of heaven, Tyr, who otherwise received the highest honours. Related to him were Forseti, son of Baldur, and Widar, who were to rule over the new world of holiness and innocence. Thus he was the Father of the Ases. On the other hand, Hönir, who gave to newly created man senses and life, and Loki, who gave him blood and blooming complexions, were Odin's brothers or comrades in primeval times. Great Niörder, his bright son Freyer and his daughter Freya belonged to another divine race, that of the Wanes; they were first brought into Asgard as hostages, but were received into the ranks of the Ases.

FRIGG AND HER MAIDENS.

After the birth of Thor, whose mother was Jörd (the Earth), daughter of the giantess Fiörgyn, Odin left the dark Earth-goddess and married bright Frigg, a younger daughter of Fiörgyn ; henceforth she shared his throne Hlidskialf, his divine wisdom and his power, becoming the joy and delight of his heart, and the mother of the Ases. She ruled with him over the fate of mortals and granted her votaries good fortune and victory, often bringing about her ends by woman's cunning. Just as in Hellas a feast was held each year in commemoration of the marriage of Zeus and Hera, so did the old Teutons in like manner hold festivity to celebrate the union of Odin and Freya.

Freya's palace was called Fensaler, that is, the hall of the sea. It probably got this name from the dwellers on the coast, who looked upon Frigg as the ruler of the sea and protector of ships. A soothing twilight always reigned, and it was adorned with pearls and gold and silver. And the goddess would bring all lovers, and husbands and wives who had been separated by an early death, to this peaceful palace, where they were reunited for ever. This belief of the old Teutons shows us that they regarded love in its truest and highest aspect, and built their hopes on being reunited after death to the objects of their affections. What we learn from the Latin annals of Armin and Thusnelda, of the high position of women as seers of future events, proves to us that noble women were always treated even by rude, fighting men, with respect and reverence ; while the romance of love is clearly shown in the Northern myth of Brynhild, who threw herself upon the burning pyre in order that she might be reunited to her beloved Sigurd.

In her gorgeous palace Frigg sits spinning, on her golden distaff,

FRIGG AND HER MAIDENS.

the silken threads, which she afterwards bestows on the most worthy housewives. The goddess' spinning-wheel was visible to man every night, for it was that shining, starry zone which we in our ignorance now point out as the Belt of Orion, but which to our ancestors was the Heaven-queen's spinning-wheel. The goddess had three friends and attendants always beside her, and with these she used to hold council on human affairs, in the hall of the moon.

Fulla or Volla was the first of Frigg's attendant-goddesses, and chief of the maidens ; according to Teutonic belief she was also the sister of the Queen of Heaven. She wore a golden circlet round her head, and beneath it her long hair floated over her shoulders. Her office was to take charge of the Queen's jewels, and to clothe her royal mistress. She listened to the prayers of sorrowful mortals, repeated them to Frigg, and advised her how best to give help.

Hlin, the second of Frigg's maidens, was the protector of all who were in danger and of those who called upon her for help in hour of need.

The messenger of the Queen of Heaven was Gna, who rode, swift as the wind, on a horse with golden trappings, over land and sea, and through the clouds that floated in the air, to bring her mistress news of the fate of mortal men.

Once as Gna was hovering over Hunaland, she saw King Rerir, a descendant of Sigi and of the race of Odin, sitting on the side of a hill. She heard him praying for a child, that his family might not be blotted out of memory ; for both he and his wife were advanced in years, and they had got no child to carry on their noble race. She told the goddess of the prayer of the king, who had often presented fine fruit as a sacrifice to the heavenly powers. Frigg smilingly gave her an apple which would ensure the fulfil-ment of the king's desire. Gna quickly remounted her horse Hoof-flinger, and hastened over land and sea, and over the country

of the wise Wanes, who gazed up at the bold rider in astonisn-
ment, and asked :

> " What flies up there, so quickly driving past ? "
> Her answer from the clouds, as rushing by :
> " I fly not, nor do drive, but hurry fast
> Hoof-flinger swift through cloud and mist and sky."

King Rerir was still seated on the hillside under the shade of
a fir-tree, when the divine messenger came down to earth at the
skirt of the wood close to where he sat. She took the form of a
hooded-crow, and flew up into the fir-tree. She heard the prince
mourning over the sad fate that had befallen him, that his family
would die out with him, and then she let the apple fall into his
lap. At first he gazed at the fruit in amazement, but soon he
understood the meaning of the divine gift, took it home with him
and gave it to his spouse to eat.

Meanwhile Gna guided her noble horse rapidly along the star-lit
road to Asgard, and told her mistress joyously of the success of
her mission. In due time the Queen of Hunaland had a son, the
great Wolsing, from whom the whole family took its name. He
was the father of brave Sigmund, the favourite of Odin, and he
in his turn of Sigurd, the fame of whose glory was spread over
every Northern and Teutonic land.

When the Queen of Heaven heard of the success that had accompanied her divine gift, she herself decided to be the bearer of the
news to the assembled gods and heroes, and determined to appear
in her most glorious array. Fulla spread out all the Queen's
jewels until they shone like stars, yet Frigg was not satisfied.
Then Fulla pointed to Odin's statue of pure gold, that stood in the
hall of the temple. She thought a worthy ornament might be
made for the goddess out of that gold, if the skilful artificers who
had made such a marvellous likeness of the Father of the gods could

only be won over. The artists were bribed with rich presents
and they at last cut away some of the gold from a place that
was covered by the folds of the floating mantle, so that the theft
could not easily be discovered. They then made the Queen a
necklace of incomparable beauty. When Frigg entered the assembly and seated herself on the throne beside Odin, she at once
made known to all present how she had saved a noble family
from extinction. Every one gazed at her beauty in amazement,
and the Father of the gods felt his heart filled anew with love
for his queen.

A short time afterwards Odin went to the hall of the temple
in which his statue was placed. His penetrating eye at once
discovered the theft that no one else had noticed, and his wrath
was immediately kindled. He sent for the goldsmiths, and as
they confessed nothing, he ordered them to be executed. Then he
commanded that the statue should be placed above the high gate
of the temple, and prepared magic runes that should give it sense
and speech, and thus enable it to accuse the perpetrator of the
deed. The Goddess-queen was greatly alarmed at all these pre-
parations. She feared the anger of her lord, and still more the
shame of her deed being proclaimed in the presence of the ruling
Ases.

Now there happened to be in the Queen's household a serving
demon of low rank, but bold and daring, who had already ventured
to show his admiration for his mistress. Fulla went to him and
assured him that the Queen was touched by his devotion, upon
which the demon declared himself willing to run any risks for her
sake. He made the temple watchmen fall into a deep sleep, tore
down the statue from above the door, and dashed it in pieces, so
that it could no longer speak or complain.

Odin saw what he was doing and guessed the reason. He
raised Gungnir, the spear of death, ready to fling at all who had

been concerned in the evil deed.   But his love for Frigg triumphed over all else ; he determined on another punishment.

He withdrew from gods and men ; he disappeared into distant regions, and with him went every blessing from heaven and earth. A false Odin took his place, who let loose the storms of winter and the Ice-giants over field and meadow.   Every green leaf withered, thick clouds hid the golden sun and the light of the moon and stars ; the earth, lakes and rivers were frozen by the raging cold which threatened to destroy all forms of life.   Every creature longed for the return of the god of blessing, and at length he came back.   Thunder and lightning made known his approach. The usurper fled before the true Odin ; and shrubs and herbs of all kinds sprouted anew over the face of the earth, which was now made young again by the warmth of spring.

In the foregoing tale, we have endeavoured as much as possible to make a conneeted narrative out of the confused, and now and then contradictory, myths regarding Frigg and her handmaids. We will only add that the myth which completes it, dates from a time when the gods had paled in the eyes of the people, and had become less exalted in character than of old.   There are many versions of it differing from one another, and it serves here to show the difference between Summer-Odin and Winter-Odin.

OTHER GODDESSES RELATED TO FRIGG.

Let us now again turn our attention to the great goddess Frigg. The Northern skalds first raised her to the throne and distinguished her from Freya or Frea, the goddess of the Wanes.   She was originally identical with her, as her name and character show. For Frigg comes from *frigen*, a Low-German word connected with *freien* in High-German, and meaning to woo, to marry, thus pointing to the character of the goddess. The old Germanic races, therefore, knew Frea alone as Queen of Heaven, and she and her husband Wodan together ruled over the world. The name Frigga or Frick was also used for her, for in Hesse, and especially in Darmstadt, people used to say fifty years ago of any fat old woman : " Sie ist so dick wie die alte Frick." (She is as thick [fat] as Old Frick.) The word *frigen* is also related to *sich freuer* (rejoice) ; thus Frigg was the goddess of joy (*Freude*). She took the place of the Earth-goddess Nerthus (mistakenly Hertha), who, Tacitus informs us, was worshipped in a sacred grove on an island in the sea. Nerthus was probably the wife of the god of heaven, in whom we recognise Zio or Tyr. He was the hidden god who according to the detailed account of Tacitus, was so reverently worshipped in a sacred grove by the Semnones, the noblest of the Swabian tribes, that the people never set foot on the ground that was consecrated to him without having their hands first bound. The Earth-goddess may also have been the wife and sister of Niörder, and separated from him when he was received amongst the Ases. In this case she belonged to the earlier race of gods, the Wanes, and her husband must have then been called Nerthus, a name afterwards changed into Niörder.

In Mecklenburg the same goddess appears under the name of Mistress Gaude or Gode, which is the feminine form of Wodan or Godan. The country people believed that she brought good luck with her wherever she went.

One story informs us that she once got a carpenter to mend a wheel of her carriage, which had broken when she was on a journey. She gave him all the chips of wood as a reward for his trouble. The man was angry at getting so paltry a remuneration, and only pocketed a few of the chips ; but next morning he saw with astonishment that they had turned to pure gold.

According to another tale, Dame Gode was a great huntress,

who together with her twenty-four daughters devoted herself to the noble pursuit of the chase day and night, on week-days and on Sundays. She was therefore made to hunt to all eternity, and her pack of hounds consisted of maidens who were turned into dogs by enchantment ; she was thus forced to take part in the Wild Hunt.

In France the goddess was called Bensocia (good neighbour, *bona socia*), and in the Netherlands, Pharaildis, *i.e.*, Frau Hilde or Vrouelden, whence the Milky Way was named Vrouelden-straat.

Hilde (*Held*, hero) signifies war, and she was a Walkyrie, who with her sisters exercised her office in the midst of the battle. Later poems make her out to be daughter of King Högni, who was carried off, while gathering magic herbs on the seashore, by bold Hedin when he was on a Wiking-raid. Her father pursued the Wiking with his war-ships, and came up with him on an island. In vain Hilde strove to prevent bloodshed. Högni had already drawn his terrible sword, Dainsleif, the wounds made by which never healed. Once more Hedin offered the king expiation and much red gold in atonement for what he had done.

His father-in-law shouted in scorn : " My sword Dainsleif, which was forged by the Dwarfs, never returns to its sheath until it has drunk a share of human blood ! "

The battle began and raged all day without being decided one way or the other.

In the evening both parties returned to their ships to strengthen themselves for the combat on the morrow.

But Hilde went to the field of battle, and by means of runes and magic signs awakened all the dead warriors and made whole their broken swords and shields.

As soon as day broke, the fight was renewed, and lasted until the darkness of night obliged the combatants to stop.

HILDE, ONE OF THE WALKYRIES.

The dead were stretched out on the battle-field as stiff as figures of stone; but before morning dawned the witch-maiden had awakened them to new battle, and so it went on unceasingly until the gods passed away.

Hilde was also known and worshipped in Germany, as is shown by the legend about the foundation of the town of Hildesheim.

One year, as soon as snow had fallen on the spot dedicated to her, King Ludwig ordered the cathedral to be built there. The Virgin Mary afterwards took her place, and several churches were built in honour of Maria am Schnee (Marie au neige) both in Germany and in France.

Nehalennia, the protectress of ships and trade, was worshipped by the Keltic and Teutonic races in a sacred grove on the island of Walcheren; she had also altars and holy places dedicated to her at Nivelles. The worship of Isa or Eisen, who was identical with Nehalennia, was even older and more wide-spread throughout Germany. St. Gertrude took her place in Christian times, and her name (Geer, *i.e.*, spear, and Trude, daughter of Thor) betrays its heathen origin.

HOLDA. OSTARA.

Once upon a time, in a lonely valley of the Tyrol, where snow-capped glaciers ever shone, there lived a cow-herd with his wife and children. He used to drive his small herd of cattle out to graze in the pastures, and now and again would shoot a chamois, for he was a skilled bowman. His cross-bow also served to protect his cattle from the beasts of prey, and the numerous bear-skins and wolf-skins that covered the floor of his cottage bore witness to his success as a hunter.

One day, when he was watching his cattle and goats on a fragrant upland pasture, he suddenly perceived a splendid chamois,

whose horns shone like the sun. He immediately seized his bow
and crept forward on hands and knees until he was within shot.
But the deer sprang from rock to rock higher up the mountain,
seeming every now and then to wait for him, as though it mocked
his pursuit. He continued the chase eagerly until he reached the
glacier which had sunk below the snow-fields.

The chamois now vanished behind some huge boulders, but at
the same time he discovered a high arched doorway in the glacier,
and in the background beyond he saw a light shining.

He went through the dark entrance boldly, and found himself in
a large hall, the walls and ceiling of which were composed of dazzling crystal, ornamented with fiery garnets. He could see flowery
meadows and shady groves through the crystal walls ; but a tall
woman was standing in the centre of the hall, her graceful limbs
draped in glancing, silvery garments, caught in at the waist by a
golden girdle, and resting on her blond curls was a coronet of car-
buncles. The flowers in her hand were blue as the eyes with which
she gently regarded the cow-herd. Beautiful maidens, their heads
crowned with Alpine roses, surrounded their mistress, and seemed
about to begin a dance. But the herdsman had no eye for any
except the goddess, and sank humbly on his knees.

Then she said in a voice that went straight to the heart of the
hearer :—

" Choose what thou thinkest the most costly of all my treasures,
silver, gold, or precious stones, or one of my maidens."

"Give me, kind goddess," he answered ; "give me only the
bunch of flowers in thy hand ; I desire no other good thing upon
the earth."

She bent her head graciously as she gave him the flowers, and
said :—

" Thou hast chosen wisely. Take them and live as long as
these flowers bloom. And here," pointing to a corn measure, "is

seed with which to sow thy land that it may bear thee many **blue flowers** such as these."

He would have embraced her knees, but a peal of thunder shook the hall and the mountain, and the vision was gone.

When the cow-herd awoke from his vision, he saw nothing but the rocks and the glacier, and the wild torrent that flowed out of it; the entrance to the palace of the goddess had vanished. The nosegay was still in his hand and beside him was the wooden measure full of seed. These tokens convinced him that what had happened was not a mere dream.

He took up his presents and his cross-bow, and descended the mountain thoughtfully to see what had become of his cattle. They were nowhere to be seen, look for them where he might, and when he went home he found nothing but want and misery. Bears and wolves had devoured his herd, and only the swift-footed goats had escaped from the beasts of prey.

A whole year had elapsed since he had left home, and yet he had thought that he had only spent a few hours chamois-hunting in the mountains. When he showed his wife the bunch of flowers, and told her that he intended to sow the seed that had been given him, she scolded him, and mocked him for his folly; but he would not be turned aside from his determination, and bore all his wife's hard words most patiently.

He ploughed up a field and sowed the seed, but there was still a great deal over; he sowed a second and a third field, and yet much seed remained. The little green sprouts soon showed in the fields, grew longer and longer, till at length the blue flowers unfolded themselves in great numbers, and even the cow-herd's wife rejoiced at the sight, so lovely were they to look upon.

The man watched over his crop day and night, and he often saw the goddess of the mountain wandering through his fields in the moonlight with her maidens, blessing them with uplifted hands.

When the flowers were all withered and the seed was ripe, she came again, and showed how the flax was to be prepared, after which she went into the cottage and taught the cow-herd's wife how to spin and weave the flax and bleach the linen, so that it became as white as newly fallen snow.

The cow-herd rapidly grew rich, and became a benefactor to his country, for he introduced the cultivation of flax throughout the land, which gave employment and wages to thousands of country-people. He saw children, grandchildren, and great-grandchildren around him, but the bunch of flowers the goddess had given him was still as fresh as ever, even when he was more than a hundred years old and very tired of life.

One morning while he was looking at his beloved flowers, they all bent down their heads, withered and dying. Then he knew that it was time to say farewell to earthly life. Leaning on his staff, he toiled painfully up the mountains. It was already evening when he reached the glacier.

The snow-fields above were shining gloriously as though in honour of the last walk of the good old man. He once more saw the vaulted doorway and the glimmering light beyond. And then he passed with good courage through the dark entrance into the bright morning which greets the weary pilgrim, when, after his earthly journey is over, he reaches Hulda's halls. The door now closed behind him, and he was seen no more on earth.

This and other traditions of the same kind are told in the Tyrol of the old Germanic goddess Hulda or Holda. Her name shows that she was a goddess of grace and mercy, and she must have been worshipped both in Germany and in Sweden, but still no traces are to be found of her at the present day in the Teutoburg Forest, where so many of the places and names point back to the old Germanic religion, nor yet do the Northern skalds give an account of her. However, German fairy legends and tales call to

HOLDA, THE KIND PROTECTRESS.

us the great goddess whose character and deeds live on in the memory of the people, and the Northern Huldra, who drew men to her by means of her wondrous song, is exactly identical with her. Her name has been derived from the old Northern Hulda, *i.e.*, Darkness ; and it has been thought that she was the impersonation of the dark side of the goddess of Earth and Death ; but the derivation which we gave before, from Huld, grace, mercy, seems more suitable.

A Northern fairy-tale makes Hulla or Hulda, queen of the Kobolds. She was a daughter of the queen of the Hulde-men, who killed first her faithless husband and then herself. She enticed wise King Odin by means of a stag, to her mansion, which was hidden in the depths of a wood. She gave him of her best, and then begged him to act as umpire in a legal dispute that had arisen between her and the other Kobolds and Thurses, about the murder of her husband. He consented to do so, and his decision made her queen of all the Kobolds and Thurses in Norseland. This tale is quite modern in its form, but it certainly is based on ancient beliefs.

A poem dating from the middle ages places Holda in the Mountain of Venus, a place that is generally supposed to be the Hörselberg in Thuringia. She was then called Mistress Venus, and held a splendid court with her women. Noble knights, amongst whom was Ritter Tannhäuser, were drawn by her into the mountain, where they lived such a gay, merry life of pleasure that they could hardly ever again free themselves from her spell and make their escape, even though thoughts of honour and duty might now and then return to them.

It was finally said of Holda, that those who were crippled in any way were restored to full strength and power by bathing in hei Quickborn (fountain of life), and that old men found their vanished youth there once more. This tradition connects her with the

I

Northern Iduna, who had charge of the apple that preserved the immortality and vigour of the Ases. But she also resembled Ostara, who was worshipped by the Saxons, Franks and other tribes.

Ostara, the goddess of Spring, of the resurrection of nature after the long death of winter, was highly honoured by all the old Teutons, nor could Christian zeal prevent her name being immortalised in the word Easter, the period of spring, at which time the Saxons in England worshipped her. The memory of these old times has long since passed away, although the " hare " still lays its " Easter-eggs." The custom is very old of giving each other coloured eggs as a present at the time when day and night became equal in length and when the frozen earth awakens to new life after the cold of winter is gone, for an egg was typical of the beginning of life. Christianity put another meaning on the old custom, by connecting it with the feast of the Resurrection of the Saviour, who, like the hidden life in the egg, slept in the grave for three days before he wakened to new life.

There are no legends about the goddess of spring. One monument alone, and that a newly discovered one, remains of the old worship, the Extern-stones, which are to be found in the Teuto-burg Forest at the northern end of the wooded hills. It is stated in the chronicle of a neighbouring village, dating from last century, that the ignorant peasantry were guilty of many misdemeanours there when doing honour to the heathen goddess Ostara. Had the clergyman only told us whether there were processions, dances, feasts, scattering of flowers, or any other kind of sacrifice, a clear light might have been shed over the manner in which the goddess was worshipped. Still, this fact proves that not only the name, but also the worship of Ostara was kept in the memories of the people for hundreds, perhaps thousands, of years, and shows how deeply rooted it was. The rocks may perhaps have been called Eastern or Eostern-stones, and may have been dedicated to Ostara. There, as elsewhere, the priests and priestesses of the goddess probably assembled in heathen times, scattered Mayflowers, lighted bonfires, slaughtered the creatures sacrificed to her, and went in procession on the first night of May, which was dedicated to her. Very much the same as this used to be done at Gambach, in Upper Hesse, where, as late as thirty years ago even, the young people went to the Easter-stones on the top of a hill, every Easter, and danced and held sports. Edicts were published in the eighth century forbidding these practices ; but in vain, the people would not give up their old faith and customs. Afterwards the priestesses were declared to be witches, the bonfires, which cast their light to great distances, were said to be of infernal origin, and the festival of May was looked upon as the witches' sabbath. Nevertheless, young men and maidens still continue, near the Meissner-Gebirg in Hesse, to carry bunches of Mayflowers and throw them into one of the caves that are to be found there. For Ostara, who gives new life to nature, is the divine protectress of youth and the giver of married happiness.

BERCHTA OR BERTA.

The dusk of evening has fallen over Berlin. A great yet silent crowd is rapidly moving through the chief street towards the royal palace, and every now and then a low whisper is heard, in which can be distinguished the words: "The King is very ill." In the palace itself yet greater silence reigns. The King's guardsmen stand motionless, the servants' steps are inaudible on the carpets of the corridors and the rooms. Now the tower clock strikes midnight; all at once a door opens, and through it glides a ghostly woman, tall of stature, queenly of bearing.

She is dressed in a trailing white garment, a white veil covers her head, below which her long flaxen hair hangs, twisted with strings of pearls; her face is deathly pale as that of a corpse. In her right hand she carries a bunch of keys, in her left a nosegay of Mayflowers. She walks solemnly down the long corridor. The tall guardsmen present arms, pages and lackeys give way before her, the guards who have just relieved their comrades open their ranks; the figure passes through them, and goes through a folding door into the royal ante-room.

"It is the White Lady; the King is about to die," whispers the officer of the watch, brushing a tear from his eye.

"The White Lady has appeared," is whispered through the crowd, and all know what that portends.

At noon the King's death was known to all. "Yes," said Master Schneckenburger, "he has been gathered to his fathers. Mistress Berchta has once more announced what was going to happen, for she can foretell everything, both bad and good. She was seen before the misfortunes of 1806, and again before the battle of Belle-Alliance. She has a key with which to open the door of life and happiness. He to whom she gives a cowslip will succeed in whatever he undertakes."

Schneckenburger was right. It was Bertha, or Berchta, who made known the King's approaching death, but she was also the prophetess of other important events. Berchta (from *percht*, shining) is almost identical with Holda, except that the latter never appears as the White Lady. Many Germanic tribes worshipped the Earth-goddess under the name of Berchta, and there are numbers of legends about her both in North and South Germany.

One evening in the year was dedicated to her, and was called Perchten-evening (30th December or 6th January), when she was supposed, as a diligent spinner, to oversee the labours of the spinning-room, or, magic staff in hand, to ride at the head of the Raging

Host, in the midst of a terrific storm. She generally lived in hollow mountains, where she, as in Thuringia, watched over and tended the "Heimchen," or souls of babes as yet unborn, and of those who died an early death. She busied herself there by ploughing up the ground under the earth, whilst the babes watered the fields. Whenever men, careless of the good she did them, disturbed her in her mountain dwelling, she left the country with her train, and after her departure the fields lost all their former fruitfulness.

Once when Berchta and her babes were passing over a meadow across the middle of which ran a fence that divided it in two, the last little child could not climb over it; its water-jar was too heavy.

A woman, who a short time before had lost her little baby, was close by, and recognised her dead darling, for whom she had wept night and day. She hastened to the child, clasped it in her arms, and would not let it go.

Then the little one said : "How warm and comfortable I feel in my mother's arms; but weep no more for me, mother, my jar is full and is growing too heavy for me. Look, mother, dost thou not see how all thy tears run into it, and how I've spilt some on my little shirt? Mistress Berchta, who loves me and kisses me, has told me that thou shouldst also come to her in time, and then we shall be together again in the beautiful garden under the hill."

Then the mother wept once more a flood of tears, and let the child go.

After that she never shed another tear, but found comfort in the thought that she would one day be with her child again.

Berchta appears in many legends as an enchantress, or as an enchanted maiden, who provided a rich treasure for him who was lucky enough to set her free from the magic spell that bound her. Still more frequently, however, she took up her abode in princely castles as the "Ahnfrau," or Ancestress of the family to whom the castle belonged.   In these stories the Goddess of Nature is hardly recognisable.

It is told that the widowed Countess Kunigunde of Orlamünd fell in love with Count Albrecht the beautiful, of Hohenzollern. He told her that four eyes stood in the way of a marriage between them, and she, thinking that he referred to her children, had them secretly murdered.   But, as the tale informs us, he had meant his parents, who disapproved of the marriage.   He felt nothing but abhorrence of the murderess when he found out what she had done, and she, repenting of her sin, made a pilgrimage to Rome, did severe penance, and afterwards founded the nunnery of the Heavenly Crown, where she died an abbess.   Her grave, as well as those of her children and of the Burggraf Albrecht, are still shown there.   From that time she appeared at the Plassenburg, near Baireuth, as the "Ahnfrau," who made known any evil that was going to happen ; later on she went to Berlin with the Count's family, and is still to be seen there as the tale at the beginning of this chapter shows.

Another account makes the apparition out to be the Countess Beatrix of Cleve, who was married to the Swan-Knight so often mentioned among the old heroes of the middle ages.   The House of Cleve was nearly related to that of Hohenzollern, and in the mysterious Swan-Knight we recognise the god of Light, who comes out of the darkness of night and returns to it again.

A more simple version refers to a Bohemian Countess, Bertha of Rosenberg.   She was unhappily married to Johann of Lichten-berg, after whose death she became the benefactress of her sub-jects, built the Castle Neuhaus, and never laid aside the white garments of widowhood as long as she lived.   In this dress she appeared, and even now appears, to the kindred families of Rosen-berg, Neuhaus and Berlin, on which occasion she prophesies either good or evil fortune.

The Germanic races carried the worship of this Earth-goddess with them to Gaul and Italy, in the former of which countries a proverbial expression refers to the underground kingdom of the goddess, by reminding people "*du temps que Berthe filait.*" It was that time of innocence and peace, of which almost every nation has its tradition, for which it longs, and to which it can only return after death.

Historical personages have also been supposed to enact the part formerly given to the Earth-mother.

A tradition of the 12th century informs us that Pepin, father of Charlemagne, wished to marry Bertrada, a Hungarian princess, who was a very good and diligent spinner. His wooing was successful, and the princess and her ladies set out on their journey to Pepin's court. The bride's marvellous beauty was only marred by her having a very large foot.

Now the chief lady-in-waiting was a wicked woman, and jealous of Bertrada ; so she gave the princess to some villains she had bribed, in order that she might be murdered in the forest, and then she put her own ugly daughter in her mistress's place. Although Pepin was disgusted with his deformed bride, he was obliged to marry her according to compact ; but soon afterwards, on finding out the deception that had been practised upon him, he put her from him.

Late one evening when out hunting, he came to a mill on the river Maine. There he saw a girl spinning busily. He recognised her as the true Bertrada by her large foot, found out how her intended murderers had taken compassion on her, and how she had finally reached the mill. He then discovered his rank to her, and entreated her to fulfil her engagement to him. The fruit of this marriage was Charlemagne.

In this tale we recognise the old myth under a modern form.

We see how Mother Earth, the protectress of souls and ancestress of man, especially of those of royal or heroic race, is thrust aside by the cunning, wintry Berchta, but is joined again by her heavenly husband, and becomes the mother of the god of Spring. Even the large foot reminds us of the goddess, who was originally supposed to show herself in the form of a swan. This is the reason why in French churches there are representations of queens with a swan's or goose's foot (*reine pédauque*).

Other French stories show Berchta in the form of Holda : how she sheds tears for her lost spouse, so bitter that the very stones are penetrated by them. Both goddesses are identical with the Northern Freya, who wept golden tears for her husband.

There is an old ballad that is still sung in the neighbourhood of Mayence, which tells of the bright, blessed kingdom of the goddess. We can give only the matter of it here, as the verses themselves have not remained in our memory.

A huntsman once stood sadly at the water's edge, and thought on his lost love. He had had a young and lovely wife, who, when he came wearied home from the chase, would welcome him with the warm kiss of love. She bare him a sweet babe, and made him perfectly happy. But ere long both were taken from his side by grim, envious death, and now he was alone. Gladly would he have died with them, but that was not to be. Three months had flown by, but his wife and child were still always in his thoughts.

One night his way led him beside a flowing stream ; he stopped still on the bank, gazed long into the water's depths, and asked :

"Is the broken heart to be made whole in a watery grave alone ? "

Thereupon sweet silvery notes fell upon his ear; and as he glanced upwards, he saw before him a beauteous, queenly woman, sitting opposite him on the other side of the stream ; she was spinning golden flax, and singing a wondrous song :

"Youth, enter thou my shining hall,
  Where joy and peace e'er rest;
When the weary heart at length finds all
  Its loved ones, 'gain 'tis blest!

The coward calls my hall the grave,
  My kiss he fears 'twere death;
But the leap is boldly made by the brave—
  His the gain by the loss of life's breath!

Youth, leave thou, then, the lonesome, des'late shore,
And boldly gain the joy enduring evermore."

The huntsman listens; do the thrilling tones come from the beauteous woman on the opposite bank, or is it from the watery deep that they proceed?

Wildly he leaps into the flood, and a fair, white arm is extended, encircling him and drawing him down beneath the water's surface, away from all earthly cares, away from all earthly distress and pain. And his loved ones greet him, his youthful wife and his babe. "See, father! how green the trees grow here, and how the coloured flowers sparkle with silver! And no one cries here, no one has any troubles!"

This tale is based upon the old heathen belief as to the life in a future state; it shows us that the conviction of our forefathers has always been, that for the virtuous death was merely a transition to a new life, to a life purer, more complete, than that on earth.

THOR, THUNAR (THUNDER).

Arwaker (Early-waker) and Alswider (All-swift), the horses of the sun, were wearily drawing the fiery chariot to its rest. The sea and the ice-clad mountains were glowing in the last rays of the setting sun. The clouds that were rising in the west received them in their lap. Then flashes of lightning darted forth from the clouds, thunder began to roll in the distance, and the waves dashed in wild fury upon the rock-bound coast of the fiord.

"Hang up the snow-shoes, lad, and take off thy fur cap; Öku-thor (Thor of the chariot) is driving over to waken old Mother Jörd. Put the jar of mead on the stone table, wife, that he may find something to drink ; and you, you lazy fellows, why are you sitting idly over the fire, instead of rubbing up the ploughshares until they shine again ? This is going to be a fruitful year, for Hlorridi (heat-bringer) has come early. Come, Thialf, pull off my fur boots."

Thus spoke the yeoman to whom Balshoff belonged, as he sat on the stone bench by the fire. But then he stopped short, and stared open-mouthed ; Thialf let the fur boots fall from his hand ; the mistress of the house dropped the jug of mead, and the farm-servants the plough. Wingthor drove over from the west in all his fury ; he struck the house with his hammer Miölnir, and the flash broke through the ridge of the roof beside the pillar that supported it, and penetrated a hundred miles below the clay floor. A sulphureous vapour filled the room ; but the yeoman, shaking off his stupefaction, rose from his stone bench, and when he saw that no more damage was done, he said :

"Wingthor has been gracious to us, and now he has gone on to fight against the Frost and Mountain Giants. Do ye not hear the blows of his hammer, the howls of the monsters in their caverns, and the crashing of their stone heads as though they were nothing but oatmeal dumplings ? But to us he has given rain, which even now is falling heavily, rain that will soon melt away the snow and prepare the soil to receive the seed we shall sow later on. The tiny sprouts will grow rapidly, and grass and herbs and the green leek will reward us for our industry. Preserve the golden ears of corn for us, O Thor, until the harvest time."

In such manner people used, in the olden time, to call on the

strong god of thunder, Thunar,—in the North, Thor. He was held
in great reverence, and was perhaps even regarded as an equal
of the God of Heaven. Traces of this are still recognisable, for
wherever he was spoken of in connection with the other gods, he
was given the place of honour in the middle. The Saxons had to
renounce Wodan, Donar, and Saxnot. In the temple of Upsala,
Thor is placed between Odin and Freyer. In "Skirnir's Journey,"
a poem of the Edda, it is said: "Odin is adverse to thee, the
Prince of the Ases (Thor) is adverse to thee, Freyer curses thee."
He retained this high position in Norway, where he fought against
the Frost and Mountain Giants, who sent the destructive east wind
over the country. And not less honour was paid him in Saxony
and Franconia. The oak was sacred to him, and his festivals were
solemnized under the shade of oak trees. When thunder-clouds
passed over the earth, Thor was said to be driving his chariot
drawn by two fierce male goats, called Tooth-cracker and Tooth-
gnasher.

Odin—not he who sat on Hlidskialf overlooking the nine worlds,
but the omnipotent God of Heaven—married Jörd, Mother Earth
and the offspring of this marriage was strong Thor, who began
even in the cradle to show his Ase-like strength by lifting ten
loads of bear-skins.

Gentle old Mother Jörd, who was known by several other names
in different parts of Germany, could not manage her strong son, so
two other beings, Wingnir (the winged), and Hlora (heat) became
his foster-parents. These were personifications of the winged
lightning. From them were derived the god's names of Wingthor
and Hlorridi.

Thor married Sif (kin), for he, the protector of households, was
himself obliged to have a well-ordered household. The beautiful
goddess had golden hair, probably because of the golden corn of
which her husband was guardian, and her son was the swift archer,

Uller, who hunted in snow-shoes every winter, and ruled over Asgard and Midgard in the cold season, while the summer Odin
was away. By the giantess, Jarnsaxa (Ironstone) Thor had two
sons, Magni (Strength) and Modi (Courage), and by his real wife
a daughter, Thrud (Strong), the names of whom all remind us of
his own characteristics.

Thor was handsome, large and well-proportioned, and strong.
A red beard covered the lower part of his face, his hair was long
and curly, his clothes were well-fitting and his arms were bare,
showing his strongly-developed muscles. In his right hand he
carried the crashing-hammer, Miölnir, whose blows caused the
destructive lightning flash and the growling thunder.

THOR AND LOKI'S JOURNEY IN
WOMEN'S CLOTHES.

THOR'S DEEDS AND JOURNEYS.

THE MAKING OF MIÖLNIR.

A gentle breeze was blowing over the rich land of Thrudheim, and the doors of Bilskirnir were standing open that the castle might be filled with the aromatic perfume of the summer flowers. Thor slept quietly in the great hall, until morning dawned and chased away the shades of night. The god then rose from his couch, but his first glance fell on his wife Sif, who looked very sad. All her golden hair had vanished in the night, and she was standing before him with a bald head, like the earth when the golden corn has been harvested. He guessed who the author of the mischief was, and rushed angrily over the hills and through the groves of Asgard until he came to spiteful Loki, whom he seized by the throat and held till his eyes almost started from his head. He would not let him go until he promised to obtain another head of hair, the same as the old one, from the dwarfs. As soon as the mischief-maker was free he hastened to Elfheim, and after paying a heavy price, brought away with him not only the hair but also Gungnir, the spear that never failed in its blow; and the ship Skidbladnir, which could sail whatever wind was blowing, and which was so cunningly made, that it could be folded up and put in the pocket when it was no longer wanted. He gave Thor the hair for his wife, and it was no sooner put upon her head than it took root and began to grow apace. To Odin he gave the spear, and to Freyer the ship, that he might go to sea with the merchants' galleys and save shipwrecked persons.

Delighted with the praise his gifts received on all sides, Loki asserted that his smiths, the sons of Iwaldur, were the best workers in metal that had ever lived. Now it happened that the Dwarf Brock was present when he said this, and Brock's brother, Sindri, was generally regarded as the best smith. So he scornfully replied that no one could beat his brother, and that he would wager his head for Sindri's fame. Brock informed his brother of the dreadful bet, but was told to be of good courage ; he was given the bellows and desired to keep on blowing the fire without stopping, so that there might be no interruption in the magic work, a circumstance which would at once bring all their efforts to naught. Sindri then put a pig-skin in the fire, and went away to draw the magic circle, and command the assistance of the hidden powers in his labours. Brock, meanwhile, worked hard at the bellows, in spite of the attacks of a fly which continually stung him on the hand till the blood flowed. When Sindri returned there was life in the fire, and he drew out of it the enormous wild boar Gullinbursti, with golden bristles, the radiance of which made the dark smithy as light as day.

The second work of art had now to be made. Sindri laid some red gold in the furnace, and Brock blew the bellows in spite of the cruel stings of the fly, until at last the ring Draupnir was formed, from which eight other rings exactly similar dropped every ninth night.

Lastly, the smith threw a bar of iron into the furnace, and desired his brother to blow steadily. Brock did as he was told, and bore the agony caused by the fly, which he knew cunning Loki had sent. But when all at once it stung him on the eyelid, and the blood ran down into his eye, he dashed his hand at it to crush it. Then the flames rose in the air and suddenly sunk again and were extinguished. Sindri rushed into the hall in terror, but his face brightened when he had looked into the furnace.

"All is well," he said; "it is finished—only the handle is somewhat short."

Then he drew a great battle-hammer out of the furnace, and gave it to his brother, as well as the two other works of art, adding:

"Go now; thou hast won the bet, and thine enemy's head also."

Brock entered the assembly of the Ases, who were sitting in council. He gave Odin the ring Draupnir, and to bright Freyer he gave the boar Gullinbursti, which he said would carry him swift as the wind through mists and clouds, and over mountains and valleys. When Thor received the hammer, and swung it in his right hand, then he, the prince of the Ases, grew tall as a giant; dark clouds piled themselves around his waist; lightning flashed from the clouds, and rolling peals of thunder shook the heights of Asgard and Midgard, terrifying both Ases and mortal men. Odin alone, to whom fear was impossible, sat unmoved upon his throne, and said:

" Miölnir is the greatest of treasures, for in the hand of my son it will protect Asgard from every assault of the giants."

So Brock won the wager and Loki's head as well, and he refused to accept anything else in exchange. But the son of Laufey had already taken refuge in flight, so Thor hastened after him, and soon brought him back.

"The head is thine, but not the neck," cried the mischief-maker, as the dwarf raised his sword.

"Then I will sew up thy great mouth," answered Brock, trying to make holes through his opponent's lips; but all in vain, the knife made no impression. So he got his brother's awl, and that did not fail. He sewed up the mouth, and Loki stood in the midst of the laughing Ases unable to speak; yet he soon found means to unfasten the string.

The hair of the earth-goddess, Sif, is the flowers and corn that grow upon the earth. These are cut down in the harvest, and the winter-demon robs the goddess of her hair, and leaves her head quite bald. But the Dwarfs who live under the earth provide her with a fresh supply of hair, and with the help of the Thunder-god punish the evil-doer.

Alwismal, the Song of Alwis.—Alwis, the King of the Dwarfs, who had travelled throughout the nine worlds and had learnt all the languages and wisdom of the dwellers therein, once went to Asgard. He met with a friendly reception there, for all the Ases knew about his palace which shone with gold and precious stones, and of his widely extended power over the underground people. He saw beautiful Thrud, Asathor's strong daughter, fell in love with her, and asked for her hand in marriage. The Ases approved of the proposal of the King of the underground treasures, and were of opinion that Thor would be pleased with the arrange-ment. So the marriage day was fixed. But Thor came home before the wedding-day, and was very wroth when he was told the news.

" Who art thou, thou pasty-faced fellow ? " he asked of the would-be bridegroom ; " Hast thou been with the dead ? Hast thou arisen from the grave to snatch the living back with thee to thy dismal kingdom ? "

Alwis now asked him who he was that pretended to have power over his bride and to be able to prevent the marriage which was already arranged ; but when he found that it was Wingthor, Thrud's father, he told him of his possessions and of his wisdom, and entreated him to consent.

Thor, in order to prove him, asked what certain words were in the different languages of men, Ases, Wanes, Jotuns, Elves, and in Helheim.

The Dwarf answered everything right; but lo! day began at that moment to break, and Alwis was touched by a ray of sunlight, whereupon he stiffened into stone, and remained on the heights of Asgard, a monument of Thor's victory.

THOR'S JOURNEY TO UTGARD.

The Hrimthurses sent out cold winds from the interior of Jotunheim over the fields of Midgard, so that the tender green shoots were blighted and the harvest spoilt. Thor, therefore, ordered his chariot to be got ready, and hastened away to force the giants to keep within bounds. Loki joined him with flattering speeches, and the Thunderer thought that it might be as well to take him with him, as he knew his way about the wilderness so well.

Thor's goats went so quickly that the travellers reached the bare rocks of the giants' country by the evening.

They saw a lonely farmhouse, and the owner offered them hospitality, but could only give them a poor supper. Thor, therefore, slew his goats and boiled them in a pot. He then invited his host and all his people to join him at supper, but commanded them to

K

throw all the bones on the skins which he had spread out on the floor, and to beware how they broke any.

Cunning Loki whispered to the farmer's son, Thialfi, that he ought to break one of the thigh bones, as the marrow in it was good to eat. Thialfi followed the evil counsel, and found that the marrow was indeed most excellent.

Next morning Thor waved his hammer over the skins and bones, and immediately the goats jumped up, but one of them was lame in the hind leg. The god was very angry, his eyes flashed, his right hand closed round the handle of his hammer, and a thunderclap shook the house to its foundations. The farmer, who had been flung upon his face, begged for mercy, and his wife and children joined him in his entreaties; he offered his son Thialfi and his daughter Röskwa in atonement for the broken thigh-bone.

Then the angry god grew calm, and accepted the expiation offered him; he left his goats and chariot behind and walked on with his companion and the sturdy children of the farmer towards Jotunheim.

They crossed high mountains, and went through deep valleys until they came to a broad sound. When they had crossed the sound, their way led them over a stony country and through a dark wood that seemed as if it would never end. The ground was covered with a grey mist, out of which an iceberg, resembling a corpse-like ghost, here and there reared its head. All was dim and uncertain, as though surrounded by enchantment.

The travellers pursued their journey all day long, Thialfi, the quickest runner in the country, always keeping in front with Thor's travelling bag.

In the evening they reached a strange, roomy inn, in which there was neither inhabitant nor food to be found; yet they lay down to rest, as they felt very hungry.

At midnight a violent earthquake shook the house, but they

succeeded in finding a place within the building that seemed to be
more secure than the rest; there Thor's companions took refuge,
whilst he, hammer in hand, kept watch by the entrance. Loud
sounds of roaring and snorting disturbed the sleep of the travellers.
The Prince of the Ases awaited the morning.

When it grew light, he perceived a man of mighty stature,
whose snoring had been the cause of all the noise they had heard.
He felt very much inclined to bless the snorer's sleep with a
goodly blow of his hammer, but at that very moment the giant
awoke.

In reply to his question, "Who art thou?" the giant answered
that his name was Skrymir, and added that he knew perfectly
well that his questioner was Asathor. As he said this, he began
to look about for his glove. And how great was the astonishment
of the Ase, when he discovered that he and his companions had
spent the night in the giant's glove, and that when they had been
startled out of their first resting-place, they had taken refuge in
the thumb.

Skrymir gave himself no further trouble about the surprise of
the strangers, but laid out his breakfast and devoured it, whilst
the travellers took some provisions for themselves out of Thor's
bag. The giant then tied up all his belongings in a bundle, threw
it over his broad back, and walked on before the others through
the wood at such a pace that they could hardly follow him. In
the evening they took up their quarters for the night under an
oak tree, the top of which reached the clouds.

The Jotun gave the travellers the remains of the food in his
bundle, because, he said, sleep was more necessary for him than
food. The strong Thunderer vainly strove to unfasten the cord tied
round the bundle. Enraged by this failure, he pulled his girdle of
strength tighter round his waist, and seizing Miölnir with both
hands, dealt a terrible blow on the head of the snoring giant, who

merely rubbed the place with his hand, and asked whether a leaf had fallen on his head.

At midnight the wood again re-echoed with his snores. Thor now hit the monster again as hard as he could on the crown. The hammer made a deep hole, but Skrymir thought that it was only an acorn that had fallen upon him, and soon began to snore again.

Towards morning the angry Ase dealt a third dreadful blow at the giant; the earth trembled, rocks fell with a horrible crash; the hammer penetrated the giant's skull, so that the end was hidden. Nevertheless, Skrymir rose quietly and said :—

"So, thou art awake already, Asathor. Look, some birds, when building their nests, have let a little bit of stick fall on my temple; it is bruised. We must part here; my way lies to the north, and yours to Utgard in the east. You will soon see Utgard-Loki's castle before you. There you will find bigger men than I. Beware lest any of you open your mouths too wide in boastful talk; for if you do, you will get into difficulties."

Skrymir went straight on through the wood, while the others turned in the direction he had pointed out to them.

About noon they came in sight of the giant's castle, which was large and shining as an iceberg. They slipped in between the bars of the postern gate, and entered the royal hall.

There sat Utgard-Loki, Prince of the Thurses, on his throne, and ranged around him on benches were his warriors and courtiers. He stared at the travellers in surprise.

"I know ye well, little people," he cried, in a voice that re-sembled the rumbling of a falling rock. "I know thee, Asathor, and guess that thou canst do more than thy appearance would justify one in supposing. Now tell me what each of you can do, for no one is allowed to sit down here without showing himself to be good for something."

First of all Loki vaunted his powers in eating.

SKRYMIR ATTACKED BY THOR WHEN ASLEEP.

"A good thing to be able to do on a journey," said the King; "for then one can eat enough at one meal to last for eight days. Logi, my cook, shall try with thee which is the better trencherman. We shall see which of you can eat the most."

A large trough was filled with meat, and the two heroes stood one at each end of it, and tried which could devour the fastest. They met in the middle; Loki had eaten one half of the meat, and Logi the other; but as the latter had at the same time disposed of the bones and the trough as well, he walked away from the table proud of his victory.

Thialfi announced that he was swift of foot, and challenged the courtiers to race with him in the lists. A young fellow named Hugin accepted the challenge. He turned back at the goal just as the farmer's son reached it.

"Well run for a stranger, by my beard," growled the Prince of the Thurses; "but now make better speed." However, Thialfi was farther behind at the second turn, and at the third he had full half the course to run when Hugin turned at the goal.

It was now time for Thor to show what he could do. He first said that he could drink a long draught. The Thurse commanded that the horn should be brought that some could empty at one draught, many at two, and the weakest at three. The Ase looked at the horn. It was long, but it was narrow, and he thought he could easily dispose of the contents. Nevertheless, the first draught hardly uncovered the rim, the second very little more, and the third a few inches at most. Much ashamed, he gave back the horn; he could drink no more.

He then spoke of his strength. Utgard-Loki told him to pick up the grey cat which was lying purring at his feet. The hammer-thrower imagined that he could fling the cat up to the ceiling; but his first attempt to lift it only made it arch its back, at the second it arched its back a little more, at the third he raised one paw from the ground; farther than that he could not move it. He heard with rage the scornful laughter with which his fruitless efforts were greeted from the benches. Lightning flashed from his eyes; he challenged the courtiers to wrestle with him in the lists.

"That will go ill with thee," said the King, stroking his beard: "try first what thou canst do here against Elli, my old nurse; she has conquered stronger men than a shrimp like thee before now."

The old woman was ready by this time, and seized strong Thor, who exerted all his strength to try and overthrow her. But she stood as immovable as a rock, and used her own strength so well, that he sank upon one knee.

"Enough," cried the Jotun. "Sit down, strangers, and enjoy my hospitality."

On the following morning the king accompanied them as far as the wood.

"Here," he said, "are the borders of my domain, which you should never have crossed had I known more about you. Let me now tell you how I have tricked you. Three times, Asathor, didst thou strike at my head; but I always shoved a mountain between me and thee. Look, dost thou see the marks made by thy hammer, three deep abysses, the last of which reaches down to the Home of the Black-Elves? The cook Logi, who measured his strength against Loki, and who devoured even the bones and the trough, was wild-fire. Hugin, was Thought, whom neither Thialfi nor any other runner could expect to overtake. The drinking horn was connected with the ocean. Thou didst drink so much that every shore was left uncovered, and the people said: 'It is ebb tide.' Thine eyes were blinded when thou didst lift the grey cat, for then thou didst swing the Midgard-snake as high as heaven, and she had nearly wriggled herself free and done irreparable injury. Elli, the nurse, who looked so weak, was old age, which none can withstand when his time has come. Go now, for this is my realm, where I have dominion over the Hrimthurses and their rocky fastnesses. Where I rule, there is no space for men to cultivate the land, yet Asathor might split the mountains and the eternal ice with his thunder."

Thor had already raised his hammer to punish the Jotun for his magic spells, but he had vanished. A bare, stone-strewed wilderness surrounded him and his companions. Columns of mist hovered here and there, out of which Jotuns were peering, now with a smile of scorn and again looking down grimly, now sinking and again rising in the air, so that the travellers did not know what was real and what enchanted. They then set out on their return to Thrudheim.

The natural myth which gave rise to this poem of the Younger Edda is very suitable for our collection. Not even the mighty Ase could make it possible for man to cultivate the soil amongst the great mountains, where rock is piled upon rock, and all are covered with ice and snow. Thialfi is the diligence which must animate the farmer, and his sister Röskwa is the quickness and activity which must attend him.

Duel with Hrungnir.—Thor passed some happy days in his halls of Bilskirnir. His fair wife Sif, who kept the house in good order, was beautiful as the May moon; her artistically-made golden hair grew daily longer, and fell over her neck and shoulders in ringlets. The god had great pleasure in his son Magni, who, although only three years old, was as tall and strong as a man. The Jotuns in the neighbourhood were all quiet, for they did not care to harm the husbandmen's crops. Still, the farmers who lived far away in valleys amid the inhospitable mountains, often called upon the helpful Ase to defend them against the monsters, who sent storms, floods, avalanches, and falling rocks, to disturb them in their peaceful labours. Thor then hastened with Miölnir to punish the peacebreakers in the east.

Allfather Odin was away on his travels, now ruling the battle of mortal men, now searching after wisdom, and now wooing the favour of women with loving words. Upon one of these journeys he arrived at the castle of the Mountain-giant, Hrungnir, where he was hospitably received. Whilst they were talking together, the Jotun remarked that Sleipnir was a good horse, but that his own horse, Gullfaxi (golden mane), was better, and that it could leap farther with its four feet than the former with its eight.

"Well," cried Odin, " I will wager my head upon my horse. Catch me if thou canst."

He jumped upon Sleipnir and galloped away, the giant pursuing him with a giant's rage.

Swift as the storm-wind, the Father of the gods galloped on far ahead. Hrungnir was not aware, in his haste, that his golden-maned horse was thundering over the bridge Bifröst until he stopped at the gates of Walhalla. Then the King of the Ases came out to meet him, and in return for his hospitality led him into the hall. To Hrungnir was given the enormous goblet, full of foaming beer, from which Thor was accustomed to drink. In his ill-humour, he emptied it in a few draughts, and asked in his intoxication for more and more.

" Ha ! " he exclaimed, "none of you know me yet. I will take Walhalla upon my back and carry it off to Jotunheim. I will throw Asgard into the abyss of Nifelhel, and strangle you all, except Freya and Sif, whom I will take home with me. I will empty all your beer barrels to the sediment. Bring me what you have. Freya shall be my cup-bearer."

The trembling goddess poured him out a bumper, but the other Ases called aloud for Thor.

The god appeared in the hall with the speed of the lightning that flashes down from the sky.

"Who has permitted the Thurse to sit down in holy Asgard ? "

he demanded in a voice of thunder. " Why does Freya give him the drinking-horn? His head shall be broken in punishment for this."

And as he said these words, his eyes sparkled and his hand closed round the shaft of his hammer.

Then Hrungnir immediately at once became sober. He stammered out that Odin had invited him to the feast, and that it would be dishonourable of Thor to attack an unarmed man. Yet he would be ready to fight with him at Griottunagard (rolling-stone, or also rock-wall) in the borders of Jotunheim.

The Ase could not withdraw from this challenge, and the Jotun made all the haste he could to reach home with a whole skin.

Everywhere and in all countries the coming duel was talked about. The Jotuns knew that their best fighting man was going to venture on a dangerous undertaking. They consulted together how they might ensure him the victory.

They made a clay man nine miles high and three miles across the chest, Möckerkalfi (Mist-wader) by name, who was to help their hero in the fight, but who had only a trembling mare's heart in his breast. The Jotun himself had a triangular heart of stone, and his skull was also of stone, and his shield and his club too.

Hrungnir and his clay squire awaited Thor at Griottunagard on the appointed day. The Ase did not waste time. He drove up in the midst of rolling thunder and flashing lightning, surrounded by clouds. His quick-footed servant, Thialfi, ran on before him, and called out to the Jotun that he was mistaken in holding his shield before him, for the god would come up out of the ground to attack him.

Then Hrungnir flung his shield under his feet and seized his club in both hand, to be in readiness to throw it, or to hit out with it. He now perceived the Ase swinging Miölnir, so he threw his club at him with fearful strength. The weapons crashed together in the middle of the lists; but the force of the hammer was so great that it splintered the club and broke the stone-head of the giant in pieces, felling him almost dead to the ground. Meanwhile a splinter from the club had penetrated Thor's forehead, so that he also fell, and as it happened, right under the leg of the falling giant. Sturdy Thialfi had in the meantime despatched the clay giant with a spade, and had broken him up into the clay from which he had been made. He now tried to help his master, but could not lift the giant's leg. Other Ases tried also, until at length the strong boy Magni came up. And he pushed aside the heavy weight as though it were a mere trifle, saying:

"What a pity it is, Father, that I did not come sooner; I could have broken that fellow's stone head with my fist."

"Thou wilt be a strong man," said Thor; "and thou shalt have the good horse Gullfaxi as a reward for helping me."

He then strove to pull the stone splinter out of his brow, but could neither move it nor could he even loosen it, so he was forced to drive home to Thrudheim with an aching head.

Loving Sif and anxious Thrud vainly endeavoured to alleviate the pain Thor was enduring. The prophetess Groa (green-making) now came to the house. She could move rocks with her magic spells, and also stop the course of wild floods. She offered to cure Thor. Then she drew her circles and sang her wondrous songs. The stone began already to shake and grow looser, and the wounded Ase hoped for a speedy cure. In order to give Groa pleasure, he told her, while she murmured her spells, that he had waded across the ice-stream Eliwagar, carrying her husband, Örwandil, on his back, and had broken off one of Örwandil's frost-bitten toes, which he had flung up into the sky, where it was now shining like a star.

"And now," he said, "he is on his way home to thee."

Scarcely were the words out of his mouth, when Groa sprang up joyfully, forgetting all about her magic spells. And so the splinter remained in Thor's forehead.

According to the poet Uhland, this is a poetical description of the splitting of the rocks by the crashing hammer of the god. Thialfi, the diligent husbandman, conquered the clay giant, the uncultivated ground, while Thor made agriculture possible among the rocks. He was hurt by the falling stones when doing this. Groa (the green-making), the sprouting power in plants, was married to Örwandil (living seed), whom Thor carried on his shoulders through the wintry ice-streams Eliwagar. Mannhardt looks upon Örwandil as lightning sparks. We refrain from noticing further the different interpretations put upon the story. The skald found the natural myth, touched the strings of his harp and sang his song with all his heart, careless whether he gave the old myth in all its particulars or not.

Journey to Hymir.—In this myth the terrors of the polar regions are described. It was in that northern realm that the Frost-giant Hymir (the dusk-maker) ruled, and in his house lived the golden, white-browed goddess of light, who had been stolen from her home, and also the nine-hundred headed grandmother, the mountains of ice and snow.

Hymir was guardian of the great brewing vat, whose depth might be counted by miles; by this was probably meant the Arctic Ocean, through which the summer god, Thor, opened a passage for seafaring men. Thor conquered the terrors of the Arctic climate before which even the bold Wikings drew back appalled, while in our days, brave North Pole voyagers face them undauntedly.

Thus Uhland explains the myth, and we feel inclined to agree with him; nevertheless, this journey to Hymir is said by other commentators to mean a descent into the Under-world. Perhaps both explanations are admissible, for all nature is dead in winter, buried under a pall of snow, and the ideas of winter and death are frequently interchangeable. Strong Thor, therefore, descended into the Under-world, conquered its terrors, as he did those of the Hrimthurses, and returned home victorious, in like manner as Herakles did in the Greek myth, which ascribes to him a heroic deed of the same kind as this.

THOR'S JOURNEY TO THRYMHEIM TO GET BACK HIS HAMMER.

Night with her starry diadem had spread her mantle over Asgard. Every creature was asleep; the Ases in their golden chambers, and the Einheriar stretched out on the benches of Walhalla after a goodly feast on the flesh of Sährimnir, and many a draught of delicious mead. They dreamt happy dreams of brave deeds and of the joys of victory.

Wingthor alone tossed restlessly about on his cushions of down. He heard in his dreams the murmur of wicked runes, and saw a gigantic hand seize hold of Miölnir. At length he was awakened by hollow peals of thunder. He snatched at the hammer which always lay by his bedside, but could not find it. Angrily he sprang to his feet and felt about for it; but it was gone; the faint light of morning showed that the place where he had laid it was empty. He shook his head wrathfully and his eyes flashed fire. His beard grew redder than ever, and the house trembled at his shout:

"Miölnir is gone; it has been stolen by enchantment."

Loki heard his cry, and said to him:

"I will get thee back thy hammer, whoever has stolen it, if Freya will lend me her Falcon-dress."

So they went to Folkwang and entered the presence of Freya. They addressed her in courteous words, and asked her to lend them her feather-garment, that they might spy out who had stolen Miölnir.

And the gentle goddess answered: "You may have it. I would lend it to you willingly, even if it were made of silver or gold."

She then took the dress out of a chest and gave it to the Ases. And now Loki flew with rhythmic strokes of his wings, high above the precincts of Asgard and the swift river Ifing, until he reached the barren mountains of Jotunheim.

Thrym, a prince of the Thurses, was sitting there on a hill. He was decorating his dogs, that ran quickly as the wind, with golden ribbons, and making the manes of his fiery horses shine.

"What news dost thou bring from Asgard, that thou comest alone to Thrymheim?" he called out to the new-comer: "how goes it with the Ases and how with the Elves?"

"Badly with both Ases and Elves," answered Loki, "for Miölnir is lost. Speak, hast thou hidden it anywhere?"

Then the Thurse laughed, and said: "I have hidden it eight miles deep in a cleft of the earth; and no one shall have it unless he brings me Freya as a bride to my halls."

Enraged at his message, Loki flew back over the Ifing river to Asgard, where Thor awaited him. He gave the message of the wicked Thurse.

Again Thor and Loki went to visit the goddess in her shining hall at Folkwang.

"Up and dress thyself, Freya," said Thor; "put on thy snowy bridal garments, and I will take thee to Thrym, prince of the Thurses."

Then the goddess' anger was kindled at this address, and she started from her throne, making the palace shake to its foundations.

"You may call me mad," she cried, "if ever I follow thee in bridal array to Thrymheim, to the Prince of the Thurses, monster that he is."

Having thus spoken, she dismissed the Ases from her presence without a word of farewell.

The Ases now all assembled on their seats of justice near the fountain of Urd, that they might consult together as to the best means of rescuing the hammer from the power of the Giants.

The first to speak was Heimdal, the god who resembled'a Want in wisdom; he said :—

"Let Thor himself put on the bridal garments, let a bunch of keys jingle at his waist, let precious stones sparkle upon his neck, let his knees be covered by the petticoats of a woman, and a veil be put before his face.

The Prince of the Ases did not approve of the advice of wise Heimdal. He would, he said, be always called a woman in future, if he ever put on female apparel. But when Loki replied that if he did not get back the hammer the giants would soon come to live in Asgard, he consented to do as the Ases entreated.

Soon afterwards he sat in his chariot dressed as a bride, and Loki, son of Laufey, in the guise of a serving maid, seated himself by his side.

The goats set off; they rushed in wild leaps through Asgard and Midgard; the earth smoked, and rocks and mountains split with loud reports wherever they went.

Thrym was sitting comfortably at the threshold of his hall. He watched his golden-horned cows coming home, he saw his large herds of black bullocks, his stores of gold and precious stones in their iron caskets.

"I have a great store of riches," he said; "the only thing wanting now is that Freya should be my wife. And to-morrow she will enter my halls; so strew the benches my men, and have plenty of food and mead in readiness, for it beseems a spacious hall like mine that the wedding should be a merry one."

Early next morning the visitors arrived, and soon afterwards his bride was sitting beside Thrym, well-veiled, as modesty and custom demanded.

The tables were laden with costly food and wine, which were a pleasure to look at as well as to eat and drink. No one could rival the bride, however. She ate a fat ox in no time, then eight huge salmon, and all the sweet cakes that were made for the women, and in addition she drank two barrels of mead. The Thurse was astonished at her hunger.

"Well," he exclaimed, "I never before saw a bride with such an appetite, nor did I ever see a girl drink mead in such a degree!"

But the serving maid assured him that her mistress had tasted neither bite nor sup for a week, so excited had she been at the thought of her wedding.

The Jotun wished to kiss his bride on hearing this, and raised her veil for the purpose; but at the sight of Freya's flaming eyes, which seemed as though they flashed fire at him, he shrank back to the end of the room.

But the wise maid calmed down his apprehensions. "My lady," she said, "has not slept for a week, and that is the reason her eyes are so fiery."

The gaunt sister of the Thurse now approached the bride to ask for a wedding present.

"Give me," she entreated, "golden rings and a pair of buckles, and thou shalt enjoy my love."

Unmoved by this appeal, the bride sat silent in her wedding array. Then the Prince, intoxicated with love and mead, commanded that the hammer should be brought from its hiding-place, that the marriage might be solemnized in the usual way.

"And then," he added, "place it in the lap of the bride."

It seemed at that moment as though the bride were stifling a laugh beneath her veil, and indeed a ferocious laugh was heard when the Prince's command had been obeyed.

Now the bride rose, and threw off her veil; it was Asathor, terrible to look upon; he raised his bare arm and held Miölnir aloft in his mighty right hand. The walls of the room tottered and cracked, a peal of thunder shook the house and a flash of lightning darted through the hall. Thrym lay stretched on the floor with a broken head; his guests and his servants fell under the blows of the hammer; not even his gaunt sister escaped. The flames made their way out through the roof; and house and hall fell with a loud crash. A smoking heap of ruins alone remained to show the place where the powerful Thrym had ruled.

The spring sun rose; it shone down upon the devastated dwelling, the broken rocks, fallen stones, torn and uprooted soil, and upon the victorious god who had conquered the power of the enemy.

The storm-clouds of anger were gone from Thor's brow. He stood upon the height and gazed at his work of destruction with a gentle and kindly look upon his face. Then he called his children of men to come and instil new life into the destruction, so that farms and dwelling houses, agriculture and commerce, civic order, law and morality should arise and flourish there. And so into this conquered land came farmers and builders, with hatchet, spade, and plough; herdsmen with their cattle and sheep, and mighty hunters to keep down the numbers of bears and wolves. And Thor was in the midst of them, setting up stones to mark the boundaries, consecrating the tilled land with his hammer; then the grateful people erected an altar to him, made a great feast in his honour, and promised him the first-fruits of their labour. After that Thor got into his chariot, followed by Loki, and together they returned to Asgard rejoicing in what they had done.

We have pointed here to the natural myth which lies at the foundation of this poem. The myth is one of the most beautiful in the Elder Edda. The poet has made free use of the materials that were at his disposal, so that the most minute details of the primitive myth can never be discovered; yet the following can be made out with certainty.

The beneficent Thunder god, who ruled over summer, was deprived of his hammer in the winter; Thrym (Thunder) hid it eight miles deep in the ground, *i.e.*, for eight months. He desired to have possession of Freya, the fair goddess of spring, in order that he might deprive man of the bright weather she brought with her. But Thor regained his hammer, and slew the Frost-giant and his followers, and his gaunt sister too, who according to Uhland was the famine that haunts rude mountain districts. Thus the god opened a new field to human industry.

JOURNEY TO GEIRÖD'S-GARD.

Loki once took Frigg's falcon-dress; he wrapped himself in it and hovered over many an abyss and broad stream until he had flown right above the barren rocks and ice of Jotunheim. He saw a chimney in the distance, out of which fire and smoke were issuing. Quickly he flew there, and perceived that the chimney belonged to a rambling grange.

This was Geiröd's-Gard, where Prince Geiröd, the Hrimthurse, dwelt with his people. The Ase was curious to know what was going on in the large hall, and fluttered down close to the window. But the Thurse caught sight of the falcon, and sent a servant out to catch it. Loki amused himself by making the man climb the high railing above which he fluttered, taking care to keep, as he thought, just out of reach; but suddenly he was caught by the leg and given to the giant.

"This is a strange-looking bird," said Geiröd, staring into the falcon's eyes as though he thought he could thus discover its character. "Tell me," he asked, addressing it, "whence thou comest, and what thou really art?"

But the bird remained silent and motionless.

So the Prince determined to tame him through hunger, and locking him up in a chest left him there for three months without food.

When he was taken out at the end of that time, Loki told who he was and begged to be set free.

At this the Thurse laughed so loud that he shook the hall and the whole grange.

"At length," he exclaimed, "I have got what I have long desired, a hostage of the Ases. I will not let thee go until thou hast sworn a holy oath to bring me Thor, the Giant-killer, without his hammer and girdle of strength, that I may fight him hand to hand. I expect that I shall conquer him as easily as I would a boy, and then I shall send him down to Hel's dark realm."

Loki promised with a holy oath to do as the giant bade, and flew quickly away.

When the cunning Ase had recovered from his fatigue, he remembered his oath. He told strong Thor that Geiröd had received him most hospitably, and that he had expressed a great wish to see the unconquerable protector of Asgard face to face, but without the terrible signs of his power, of which he was much afraid. Loki went on to say that there were strange things to be seen at the giant's house which were not to be seen elsewhere. Thor listened to the tempter, and at once set out on his journey, accompanied by Loki.

On his way to Geiröds-gard he met the giantess Grid, by whom Odin had once had a son named Widar, the silent. She told him what the true character of Geiröd was, and lent him her girdle of strength, and her staff and iron glove as a defence against the giant.

The day after this, he and Loki reached the broad river Wimur, which stretched out before them like a sea, and was so wide that the other shore was invisible. When Thor began to wade across, steadying himself by means of his staff, the water rose, and the waves beat wildly against his shoulders.

"Do not rise, Wimur," he cried, "for I must wade over to the giant's house."

Then he saw Geiröd's daughter, Gialp, standing in the cleft of a rock and making the water rise. He forced her to flee by throwing a great stone at her, and afterwards got safely over to the other bank, which he managed to climb, swinging himself up by means of a service tree. Loki also got safely over, for he clung to Thor's girdle the whole way.

When the travellers saw the chimney with the fire issuing from it, and the castle high as a mountain just in front of them, they knew that they had got to the end of their journey.

They went into the entrance hall. Thor seated himself wearily upon the only chair that was to be seen. But he soon discovered that it was rising higher and higher, so that he was in danger of being crushed against the ceiling. He pressed the end of his staff against the beams that ran across the top of the hall, and with all his Ase-strength tried to force the chair down again. A terrible crack and a cry of pain told him that he had hurt some living creature in his struggles. Gialp and Greip, Geiröd's daughters, had raised the chair on which he was sitting, and they now lay under it with broken backs, victims of their own cunning.

A monster serving-man now challenged Thor to a fencing bout in the great hall. On entering it the Ase saw with amazement that fires were burning all round the walls, the flames and smoke of which rose through the chimney he had seen before.

Instead of giving him courteous greeting, the Jotun king flung an iron wedge at him, which he had taken red hot out of the furnace with a pair of tongs. But Thor caught it in his iron glove and threw it back with such impetus that it broke through the brazen breastplate and body of the Jotun, and then crashed through the wall, burying itself deep in the earth on the other side of it. Thor looked down on the cowering giant who had at once turned into stone. He set him up as a monument of his victory, and there the petrified monster remained for centuries, reminding succeeding generations of men of the great deeds done by Asathor.

This is said to be another of the natural myths which tell how the beneficent god of summer conquered the destructive tempest with his own weapons ; the two daughters are supposed to be personifications of the mountain torrents which caused rivers to overflow.

According to some, however, this legend, like the last one, describes a descent of the god into the Underworld, and there is also a similar one related by Saxo Grammaticus, of which Thorkill is the hero.

But we are of opinion that it is far more likely to have been in the volcanic island of Iceland that Thor was victorious over the demon. The island was known to the skalds, from the descriptions of bold sailors, long before its colonization by the Northmen. Tales of volcanic eruptions and hot springs must have excited the imagination of the poets extremely. Thus perhaps arose the myth of Thor's journey to Geiröds-gard, in which the god conquers the demon of subterranean fire. This view is supported by the shape of a rock near Haukadal, where, within a circle of 900 feet, are geysers and strocks. The rock is said to resemble a gigantic man cowering down, his body broken in the middle.

THE HARBARD LAY.

In this poem Odin acts the part of a ferryman, under the name of Harbard, refuses to row Thor, the god of agriculture, over the river, and sends him on his way with opprobrious words.

The reason was, that Odin was the god of the spirit and the warlike courage which animated the nobles and their retainers The proud warriors and skalds despised the peaceful peasantry who remained quietly at home, lived upon herrings and oatmeal porridge, and hated the devastation caused by war; while they, on the contrary, were continually fighting for wealth and glory, and hoped to rise to Odin's halls after death upon the field of battle.

This contempt for the tiller of the soil is clearly shown in the Lay, which makes the protector of agriculture play a very pitiful part. The myth had its rise in later times, when the old faith in the gods and deep reverence for them had already begun to decay.

The bold Wikings did not hesitate to say that they trusted more in their own good swords than in the help of Odin and Asathor. The Lay was perhaps composed at that time, but still, it rested on an older one, in which the myth of agriculture, of the apparent death of Fiörgyn or Jörd, mother of Thor, through the devastation caused by war, and of the renewed life of the Earth-goddess, were more clearly described.

IRMIN.

As we have before remarked, the Prince of the Ases was worshipped as one of the holy ones by the Teutonic race; it is probable that he was also adored under the name of Irmin, and that the different Irmin-columns were dedicated to him.   But Irmin means universal, and it was to the universal, omnipotent god that the Irmin-columns were erected.   It was he who helped the Teutons to victory in their battles against the Romans; for this reason the celebrated Irmin-column, which was destroyed nearly 800 years later by Charlemagne, was set up in his honour at Osning (in the Teutoburg Forest).   It also reminds us of the hero Armin, who was held in great reverence, and whose name and character were in process of time confounded with those of the god.

Irmin was also supposed to be identical with the mythical hero Iring, who, when the Franks and the Saxons were fighting against the Thuringians, traitorously slew his lord, Irminfried, and then killed the false-hearted ruler of the Franks.   After this he cut his way through the ranks of the enemy, sword in hand, and did many other heroic deeds.   If this hero was the same as Irmin, he was very different from Thor, whose nature in all the myths regarding him was always true-hearted, and never cunning. But the legend also makes out the traitor to have been different from the god, for, after their victory, the Saxons erected a pillar to Irmin, and not to the Thuringian Iring.

Irmin was the common god of many tribes, and some philologists derive the name " German " from him.   He was the guardian deity of the Thuringians, Katti, and Cherusci, and showered down his blessings upon them as he drove over the firmament of heaven in the Irmin-wain (Great Bear or Charles' Wain).   The Milky-way, Iring or Irmin-road, the way of souls, was also sacred to him, and thus he was the ruler of souls, and identical with Aryama, the national god of all the Aryan races in the oldest times.   The Kelts worshipped the same god under the names of Erimon and Erin, whence Ireland and the Irish are called after him.   The chariot in which he drove through the heavens showed

CHAINING OF THE FENRIS WOLF.

his relationship to Thor according to the oldest ideas; but still Odin, the Leader of souls, had much in common with him. Tyr, the ancient god of heaven, the sword-god, was, however, yet more nearly kin to him, because he was depicted in warlike array, and because the monuments of victory, the Irmin-columns, were called after him. Several places have also derived their names from him.

TYR OR ZIO.

Who is there, who, after a hard day's work, has not rejoiced to see the approach of quiet Mother Night, when, wrapped in her starry mantle, she brings back peace to the world which has been robbed of it by restless Day?

This feeling of peace has often been destroyed by a sound that has something mysterious and strange about it. It is only the long-drawn howl of a dog, a sound that is heard most frequently when the moon is shining brightly; but it has something grue-some in it, and this accounts for the popular belief that it betokens the death of the person who hears it.

A circumstance of this kind happened once upon a time within the holy precincts of Asgard.

Mani (the moon) was following Mother Night merrily in his chariot, when suddenly he started and his happy face became clouded, for out of a great abyss there arose a howling noise which quickly swelled to a dreadful roar, so that the whole earth trembled as after a peal of thunder.

The Ases were awakened by it, and the Einheriar snatched at their weapons, for they thought that Ragnarök had come. Amongst them stood Tyr, tall and slender as a pine, and unmoved by the terrors that they had expected.

" Fenris," he said, " has been wakened by the moon, and wants something to eat; I will go and feed him."

Then he set out in the night, laden with living and dead animals with which to appease the monster's rapacity. Once more the terrible roar was heard, then it seemed that the monster was quieted ; only the cracking and crunching of the bones of the animals he devoured could now be heard.

In the morning the Ases held council as to what was to be done ; for the Wolf was slinking about, casting greedy looks at Asgard, as though he were devising how to break into the castles of the gods and carry off the spoil. They saw how gigantic he had grown, and knew that he daily increased in size and strength.

Heimdal pointed at Thor's hammer, and at Gungnir, the death-spear, in Odin's hand ; but Allfather said gravely :

" The black blood of the monster may not soil the sacred courts of the gods. A chain must be made, so strong that it cannot be broken ; then let him be bound with it, that his rage may be held in check."

The word was spoken, the work must be done. The Ases forged the chain Leuthing as quickly as they could, and took it to the Lyngwi island, where the Wolf, enticed by Tyr, followed them willingly.

The Wolf peacefully allowed himself to be bound, for he knew his own strength. When he was fully chained, he twisted and stretched himself, and the iron-ropes broke in pieces like weak thread.

A second chain, called Droma, much stronger than the first, was made, and he bore it for a moment ; then he shook himself violently, and it fell clattering to the ground, broken to pieces.

The Ases stood round him silent and not knowing what to do, while Fenris increased his strength by devouring the food that had been thrown to him.

Wishfather now sent Skirnir, a young but wise and able servant of Freyer, to the Home of the Black-Elves, to get the Elves, who were versed in magic lore, and who lived in the bowels of the earth, to make fetters that should bind the Destroyer.

The underground people made a chain, small and slight as a silken thread, which they called Gleipnir. They said that it would grow stronger and stronger the more the prisoner strove to free himself from it.

Skirnir took the chain to the Ases. The All-Devourer resisted, and opened his mighty jaws threatening to swallow up all who tried to bind him; for he guessed that there was magic power concealed in the slight fetters.

Then brave Tyr came forward, petted and stroked the monster, and put his right hand into his jaws. Fenris thought this a sign that no evil was meant, so he allowed the slender chain to be bound around his neck and feet.

When this was done, he stretched himself violently, endeavouring to break his bonds, but they only became the stronger and cut into his skin and flesh. He had already bitten off Tyr's hand, and now he opened his blood-red jaws to seize the god himself and the other Ases too. But they feared the wild beast no longer; they thrust a sharp sword into his gaping mouth till the point penetrated the palate above and prevented him biting.

Then they fastened Gleipnir to two great rocks, that the Wolf might not get away. In vain the monster howled day and night while the blood ran down between his jaws and collected in the river Wan ; he could not break his bonds.

Thus is crime, which threatens to corrupt the human race, bound by the apparently slight fetters of law, and as the power of the Wolf was broken by the sword, that of crime is kept under by the awards of justice. When a people no longer heeds the law, and throws aside all civic order, crime frees itself from its fetters, and the nation rushes to its ruin as surely as Gleipnir would be broken in the Twilight of the Gods, as surely as the All-Devourer would become freed from his chains and from the sword.

Tyr was called Tius by the Goths, Tio or Zio by the Anglo-Saxons, and the same by the Suevi, a tribe of whom, the Jut-hungen, lived beside the Lake of Constance. They were called Ziowari (servants of Zio), because they regarded this god as their guardian deity; the name of their chief town was Ziesburg (now Augsburg). The rune that stands for it, and is called after the god, is the sign of the sword. It bears the names of Tius, Tio, in Old High-German Zio, and besides these, is known as Eor, Erch, Erich, and in old Saxon Er, Eru, Heru or Cheru. These different appellations were all borne by the god, whose worship was so wide-spread.

Moreover the religion of the Suevi acknowledged a goddess Zisu, as is proved from the fragment of a Latin chronicle. She had a temple in Augsburg, and was of a warlike nature ; she must there-fore have been the female representative of the god Zio or Tyr. This god was the expression in ancient times of the impression that nature as a whole made upon the minds of those who were influenced by her. He was without form, and originally without a a name. When the Romans first knew the Germanic race he had already become a personality and was endowed with attributes, for they compared him with their own Mars, and therefore recog-nised him to be the god of war. Thus he had lost his original signification.

Tyr or Tius, meant brightness, glory, then the shining firmament, and was derived from the same root as the Hindu Djaus, the Greek Zeus, and the Roman Jupiter (Diu-piter, Dies-pater). Rays of sunlight and forked lightning both come from the sky, and were typified in arrows and deadly missiles. In the middle ages arrows were still called rays in German. Hence an arrow became the attribute and also the symbol of the omnipotent god of

TYR, THE SWORD GOD.

heaven; in later times a sword took the place of the arrow as it was a stronger weapon in battle. This symbol remained to him in the rune and also in the groves which were dedicated to him. When his place was afterwards given to Wodan and Thor as the ruling gods of heaven, Tyr was looked upon as the god of battles, whose help must be entreated during the fight and whose rune of victory was scratched on the handles and blades of swords while ejaculating the name of the god.

Tyr was held in much less honour in the time of the skalds; he was then regarded as the son of Odin and the god of unnatural warfare that could never be appeased. Odin, the god of the mind, of martial courage and of poetic enthusiasm, had taken his place as the ideal of Kings and brave Jarls. Thor also, the god of the peasant, the benefactor of mankind, helped to force him into the background and gained some of the devotion Tyr had lost.

HERU OR CHERU, SAXNOT.

Nearly related to the warlike Tyr, perhaps identical with him, were Heru or Cheru and Saxnot. They were essentially German sword-gods, and were not known to the northern skalds. Their worship was wide-spread; for the Alanes, Quades, Getes and Markomanns paid divine honours to the sword, and even the Scythians, as Herodotus tells us, planted it in a high pyramidal heap of brush-wood, and called upon it as the symbol of the divinity. Many legends are still in existence about it, one of which we give as an example.

Cheru's sword was made in the mysterious smithy of the Dwarfs, whose artistic workmanship was celebrated among Ases and men. The sons of Iwaldi, who had made Odin's spear, and Sindri, who had forged Miölnir, had united their efforts in making the marvellous weapon on which the fate of kings and nations was to hang.

M

The zealous master-smiths worked busily within the earth, when Sökwabek was built under the flowing river, until at length the shining sword was completed, which Cheru the mighty god received.

This sword shone every morning on the high-place of the anctuary, sending forth its light afar when dawn arose, like a flame of fire; but one day its place was empty and the rosy light of morning only shone upon the altar from which the god had disappeared.

The priests and nobles sought the advice of the wise woman. This was the inscrutable answer they received.

"The Norns wandered on the ways of night; the moon had hidden his face; they laced the threads, strong and powerful, of gods and men, that none might break. One towards the east, the other towards the west, and one towards the south; the black thread towards the north. They spake to Cheru: ' Go, choose out the ruler, the lord of the earth; give him the two-edged sword to his own hurt.' He has it, he holds it in his hands; but yet Cheru the lord will bring it back after a time."

Startled at this dark oracle, the men begged for an explanation; but the maiden of the tower gave no reply. Meanwhile the story relates the course of events, and throws the only light that is given upon the riddle.

Vitellius, the Roman prefect of the Lower Rhine, was supping past midnight in his house at Cologne, for he liked the pleasures of the table better than all the glory and all the diadems in the world.

When he was told that a stranger, bearing important news from Germany, wanted to speak to him, he rose impatiently. He desired to get rid of him as soon as possible; but when he entered the anteroom, he found himself in the presence of a man of such distinguished appearance, that he could not treat him discourteously. He would have at once taken him for one of the Immortals, if his self-indulgent life had not long ago destroyed his faith in the religion of his ancestors.

The stranger gave him a sword of beautiful workmanship, and said :

"Take this weapon; keep it carefully and use it well, and it will bring thee glory and empire. All hail, Cæsar Augustus!"

The prefect examined the sword; when he looked up, the stranger was gone, and the guard had neither seen him come nor go. He returned to the supper-room and told what had happened. He drew the sword out of its sheath, and it was as though a flash of lightning passed through the room.

Immediately a voice exclaimed, but whether in the room or not, no one could say : "That is the sword of the divine Cæsar! All hail, Vitellius! All hail, Emperor!"

The guests at the supper-table joined in the cry and spread abroad the news; next morning the legions greeted Vitellius as Emperor. Messengers were despatched on horseback to the other provinces, and Fortune seemed to have chosen him as her favourite. His general conquered the army of his opponent, Rome opened her doors to him and the whole East acknowledged his sway.

"It was the sword of the divine Cæsar that made me master of the world," said the Emperor, as he seated himself at table to enjoy the delicacies which had been imported by land and water from distant countries. He ceased to care for the sword; he left it standing in a corner of the peristylium, where a Teutonic soldier of the body-guard found it and took it in exchange for his own clumsy old weapon.

The new possessor of the sword watched the conduct of the Emperor with displeasure, for Vitellius cared for nothing but the pleasures of eating and drinking; he paid no attention to the affairs of the Empire, or to the wants of the soldiers; he took no notice when far away in Asia brave Vespasian had been proclaimed Cæsar by his legions.

The German soldier left the Emperor's service and mixed himself with the idle populace. Meanwhile one misfortune after another befel the gluttonous Emperor. Provinces, generals, armies forsook him; the enemy's troops approached the capital; then Vitellius had recourse to the sword which had before brought him victory; but instead of it he found only an old and useless weapon.

Now all his courage forsook him; he wished to escape, and crept away to bury himself in a corner of the palace. The populace tore him from his hiding-place, dragged him through the streets, and when he reached the foot of the Capitol, the German soldier stabbed him to death with the sword of Cheru or of the divine Cæsar. In this manner was the prophecy of the wise woman fulfilled: "to his own hurt."

Afterwards the German soldier left Rome and went to Pannonia, where he re-entered the Roman service. He fought in many battles and was victorious in all, and soon became so famous that he was made centurion, and then tribune. When he grew old and was incapable of further service, he made a hole on the bank of the Danube, hid the good sword in it, and covered it up again with earth. Then he built himself a hut and lived there until his end. On his death-bed, he told the neighbours who had assembled round him, of his battles, and how he had got possession of the sword of Cheru; but he did not betray the place where he had hidden it, yet the saying that whoever should find the sword would become ruler of the world, remained current among the people from generation to generation.

Centuries came and went. The storm of the migration of races swept over the Roman empire; the Germanic races shared the spoil amongst them; the nomads of Asia, the wild Huns, made their way over from the East, like the waves of a sea, in order to have a share in the booty. Attila, or Etzel, raised his blood-besprinkled banner in the desire for land and military fame, but his efforts were fruitless for a long time.

As Attila was once riding with his troopers along the banks of the Danube, he busied himself with framing in his own mind gigantic plans of gaining for himself the empire of the world. He happened to look up and saw a peasant driving a lame cow and carrying a beautifully made sword under his arm. On being questioned, the man replied that his cow had hurt her foot against something sharp that was hidden in the grass, and that when he sought for the cause of the injury he found and dug up the sword.

The king desired that the sword should be brought to him, and drew it out of its sheath with joyful emotion; its bright blade shone fiery red in the evening light and all present stared at it in amazement.

But Attila, holding up the shining weapon in his strong hand, exclaimed :

" It is the sword of the war-god with which I shall conquer the world."

Having said this, he galloped away to the camp, and soon afterwards marched on to battles and victory. Whenever he drew the sword of the war-god the earth trembled from the east to the very west.

After his last campaign in Italy he married the beautiful Ildiko, daughter of the King of Burgundy whom he had slain. The youthful bride adorned herself unwillingly for the wedding she hated.

An old woman came to her secretly, and gave her the sword with which to revenge her father's death.

At length the king entered the bridal chamber in a state of in-toxication and threw himself upon his couch. Ildiko now drew the weapon from under her dress and stabbed him to the heart with its sharp blade.

The rule of the Huns came to an end with the death of Attila, and the Germanic races chased these hordes back to the steppes whence they came ; but tradition does not inform us whether these later deeds of war were done with the help of the miraculous sword. Yet it tells us of many strange things performed by means of it in the middle ages, and of how Duke Alba buried it in the earth after the battle of Mühlberg.

HEIMDAL (RIGER).

Once upon a time, when there was peace in the worlds, Riger arose and set out to visit his children of men, to see how they lived and what they did.

He walked along the green road, and arrived at last at a badly built house with a low roof. On the wooden bench beside the hearth were seated a man and his wife.

Ai and Edda (great-grandfather and great-grandmother) were their names, and they were very poorly clad. Riger addressed them kindly, seated himself between them, and ate with them of their coarse bran cakes, and their porridge in earthenware dishes.

The Ase remained in the cottage for three days and three nights, giving good counsel to them, and then went on from the sea-sand to the better ground for cultivation.

Nine moons after his departure a little boy was born to Ai and Edda, whose skin was of a dark colour and whose forehead was low. His parents called the lad Thrali. He grew and flourished, and soon learnt to use his strength. He tied up bundles with his muscular arms, and carried heavy weights upon his back all day long.

When he had grown to man's estate, he married a girl with black feet and sunburnt hands, called Thyr, who worked with the great- est diligence. From them are descended the race of Thralls.

Meanwhile Riger pursued his journey. He came to a roomy, well-built house in the middle of a cultivated field. There he found Afi and Amma (grandfather and grandmother) neatly dressed and working busily. The husband was making a loom, and the wife was spinning snowy linen thread on her wheel. A pot of good food was bubbling on the fire. Amma soon filled the plates, and at the same time gave her guest a cup of foaming beer as was the custom of the free-born farmer. Riger gave them much good advice regarding the management of house and land ; and after remaining with them for three days and three nights, he set out again along the road which ran through shady groves and across green meadows.

Nine moons passed, and then came a happy time, for a little boy was born to the great delight of his parents. He was called Karl (lad), and grew and flourished ; rosy were his cheeks, and bright and clear his eyes.

The boy soon learnt to drive the plough, to yoke the oxen and make carts in the same way as his father. In course of time he married Snör (cord), who was rich in keys and wore finely-woven dresses ; and he brought her home to his new house. Sons and daughters were born of this marriage ; all grew up active, merry, and free, and dwelt upon their own land.

Meanwhile Riger walked on through beautiful fields and bloom- ing gardens up to the manor house on the top of a sloping hill. The door with its shining handle was not locked, so he entered the richly furnished hall. The floors were carpeted, and the father and mother were sitting on cushions, dressed in silken garments and playing with delicate toys.

Then the master of the house tried his bow, made arrows and whetted his sword, while his wife came out to watch him in a blue·

dress with a long train, and with a kerchief crossed over her white neck and shoulders.

Riger seated himself between them. He knew how to advise them for the glory and weal of their house.

Afterwards the lady spread the table with a beflowered linen cloth; she brought in well-cooked dishes of game and poultry, and filled the golden beakers and jugs with sparkling wine. They drank and talked till night-fall, and then Riger was shown his comfortable bed.

He remained with his hosts for three days and three nights, and then went away to continue his journey.

Nine moons passed, and a son was born in the manor house, fair-haired, with beautiful rosy cheeks and eyes like shining stars.

He was called Jarl; he grew and flourished, learnt to draw the sword, to throw the spear, to bend the bow, to carry the shield, to ride the horse, and to swim across the Sound. The boy learnt even more than this as he grew older, for Riger came to him out of the dark grove, and taught him to understand the runes, inspiring him at the same time to do deeds which should bring him and his house honour and glory.

Then Jarl went out to battle, conquered the enemy, and won for himself renown and booty, castles and land, rewarding his companions in arms generously with golden clasps and rings.

He became a great ruler, but still he felt sad and lonely in his luxurious hall. So he sent messengers to ask for the hand of Lady Erna, the slender-waisted. His offer was accepted, and the noble maiden entered his shining halls where the Earl received her with joy. They grew to love each other and lived together to a good old age.

Sons and daughters came of this marriage, and increased the number of the Jarls. The youngest son, Konur, understood the runes, both of the present and the future, and also the language of birds. Besides this, he was a mighty warrior, and afterwards became the first King of Denmark. This is what the " Rigsmal," a poem of the Edda, teaches us of the beginning of class distinctions.

When Riger (or Heimdal) had finished his labours he mounted his horse, Gulltop (golden-mane), and rode home to Himinbiörg to fulfil his duty as watchman.

He drank sweet mead late each night, for all things in Asgard and without it were sunk in sleep. At midnight he once heard a noise of footsteps, but so faint was the sound that no ear but his could have heard it. It came from Folkwang, where Freya, the goddess of love and beauty, dwelt.

Heimdal cast a penetrating glance in the direction whence the sound came, and saw the sleeping goddess resting upon her couch. She was lying on her side, one arm resting upon her shining necklace, Brisingamen. Loki was standing beside her bed gazing covetously at the ornament. He seemed in doubt as to how he could get possession of it. He murmured magic spells, and lo! he grew visibly smaller and smaller. At last he became a tiny little creature, with bristles and a sharp set of teeth, a creature that thirsts for blood and attacks both gods and men ; in the form of a flea he jumped upon the bed, and slipped beneath the sheets ; he stung the sleeping goddess in the side so that she turned. The necklace was now free, and the cunning Ase, regaining his natural form, untied the ribbon that fastened it round her neck, and made off with it.

The faithful watchman on the heavenly tower was very wroth with the night-thief. He drew his sharp sword, and, as he had his seven-league boots on, came up with him in a few strides. He struck out at the robber, but his sword only went through a pillar of fire that towered up into the sky in which Loki's form had disappeared.

In a moment Heimdal rose in the shape of a cloud, from which such a torrent of rain descended that it threatened to extinguish the fire.

Loki immediately changed himself into a polar bear, that opened its mouth and drank up the rain. Before he could escape he was attacked by Heimdal as a still larger bear.

Loki fled from the deadly embrace in the form of a seal, but his flight was useless, for he was caught by another larger seal.

The two creatures fought furiously; they bit and scratched each other till the waters were stained with their blood. After a long and fierce struggle, Heimdal was victorious, and Loki slipped out of his torn and mangled seal's skin; but when Heimdal whirled his sword round his head, he begged for mercy and gave up the necklace to his opponent.

Heimdal stood leaning on his sword and holding Brisingamen in his left hand, rejoicing in his victory in spite of the pain his wounds caused him. But Iduna, Bragi's lovely wife, came to him and gave him an apple of eternal youth. As soon as he had tasted it, his wounds were healed and he ceased to suffer pain. He bade the goddess take the necklace back to Freya.

Then he returned to Himinbiörg, mounted his good horse Gulltop and rode down Iring's road, which men now call the Milky Way; immediately the black storm-clouds vanished and the shining stars lighted up the expanse of heaven in the same way that Brisingamen did Asgard's halls, until day came and called up gods and men to their work. For Heimdal is the same as Heimdellinger for Heimdäglinger, he who brought day to the home of the world. His name Riger shows that he was also related to the German Erich, Erk, Heru or Cheru, the sword-god, and consequently to Tyr or Zio. The Edda calls him the Sword-Ase, and makes him wander on the green ways of earth, as Iring did on the Milky Way, which was called after him. Certain roads bore the same name, such as those which ran through England from south to north, and the Irmin-streets in Germany that led to and from the Irmin-columns; thus Riger resembled the universal god, the giver of victory.

Riger's wanderings reminds us of Örwandil, whom Thor carried through the ice-streams Eliwagar. He was identical with the mythical hero Orendel, a son of King Eigel of Treves, whose travels and adventures on every sea have much resemblance to those of Odysseus. It is very doubtful whether these stories were known to the Teutons at the time of Tacitus, as this author mentions that the Hellenic hero had been in Germany, and had founded the town of Asciburgum (Ase-burg). It was rather to the poets of the middle ages that dark rumours of the Odyssee came.

Heimdal was born of nine mothers (the wave-maidens), whose names are taken from waves and cliffs; he was nursed and strengthened by Mother Earth, the cold sea and the rays of the sun; hence he appears as a god of heaven, raised aloft by the waves of the sea, which afterwards fall to the earth as fruitful rain or dew. This was his position in the natural myth. The skalds made him out to be the watchman of Asgard, to whom wa entrusted the care of Bifröst, the rainbow-bridge, that all attack of the giants might be prevented.

BRAGI AND HEIMDAL RECEIVING THE WARRIORS IN WALHALLA.

BRAGI AND IDUNA.

In the beginning the silence of death rested upon the immeasurable ocean, not a breath of wind stirred the air, not a wave rose on the surface of the deep; everything was motionless, dumb, without breath or life.

A vessel, the ship of the Dwarfs, crossed the silent waste of water. Bragi, the divine singer, was lying on the deck asleep, sunk in the dream of life; he was without spot or blemish, and his golden-stringed harp lay at his side. When the vessel glided over the threshold of Nain, the Dwarf of Death, the god awoke, touched the strings of his harp and sang a song that echoed throughout the nine worlds, describing the rapture of existence, the rage of battle and the charm of victory, and the joy and happiness of love. This song wakened dumb nature out of her trance.

Whether the god of poetry were the son of Odin or not, we cannot tell ; the skalds do not inform us. But poetry cannot die, it always rises out of death to a new life and rejoices the hearts of both gods and men.

Bragi landed on the shore, singing his noble song about the awakening of nature and the blossoming of new life ; and he wandered through the growing, budding woods as he sang. Then Iduna rose before him from amongst the grasses, flowers and foliage, the goddess of immortal youth, the youngest daughter of Iwaldi, the Dwarf, who hid life in the deep and afterwards sent it again to the upper world when the right time had come.

Iduna was beautiful in her crown of flowers and leaves ; she was beautiful as the dawn. When the god saw her, his song of love became more glowing and intense. He stretched out his arms and she sank upon his breast, for the poet must needs marry youth and beauty.

After they were united, they went to the blessed ever-green heights of Asgard, where the Ases received them with joy. Then Iduna gave them to eat of the apple of ever-renewed youth.

When the gods and Einheriar had eaten their fill of the flesh of Sährimnir, Bragi touched the strings of his harp and sang the praises of the heroes. But this pleasant life in Asgard, and the married happiness of the divine poet, were once broken by a severe trial, as we shall presently see.

Odin, Hönir and Loki were travelling about the world together to see what were the joys and sorrows, works and labours of the dwellers upon earth. They went a long way, and at length came to a densely wooded mountain where there was nothing to eat. They could find no hospitable house in which to take shelter; could hear no friendly voice calling to them. The autumn wind was blowing the tops of the oaks and firs.

When they reached the valley, they saw a herd of cattle grazing in the meadow. They caught one of the animals and slaughtered it; they cut it up and prepared to cook it for their supper. The fire, kindled by Loki, blazed up, and they thought the beef would soon be cooked. But when they looked to see, it was still quite raw. This happened a second and a third time; the Ases were astonished and wondered what to do.

Suddenly they heard a voice above them saying that he who prevented the beef from cooking was sitting above them in a branch of the tree. On looking up they saw a gigantic eagle through the leaves of the oak, busily engaged in trying to put out the fire by flapping his wings. He promised to allow them to cook their supper if they would give him some of it. When they had agreed to do so, he flew down, fanned the fire, and very soon supper was ready.

They all sat down together, but the eagle ate so quickly that it seemed as though he would devour the whole bullock. Loki was dreadfully hungry, and getting into a rage, snatched up a stake and stabbed at the gigantic bird with it. The eagle flew up into the air when he felt the blow. The stake had fastened itself to the feathers of the bird and Loki's hands were glued to the other end.

The eagle flew so low that Loki's feet dragged along the ground and hit against any stones and stumps that might be in the way, while his arms felt as if they were dislocated. He shrieked and groaned and begged for mercy of the Storm-giant, who, as he well knew, was hidden under the eagle's dress.

"Very well," said the giant, "I will set thee free if thou wilt promise to bring me Iduna and her golden apples."

Loki swore to do so, and, as soon as he was set free, limped back to his companions. Under the circumstances the travellers determined to go home, and they must have been provided with seven-league boots, for they arrived at Asgard on the following day.

Beautiful Iduna was going about her household duties, dressed in green and wearing a garland of leaves, the crown of unfading youth. Bragi was away from home journeying as a minstrel. She collected her apples, which she usually gave the Ases at breakfast time.

At this moment Loki came up to her quickly, and looking round to see that no one was near, whispered :

"Gentle and lovely goddess, follow me quickly out of the castle gate, for I have discovered a strange tree covered with golden fruit like thine."

This was a request the goddess could not decline. She put some of her apples in a crystal dish and followed the traitor through Asgard, and on into the dark wood.

All at once the Storm-wind roared through the trees ; and Thiassi, the giant in the eagle's dress, rushed up, caught the terrified goddess in his talons, and flew with her to dreary wintry Thrymheim, where spring flowers cannot bloom, not yet can youth survive.

Loki slunk back to Asgard, and quietly kept his secret about Iduna to himself. "The longer hence they notice it, the better," he cunningly thought to himself.

The Ases for a long time did not know that Iduna had been stolen ; they thought she had gone away on a journey. But when days and weeks had passed their hair began to turn grey, the colour left their cheeks and their faces showed the folds and wrinkles of age. The goddesses, even Freya herself, discovered signs of approaching old age, when they looked at their faces in the mirror of a clear stream.

They all asked for Iduna and sought her high and low. The last time she was seen, she was walking with Loki. The cunning Ase was questioned; his lies did not help him; Thor threatened to break all his limbs, and raised his hammer for the purpose: then Loki confessed, and promised to bring back the giver of youth, if Freya would lend him her falcon-dress.

The request was granted, and he flew away at once to Thrymheim, the dwelling of the Storm-giant Thiassi.

The giant was at sea, and Iduna was sitting lonely and sad in an uncomfortable room, made of roughly hewn logs. Loki told her to be of good courage and changed her into a nut.

Then he flew over rocks and chasms with his light burden towards Asenheim.

Meanwhile the giant came home from his sea voyage. He had always hitherto begged his prisoner in vain to give him a slice of the apple of youth, that his horrible deformity might be transformed into the beauty of youth. As soon as he discovered Iduna's flight, he put on his eagle's dress and rushed after the fugitives with the speed of the storm.

The Ases watched the wild chase anxiously. They collected shavings and bits of wood before the fortress, and when the falcon had reached the shelter of the wall with his charge, they set fire to the wood, and the flames towered up into the air, singeing the wings of the pursuing eagle and bringing him to the ground.

Thiassi was then slain, but Thor threw his eyes up into the heavens where they shone henceforth as stars every night.

On his return, Bragi found his wife at home and heard from her all that had happened. He saw how Skadi, daughter of the Storm-giant, appeared in helmet and chain armour to avenge her father's death. And he afterwards told the whole story, ending with how Ögir, the god of the sea, had made expiation to the warlike maiden.

It is interesting to see how the genius of Odin's skalds united the god of poetry in marriage with the goddess of spring, the giver of renewed youth, and interwove the changes of the seasons into the myth. Bragi, who came out of the unknown distance, awoke mental life and also nature out of their trances; Iduna, who brought spring and youth into the world, became his wife. She gave the Ases the golden fruit of renewed youth, a fruit which was perhaps identical with the golden fruit that the Grecian hero Herakles carried away from the Hesperides.

In the same way as the autumn winds tear the leaves from the trees, the Storm-giant stole Iduna, and as the green meadows are covered with ice and snow in winter, so Iduna had to spend some time in the giant's uncomfortable house, while the gods themselves grew old and their hair turned grey.

Then Loki, probably the south wind, had to go and set Iduna free. The Storm-giant had gone on a voyage to the north, where his power lasted until the coming of spring. So the imprisoned spring was delivered from its bonds, and when the giant made his way into Asgard he was slain; *i.e.*, the storms of winter were confined within certain bounds.

ULLER.

Uller appears in the Edda as the cheery and sturdy god of winter, who, caring nothing for wind or snowstorm, used to go out on long journeys on his skates or snow-shoes.

Whenever he reached a lake or fiord which was not frozen, he transformed his shoes into a boat, and, making the winds and waves obey him, passed over to the other side.

Snow-shoes, as they are still worn in Norway and Iceland, are light shoes, very large and shaped like a boat turning up at the ends. With their help it is easy to slide quickly down hill, and

N

they may have been the shoes alluded to in the stories of Uller; still, skates were also used at that time to glide over the frozen lakes. These shoes were also compared with a shield; thus the shield is called Uller's ship in several places.

When the god skated over the ice, he always carried with him his shield, deadly arrows, and bow made of the yew-tree. The pliable wood of the yew was the most suitable for making bows for use either in hunting or in war. Uller, therefore, lived in the palace Ydalir, the yew-vale.

As he protected plants and seeds from the severe attacks of the frosts of the north by covering the ground with a coating of snow, he was regarded as the benefactor of mortal men, and was called the friend of Baldur, the giver of every blessing and joy.

Once when out hunting, Uller saw beautiful Skadi, the bold huntress, of whom we shall have more to tell further on. He fell in love with her, and as she was by this time separated from her first husband, Niörder, she willingly consented to marry him. At the wedding the storms all played dance music in every tune, for the time when the day and night were of equal length in autumn was past, and winter, the happiest time for marriage, had begun.

Vulder with the Anglo-Saxons meant divine glory, or even God himself, and it seems that the Northern god Uller was thus characterised in heathen times. This was perhaps a consequence of the glory of the Northern winter night, which is often brilliantly lighted by the snow, the dazzling ice, and the Aurora borealis, the great Northern Light.

ULLER, THE BOWMAN.

PART SIXTH.

THE WANES.

DISUNION had shown itself amongst the gods, as on earth amongst men, for the sake of power and gold. The Wanes came up against Asgard in numbers like the stars of heaven, and crowded over the broken wall into the holy precincts.

The Ases had no Einheriar to help them as yet, for this was the first war which was to decide the government of the world. Spears hurtled through the air, swords rattled against helmets and coats-of-mail. The fallen warriors felt the pang of their wounds, but not the agony of death, for the wounds soon closed again, and they stood up anew to do battle with the foe.

Weapons did not suffice ; the warriors broke off pieces of rock and the tops of mountains, tore pines and oaks up by their roots and flung them at each other. Thunder rolled ; the sun hid its face ; universal destruction threatened to overwhelm the world, and the Jotuns looked on at the battle with delight, holding themselves ready to fall upon both victor and vanquished, and complete the work of destruction.

Then Allfather appeared, mighty and glorious, wearing his golden helmet, and swinging the spear of death, and commanded that there should be a truce.

The fiery warriors obeyed his behest ; they bowed their stubboi n heads, and lowered their uplifted weapons, as they listened to the words of the King : " Let there be peace henceforth in heaven and upon earth, and let a treaty be made between the divine Powers, that neither may in future interfere with the province of the other, but that each race of gods may do its utmost for the weal and happiness of mortal men, who offer sacrifices and gifts as be seems them."

In this way a Milton would probably have described the conclusion of the battle of the gods ; but the Edda, in addition to this, relates how the Ases and Wanes each gave hostages to the other in token of good faith.

Hönir, Odin's brother, who had in the olden time given man mind and senses, was sent to the Wanes, who in their turn made over to the Ases Niörder, the unspotted Prince of men, with his children Freyer and Freya, who were held in equal reverence with himself.

The wise Mimir accompanied Hönir to Wanaheim. But the Wanes slew him and sent his head to the Ases. Odin, however, restored it to life with his magic runes, that it might always confer with him about the Past and the riddles of the Future, as in the old time when after pledging his eye to Mimir he was permitted to drink of the fountain of wisdom. He did not return evil with evil, but included Niörder and his children amongst the ranks of the Ases, so that they lived in honour whilst the rest of their race were almost entirely forgotten.

The Wanes, of whose worship but few and uncertain traces remain in German traditions, are supposed to have been the gods of feeling and of the senses. Professor Simrock has shown that very probably that they were not essentially different from the Ases, but that they were worshipped by other tribes than the Ases, presumably by those of the Suevi, who were dwellers by the sea, for the Aestyer and especially the Suiones, Suevian tribes, principally adored Freyer, Freya, and Niörder. It is also supposed that they may have been the gods of tribes which had been forced back and partially subjected to the conqueror, who at length threw off the yoke of the victor and in renewed battle broke down part of the fortifications of Asgard, but afterwards came to reasonable terms with the enemy. This uncertain hypothesis would quite, explain the war with the Wanes, and show it to have been a war of races.

Some writers explain the Wanes to have been the priestly class and the war to have been a struggle between ecclesiastical and temporal power, such as raged between Pope and Kaiser all through the middle ages, and which is perhaps not even yet at an end. This cannot be called an altogether unjustifiable hypothesis, for in the Edda we find many references to the wise Wanes, and wisdom could not well be an attribute of the gods of sensuous impulse, whilst it might quite easily be found amongst the priests. So much only is certain, however, that with the exception of the three Wanes received into Asenheim, no other gods of that race take part in any of the mythical occurrences. It was not supposed that Wanaheim would disappear in the universal destruction of nature; for when the world was to be renewed, Hönir would be allowed to choose whether he would enter the blessed Gimil, or remain in Wanaheim.

NIÖRDER AND SKADI.

The Prince of men, as Niörder was called, was, according to tradition, tall and stately and of matchless beauty. He was as famous for his wisdom and goodness as for his wealth. Therefore he listened to those who prayed him to bless their labours, especially attending to those who were engaged in seafaring and mercantile pursuits.

He lived at Noatun (seaport), where he delighted to hear the dash of the waves and the song of swans. The swan, which only sings when it is dying, was looked upon as the bird of the Underworld divinities. Hence Niörder seems to have had some connection with them. Moreover, he was regarded as the ruler of the calm, peaceful ocean. When wild Ögir excited the sea to rise foaming and dashing against the ships, threatening to engulf them, Niörder calmed its fury with magic spells, and sent a favourable wind to the assistance of the mariners. He did not wear Ögir's helmet, of which all living creatures were afraid, but a hat trimmed with shells, above which waved a heron's plume. A sea-green tunic clothed his slender figure, leaving the lower part of his well-formed legs uncovered. To this circumstance he owed his marriage to his second wife, beautiful Skadi. His residence in Asenheim had separated him from his first wife Nerthus, Mother Earth, who was also his sister, and he therefore lived unmarried in remote Noatun, until he was wed to Skadi.

Then, as we have already told, gentle Iduna was stolen away, was set free by Loki, and the storm-giant Thiassi was slain by the Ases.

After this, Skadi, the giant's warlike daughter, armed herself in her native Thrymheim with helmet and chain-mail, with spear and deadly arrows, and appeared before Asgard demanding vengeance. She looked gloriously beautiful in her shining armour, and the Ases did not wish to fight with the noble maiden, whose wrath seemed just in their eyes. They offered her expiation for her father's death, but she would not listen to their friendly words; she raised her spear to hurl it at one of those who had been accomplice in his death.

Then cunning Loki came forward, bowed low before her, and sprang now to the right hand, now to the left, and then danced backwards and forwards, while a long-horned, long-bearded goat made the same movements behind him, for he had fastened the creature to himself with an invisible cord. When at length he threw himself on his knees before her like a lover, and the goat, bleating mournfully, followed his example, Skadi burst into a fit of laughter. Her anger passed away, and she allowed herself to listen to terms.

Meanwhile it had grown dark, and Odin said, as he pointed to the sky,—

" Look, there are thy father's eyes which I have placed in the firmament of heaven that they may henceforth look down upon thee as stars. As for thee, thou shalt become one of us, and shalt choose thyself a husband from amongst us, but thine eyes must be so covered with a veil that thou mayest only see the feet of the assembled gods."

She gazed about her in astonishment, and as she did so, her eyes fell upon Baldur, who stood before her in his divine beauty, for he shone amongst the Ases like the morning star amongst the paling stars of night. She hoped to recognise him even if she only saw the hem of his garment. Her eyes were then partially bandaged, and the gods formed a circle round her. She looked around her on the ground, and perceived amongst them a foot of remarkable beauty.

"I choose thee," she said, "thou art Baldur."

She tore the bandage from her eyes, and—it was not Baldur, it was Niörder whom she had chosen ; and he was slender, stately, gentle and pleasant to look upon.

The word was spoken ; the choice was made ; the marriage was solemnized with much pomp. The great huntress found her life with her husband in heavenly Asgard a very happy one. The golden wood Glasir was full of melody as she walked through it ; the Einheriar rose from their seats when she entered Walhalla ; the goddesses gave her ornaments to wear, and the Ases delighted in doing her honour.   Thus the honeymoon passed, and then she followed her husband to Noatun, his castle by the sea.

She liked the life she led there at first, but soon she began to long for her native Thrymheim, for the sounds of the forests, in which she had been accustomed to hunt, and the frozen meres on which she used to skate.

She hated to hear the beat of the waves upon the shore, the groans and barking of the seals, and to see the fish leap ; while the hoarse cries of the gulls often wakened her out of her sleep. She could bear it no longer, and told her husband she must either go back to Thrymheim or she must die.

Niörder listened to her kindly, and proposed that he should spend nine nights with her at Thrymheim, and that she should then live three nights with him at Noatun, and so on until Ragnarök should come.   She gladly consented, and this plan of life was kept up for some time to the satisfaction of both.

But in course of time Niörder himself grew weary of Thrymheim.   The howling of the wolves, the bellowing of the buffaloes, and the growling of the bears were as hateful to him as the noises of the sea-side were to his wife.   They therefore had themselves set free from the marriage tie, and each dwelt in his and her own land.

Niörder was patron of the fisheries, and also of ships and trade. Skadi continued to hunt as before, and ruled with her bow and arrows over the beasts and birds that lived in the forest.   Some time after her separation from Niörder, she married wintry Uller, who was much better suited to her in character.

Simrock rightly maintains with regard to the origin and interpretation of this myth, that Niörder was a beneficent summer-god, who helped the harvest to ripen, and was the giver of material well-being, who taught men how to cultivate the vine and other kinds of husbandry.   He was perhaps the masculine counterpart

NIÓRDER AND SKADI ON THEIR WAY TO NOATUN.

of the Earth-goddess Nerthus, who, probably, was both his wife and his sister in Wanaland. As he was also interested in commercial undertakings and voyages, the Edda shows him to have been essentially the ruler of the sea and peace-maker with the storms. Skadi, too, was connected with the Earth-goddess, but only in her wintry dress.

Winter, regarded in its pleasantest aspect, gained a form and personality in the consciousness of the people ; and so beautiful Skadi appeared in the songs of the skalds. This myth is a creation of Norse genius, not of that of any particular poets. It proves that in these poems, the Giants, Ases and Wanes were not inimical Powers diametrically opposed to one another, but that they could at one time live on friendly and intimate terms together.

FREYER OR FRO.

The Edda informs us that Freyer was the son of Niörder. He and his sister Freya left Wanaland with their father, and were received amongst the number of the Ases.

It appears, however, that he was known in still older times than that, having been held in great reverence as the sun-god by the Scandinavians, and probably by the Southern Germans also ; as such he made the fields fruitful, blessed households and marriage and family life.

We learn in the Edda, as has been already related, that immediately before the wager between Loki and the dwarf Brock, Freyer received the ship Skidbladnir, which could sail in any wished-for direction, and which, when no longer wanted, could be folded up and put in the pocket. And then he was given the boar Gullinbursti, one of the three works of art made by Sindri, brother of Brock ; this boar drew the god's chariot, and was at times ridden by him ; it would bear him through woods and over meadows, its golden bristles rendering the darkest night as light as day.

In the ship we recognise the clouds, which always have a favourable wind when they scurry across the sky, and in the boar we see the sun's golden light. Blodhughofi, a horse swift as the wind, was at his command whenever he rode to join the council of the Ases.

Yule-tide, which was sacred to this god, takes its name from the wheel of the sun, for *jul* or *giuli,* means wheel (hveohl). This festival, for which the sun-god awakes and lights up his wheel once more, was kept by all the Teutonic races. The special dish that appeared at these feasts was a boar's head, such as is still seen on the dinner tables at Christmas time in the University of Oxford.

To Freyer was awarded the Home of the Light-Elves by the gods as a 'fit gift on his cutting his first tooth, for the god of sunshine and fruitful harvests must necessarily rule over the kingdom of the Light-Elves.

According to one legend, Freyer once took a human form, and ruled over Sweden under the name of Fiölnir. At the invitation of King Frodi, he went to Hledra (Zealand), to take part in a great feast prepared in his honour. When there, he fell into an enormous butt of mead, and was drowned, in like manner as the sun-god sinks every evening into the rosy waves of the sea.

He appeared amongst the Danes as Fridleif (peace-giver), the son or grandson of Hadding, and governed the people with a strong hand. In vain he sent messengers to ask for the hand of fair Freygerda, King Amund's daughter. As Amund received his offer with scorn, Fridleif organized an expedition to force him to consent to the marriage.

One evening as the lover sat thinking beside a pond in a wood, he heard the swans singing to the murmuring waters :

> " Heartless the robber has stolen thy lover :
> Tarry not, hasten the giant to slay

Lurking in caverns his treasure to cover ;
Gerda is mourning thy weary delay."

Scarcely was the song ended, when Fridleif perceived a giant taller than the highest tree preparing to throw his stone club at him.

The battle immediately began ; and Fridleif first hewed off one of the monster's legs, and then, when he had fallen to the ground, his three heads.

The victor found Freygerda and a great treasure of gold hidden away in the cave the Jotun had inhabited.

Soon afterwards Fridleif married the princess, and on his way home the hero succeeded in killing a terrible dragon, in whose cavern he discovered a still greater hoard of gold.

A son was born of this marriage named Frodi. He succeeded his father on the Danish throne, and bestowed blessings upon his people, such as only a god can give to mortal man.

So great was the public safety in his reign that the king had golden chains and jewels kept day and night in the open air, and no one dared to touch them. The traveller then always found a hearty welcome throughout the kingdom, for there was no lack of food in the country : the fields bore double harvests, and the king was ever willing to relieve want wherever his help was needed. This peaceful state was accounted by all as the greatest of blessings, and in honour of Frodi was ever afterwards called the Peace of Frodi. The king felt very happy, whether drinking sweet mead upon his high throne in the hall of his fathers, or making inroads upon the neighbouring tribes, followed by his retainers.

* Among his treasures were two quern stones ; nothing much to look at, simply two common mill stones in appearance, and no

* The following legend is quoted from the charming book, entitled, " Wonderful Stories from Northern Lands," by Julia Goddard (London : Longmans, 1871).

one who did not know what they could do would think of taking any notice of them. Nevertheless, these quern stones were of more worth than anything that King Frodi had, for they could produce anything that the grinder of the quern or handmill wished for. They would bring gold, silver, precious stones, anything and everything; and besides this they could grind love, joy, peace; therefore it is not too much to say that these stones were worth more than all the treasures of the king put together.

At least they would have been if he could have made use of them, but they were so heavy that few could be found to turn the quern, and just at the time of which I am speaking there was no one at all in the land of Gotland able to work away at the quern handle.

Now the more King Frodi pondered over his wonderful quern stones, the greater became his desire to use them, and he sought throughout the land from north to south, from east to west, if perchance he might find some one strong enough to help him in his need. But all to no purpose, and he was utterly in despair when, by good luck, he happened to go on a visit to the King of Sweden, and to hear of two slave-women of great size and strength. "Surely," thought Frodi, "these are just the women to grind at my quern Grotti" (for so it was called), and he asked the king to be allowed to see them.

So the king ordered the slaves to be brought before Frodi, and when Frodi saw them his spirits rose, for certainly Menia and Fenia were strong-looking women. They were eight feet in height, and broader across the shoulders than any of Frodi's warriors, and the muscles of their arms stood out like cords. And they lifted heavy weights, threw heavy javelins, and did so many feats of strength that Frodi felt quite sure that they would be able to turn the quern handle.

"I will buy these slaves," said he, "and take them with me to Gotland."

Menia and Fenia stood with their arms folded and their proud heads bowed down, whilst Frodi counted out the gold to the seller. They were slaves; with money had they been bought, with money were they sold again. What cared Frodi who was their father, or how they had come into the land of Sweden?

And he took them home with him and bade them grind at the quern. Now he should be able to test the power of the wonderful stones.

"Grind, grind, Menia and Fenia, let me see whether ye have strength for the work."

So spake King Frodi, and the huge women lifted the heavy stones as though they had been pebbles.

"What shall we grind?" asked the slaves.

"Gold, gold, peace and wealth for Frodi."

Gold! gold! the land was filled with riches. Treasure in the king's palace, treasure in the coffers of his subjects—gold! gold! There were no poor in the land, no beggars in the streets, no children crying for bread. All honour to the quern stones!

Peace! peace! no more war in the land, Frodi is at peace with every one. And more than that, there was peace in all countries where Frodi's name was known, even to the far south; and every-one talked of Frodi's Peace. Praise be to the quern stones!

Wealth! yes, everything went well. Not one of the counsels of King Frodi failed. There was not a green field that did not yield a rich crop; not a tree but bent beneath its weight of fruit; not a stream that ran dry; not a vessel that sailed from the harbours of Gotland that came not back, after a fair voyage, in safety to its haven. There was good luck everywhere.

"Grind on, grind on, Menia and Fenia! good fortune is mine," said King Frodi.

And the slaves ground on.

o

"When shall we rest, when may we rest, King Frodi? It is weary work toiling day and night."

" No longer than whilst the cuckoo is silent in the spring."

" Never ceasing is the cry of the cuckoo in the groves ; may we not rest longer ? "

" Not longer," answered King Frodi, "than whilst the verse of a song is sung."

"That is but little!" sighed Menia and Fenia, and they toiled on. Their arms were weary, and their eyes heavy, they would fain have slept ; but Frodi would not let them have any sleep. They were but slaves who must obey their master, so they toiled on, still grinding peace and wealth to Frodi—

> "To Frodi and his queen
>   Joy and peace—
> May plenty in the land
>   Still increase,
> Frodi and his queen
>   From dangers keep ;
> May they on beds of down
>   Sweetly sleep.
> No sword be drawn
>   In Gotland old,
> By murderer bold.
>   No harm befall
> The high or low—
>   To none be woe,
> Good luck to all.
>   Good luck to all,
> We grind, we grind
>   No rest we find,
>   For rest we call."

Thus sang the two giant women ; then they begged again, " Give us rest, O Frodi !"

But still Frodi answered, " Rest whilst the verse of a song is sung, or as long as the cuckoo is silent in the spring."

No longer would the king give them.

Yet Frodi was deemed a good king, but gold and good luck were hardening his heart.

Menia and Fenia went on grinding and their wrath grew deeper and deeper, and thus at last they spoke.

First said Fenia, " Thou wert not wise, O Frodi. Thou didst buy us because like giants we towered above the other slaves because we were strong and hardy and could lift heavy burdens."

And Menia took up the wail : " Are we not of the race of the mountain giants ? Are not our kindred greater than thine, O Frodi ? The quern had never left the grey fell but for the giants' daughters. Never, never should we have ground as we have done, had it not been that we remembered from what race we sprang."

Then answered Menia : " Nine long winters saw us training to feats of strength, nine long winters of wearisome labour. Deep down in the earth we toiled and toiled until we could move the high mountain from its foundations. We are weird women, O Frodi. We can see far into the future. Our eyes have looked upon the quern before. In the giants' house we whirled it until the earth shook, and hoarse thunder resounded through the caverns. Thou art not wise, O Frodi. O Frodi thou art not wise ! "

But Frodi heard them not ; he was sleeping the sweet sleep that the quern stones had ground for him.

" Strong are we indeed," laughed Fenia, sorrowfully, "strong to contend with the puny men. We, whose pastime in Sweden was to tame the fiercest bears, so that they ate from our hands. We who fought with mighty warriors and came off conquerors. We who helped one prince and put down another. Well we fought, and many were the wounds we received from sharp spears and flashing swords. Frodi knows not our power, or he would scarce have brought us to his palace to treat us thus   Here no one has compassion upon us. Cold are the skies above us, and the pitiless wind beats upon our breast. Cold is the ground on which we stand, and the keen frost bites our feet. Ah, there are none to pity us. No one cares for the slaves. We grind for ever an enemy's quern, and he gives us no rest. Grind, grind; I am weary of grinding; I must have rest."

"Nay," returned Menia, "talk not of rest until Frodi is content with what we bring him."

Then Fenia started: "If he gives us no rest, let us take it ourselves. Why should we any longer grind good for him who only gives us evil? We can grind what we please, let us revenge ourselves."

Then Menia turned the handle quicker than ever, and in a wild voice she sang:

> "I see a ship come sailing
> With warriors bold aboard,
> There's many a one that in Danish blood
> Would be glad to dip his sword.
> Say shall we grind them hither?
> Say shall they land to-night?
> Say shall they set the palace a-fire?
> Say shall they win the fight?"

Then called Fenia in a voice of thunder through the midnight air: "Frodi, Frodi, awake, awake! Wilt thou not listen to us? Have mercy and let us rest our weary limbs."

But all was still, and Frodi gave no answer to the cry.

"Nay," answered Menia. "He will not hearken. Little he cares for the worn-out slaves. Revenge, revenge!"

And Frodi slept, not dreaming of the evil that was coming upon him.

And again Fenia shouted: "Frodi, Frodi, awake! The beacon is blazing. Danger is nigh. Wilt thou not spare?"

But Frodi gave no answer, and the giant women toiled on.

" O Frodi, Frodi, we cannot bear our weariness."

And still no answer came.

" Frodi, Frodi, danger is nigh thee. Well-manned ships are gliding over the sea. It is Mysinger who comes, his white sail flutters in the wind. His flag is unfurled. Frodi, Frodi, awake, awake! thou shalt be king no longer."

And as the giant women ground, the words they spake came to pass ; they were grinding revenge for themselves, and brought the enemy nearer and nearer.

" Ho! hearken to the herald! Frodi, Frodi, the town is on fire. The palaces will soon be ruined heaps. Grind, Menia, ever more swiftly, until we grind death to Frodi."

And Menia and Fenia ground and ground till Mysinger and his followers landed from the ships. They ground until they had reached the palace.

" To arms, to arms," shouted the warders, but it was too late. The Gotlanders armed themselves ; but who could stand against the army that the slave women were grinding against them ?

Not long did the struggle last. Frodi and his Gotlanders fought bravely, but the sea-king and his allies were mightier, for the giantesses were in giant mood, and turned the handle faster and faster, until down fell the quern stones. Then sank Frodi pierced with wounds, and the fight was over. The army that Menia and Fenia had ground to help Mysinger vanished , and Mysinger and his men alone were left conquerors on the bloody field.

They loaded their ships with treasure, and Mysinger took with him, Menia, Fenia, and the quern stones.

But, alas! Mysinger was no wiser than King Frodi had been.

Gold, however, was not his first thought ; he had enough of that, but he wanted something else that just then was more to him than gold.

There was no salt on board the sea-king's vessels; so he said, "Grind salt."

And Menia and Fenia ground salt for Mysinger.

At midnight they asked if they had ground enough.

And Mysinger bade them grind on.

And so they ground and ground until the ship was so heavy with salt that it sank, and the sea-king and all his men were drowned.

Where the quern stones went down there is to this day a great whirlpool, and the waters of the sea have been salt ever since.

SKIRNIR CONJURES GERDA TO
FOLLOW HIM.

FREYER AND GERDA.

Once when Freyer, the summer god, had tried in vain to
melt the snow and ice of winter,
he ascended Hlidskialf to see
whether he could find out the
reason why his efforts were useless.
He looked towards the east, the west and the south; at last he
turned to the north, and there he saw a maiden, taller and more
beautiful than any he had ever before beheld. Her arms shone
like the radiant beams of the sun, and heaven and earth were
resplendent with her beauty. But the vision did not last long, for
she opened the door of her dwelling, and soon had disappeared.

In vain he hoped for her return, but she came not; her image only remained fixed in his soul, filling it with the pangs of hopeless love.

He no more joined the merry feasts in Odin's joyous hall, nor did he mingle with the other gods in their familiar talk; he sought solitude, and was ever gloomy and morose.

His father Niörder grieved to see his son's sad listless manner, and wondered what was the cause of it. He entreated Skirnir, Freyer's faithful servant, wisely to search out the source of his master's gnawing grief.

So Skirnir went to his lord: "Tell me, O mighty ruler of nations, what I fain would know, why thou thus lonesome and full of sadness dost ever linger in the spacious hall?"

Freyer answered: "Thou art young in years and in experience; how then couldst thou fathom my grief? The sun shines every day on happy people, but his light can bring no joy to the sad at heart."

Yet Skirnir did not cease in his efforts. He reminded Freyer of their happy boyhood, of their merry games, and of the time when they had never had a secret from each other.

Freyer was touched by his devotion and told him of his undying love and of its hopelessness.

"Give me," said Skirnir, "thy good horse to bear me through my journey; give me thy trusty sword that fights of its own accord against the Frost-giant's power, and I will woo the maiden for thee. I foresee that my mission will be successful."

Soon afterwards Skirnir leaped into the saddle, the good sword at his side.

"Up," he cried, "haste thee, Red horse, on thy way over the steep mountain, for darkness approaches, that time which brings help and comfort to the Jotuns. But we shall make our journey safely if only we can escape the clutches of the giant."

The good horse galloped swiftly over hill and dale, as the eagle flies over the tops of the tall pines ; and Skirnir soon perceived the wide demesne of the Frost-giant.

A high hedge, guarded by fierce dogs, surrounded the bower of the beautiful maiden, and within was a circle of flames that shot all round the building. At one side was leaning the herdsman who watched over the stately herd of cattle.

Skirnir turned to him and asked him how he was to pass the dogs and the fire, and so reach the hall of the noble maiden.

"Art thou already dead ?" asked the herdsman ; "or dost thou feel death in thy heart ? No living man is permitted to enter the dwelling."

"Boldness befits a traveller better than fear. The days of my life are all numbered, and no one can shorten them against the will of the Norns."

With these words Skirnir drove his spurs into his horse, which thundered over the fierce dogs, the high hedge and the flames, making the whole grange tremble to its foundations.

Gerda was sitting in her hall, and asked her women in startled tones why Gymirsgard was quaking so strangely.

One of her maidens informed her that a man, who had just ridden up to the door, demanded admittance.

Gerda bade her bring the man into her presence, and ordered that sweet mead should be given her guest, although she had a foreboding that he brought unwelcome tidings, or was perhaps the murderer of her brother Beli.

When the stranger had drunk of the mead offered him, she asked,—

"Art thou an Elf, or an Ase, or one of the wise Wanes, that thou, mad rider that thou art, hast dared to force thy way through Wafurlogi and thus enter our halls ?"

"I am no Elf, nor yet am I an Ase, nor do I belong to the race of wise Wanes," replied the stranger. " I bring thee eleven apples of pure gold as a bridal gift, in order that thou mayst own that there is none so dear to thee as Freyer, who yearns for thy love in return."

But she answered : " I will not take thy golden apples, nor shall bonds of union ever link my fate to that of thy master, Freyer.

"Then I will add the golden ring that the Dwarfs made," he continued ; " that ring from which eight new ones drop each ninth night."

" Gymir's daughter needs no golden rings," she replied ; "her father's treasures are enough for her."

" Look, proud maiden," he cried in anger, " look at the shining sword in my right hand ; with it will I strike if thou dost still refuse him."

" Neither will I submit to force," she answered unabashed, " nor will I accept the love of any man ; and I know that Gymir is armed and ready to punish thy daring."

Then Skirnir rose from his seat in wrath, and replied to her in these words :

" Maiden, seest thou this sword in my hand ? With it I shall slay the old Jotun, thy father, if he dares offer me battle. But thee I shall conquer by means of my magic wand. Hearken to the words which I trace in runic staves : —

> On an eagle's mount thou shalt early sit,
> Looking and turned towards Hel.
> Food shall to thee more loathsome be than is to any one
> The glistening serpent among men.
>
> Solitude, horror, bonds and impatience,
> Shall thy tears with grief augment.
> Sit thee down, and I will tell thee
> Of a whelming flood of care, and of a double grief.
>
> Terrors shall bow thee down the live-long day
> In the Jotun's courts, in thy chamber lone;
> To the Hrimthurses' halls thou shalt each day.

Crawl exhausted, joyless crawl ;
Wail for pastime shalt thou have,
And tears and misery.

With three-headed Thurse thou shalt be ever bound,
Or be without a mate.
To the wold I have been, to the humid grove,
A magic wand to get ; a magic wand I got.

Wroth with thee shall Odin be, and wroth the Ase's Prince ;
And Freyer too shall loathe thee.
Flee, wicked maid, e'en ere thou shalt have felt
The gods' dire vengeance.

List, ye Jotuns, list, ye Thurses,
Sons of Suttung ! also ye, ye Ases' selves !
How I forbid, how I prohibit
Man's joy unto the damsel,
Man's converse to the damsel.

Abridged from the " Edda."

Skirnir ceased and took his knife to cut the runes from the
magic wand on which they were carved.

Gerda cried shudderingly :

" Turn away the fulfilment of thy curse, O hero ! Take from
my hand this icy cup filled with old mead ! I never thought that
it had been my lot to love one of the Ases' race. Listen to the
words I speak most grudgingly,—

' Barri the grove is named, which we both know,
The grove of tranquil paths :
Nine nights from now to Niörd's son
Gerd there will grant delight.'"

Overjoyed at his success, Skirnir mounted his horse, and hastened to tell his master the good news.

Freyer rejoiced, yet cried, impatiently,
Long is one night, yet longer two will be ;
How shall I nine endure ?
Often has a month to me seemed less
Than half a night of longing.

Freyer met Gerda at the appointed time in the grove Barri, and their wedding was solemnized, wakening the earth out of winter's sleep, and dressing her in bridal raiment of spring blossoms.

This, as the poem teaches us, happens every year ; the bright god of summer slays Beli, the snow-covered giant of wintry storms, and woos fair Gerda, the Earth, who, herself of the race of giants, is held in bonds of ice by her father Gymir.

Gymir was the same as Hymir, the Frost-giant conquered by Thor ; he was also related to Ögir, god of the blustering, wintry sea. Freyer gives his good sword, the ray of sunshine, to his servant Skirnir, that he may force the unwilling Gerda to become his bride. The messenger, in the oldest tradition the god himself, offers the unwilling maiden the golden ring from which eight other rings drop each ninth night, even as the corn that is sown late in autumn grows and ripens in nine months. He threatens the hard-hearted girl with runes which he carves on a magic wand, and which his curse makes powerful for evil. His curse dooms her to marry Hrimgrimnir, or be buried alone under the ice of winter. Just as he is about to cut off the runes, that his curse may be fulfilled, fair Gerda yields to necessity and marries Freyer.

Skirnir's Journey is one of the most beautiful poems of the Edda, and certainly the ideas to which it gave rise in the mind of the poet are no less interesting. They are to be met with in other myths, and they also occur in fairy-tales and the heroic epics ; as, for instance, in the story of the Sleeping Beauty in the Wood, who is kept in the bondage of slumber by the chill embrace of winter, and wakened to new life by the warm kiss of the sun-prince.

A similar tale is current in Denmark.

Young Swendal was playing with a ball, and the ball flew out of his hands far away into the ladies' chamber. He went after it ; he came back again with love in his heart, for he had seen there a lovely damsel, whose picture had fixed itself upon his soul.

Hark! he heard voices calling to him ; he thought it was his sister and his step-mother.

"Hark ye, young Swendal," they said; "fling not thy ball at me ; fling it rather at the fair maiden whom thou dost love. Nor shalt thou longer have peace or sleep, until thou hast released the blooming girl, lying oppressed by heavy grief."

No sooner had he heard the words than he donned his fur-cloak, and entered the chamber where the court was assembled.

He told them he would go into the mountains to ask his mother what he was to do, that he might free the grieving maiden

They praised his errand, and he set out, and reached the mountain where his mother had been slumbering peacefully for many a year.

As he entered, the walls and marble boulders burst asunder, the earth opened, and a voice cried out:

"Who is it that wakens the weary sleeper? Can I not rest in peace beneath the dark ground?"

"Mother," he answered, "it is thy son that comes to seek thy counsel, as they told me that no longer should I have peace or sleep until I should release the blooming maiden who has suffered thraldom this many a long day."

Thereupon the voice spake,—

"Take, then, thy mother's last gifts, young Swendal, and set out that thou mayst find that which thy heart is yearning for."

And suddenly there lay before him a sword, and without there neighed a noble steed.

It was the sword that ever carries victory with it, and the stallion that gallops over land and sea, and never wearies!

Young Swendal girt the sword around his waist, mounted the steed, and rode away over the vast ocean, through green woodlands beyond, until he reached the castle where the maiden was imprisoned and endured her bitter fate.

He begged admittance of the surly keeper that sat outside the gate, promising him courtly honours when he should be king.

The keeper replied morosely that the gate was of steel and the walls of solid marble, and inside a fierce lion and a grim bear kept watch, to tear to pieces any intruding stranger, unless it were young Swendal.

When the rider heard these words, his heart gladdened, and, setting deep the spurs into his noble steed, he leaped right into the court-yard. The ferocious beasts crouched humbly at his feet, and the lime-tree with its golden leaves bent to the ground before him for he was the long-awaited master.

The longing maiden heard the tinkling of the rider's spurs, and awoke from her death-like slumber. Her heart was filled with the thought of her bold redeemer; she ran to the gate and sank into the arms of young Swendal.

FREYA, FREA, OR FROUWA.

Through the shady forest once strode a powerful young huntsman. His eyes beamed with the fire of his soul, and his strong manly frame was clad in a light hunting dress, decked with eagle's feathers; his broad, trusty sword clanked in its sheath as he went, and in his right hand he bore a spear.

Several attendants followed him, and two large greyhounds sprang round him with mighty bounds. Suddenly they stopped, threw back their heads and began barking loudly, then disappeared in the dense bushes hard by.

A loud, fearful roar came out from where the hounds had entered the underwood, and the bushes creaked and groaned, as though trampled under the foot of some enormous giant, and a monstrous wild ox of untold proportions rushed out, chasing the hounds.

As soon as it reached the open space where the huntsman and his followers stood, it lowered its monstrous head, and, catching one of the dogs round the neck in its rounded horns, hurled it high into the sky. But at the same moment the huntsman's spear hissed through the air, and entered deep into the ox's fleshy neck.

The monster turned fiercely towards its new opponent, but the huntsman did not budge from his place. All would have thought him lost, so unequal did the chances seem, so terrible did the giant ox appear.

Calm and collected, the bold youth awaited the onslaught of the monster, then seized it by the horns, and, straining his whole strength into his shoulders, with superhuman power, overthrew it on its back. Before it could rise again the huntsman's foot pressed heavily upon its throat, and soon his trusty sword put an end to the battle, a stifled roar telling that the life flame of the monstrous ox had at length gone out.

The huntsman's followers had not shared in the fight, for they knew their master and his mighty strength, and had no fear for the result. They now went silently to their work, took off the wild ox's skin from his steaming carcase, and bore it to their master's castle. He, however, laid himself down under the shade of an oak-tree close by, and sank into a deep reverie.

A rustling sound in the neighbouring ferns woke him from his dreams, and, when he looked up, the tall figure of a woman stood before him, encircled by an unearthly shimmering light.

A snowy, trailing garment, bound by a golden girdle, draped her wondrous limbs; her flaxen locks shone through the transparent web that covered her head, and rich golden ornaments decked her neck and shoulders.

The young noble gazed in wonderment at his unknown visitor;

he knew not whether he was awake or whether he still slept, or whether the figure was but a creation of his own unconscious mind. But the more he looked at it the clearer did it become. It did not vanish; it was full of life.

"Hero of the Wolsings," Freya began, and her voice sounded not of the earth, but rang clear as a silver bell: "offspring of the Wolsing race, why dost thou discolour thy blade with mere ox blood? Rather should it be tinged with the dragon's blood. he that lurks in Asgard's holy groves, and drains the mind and marrow of mankind with eager jaws. Dost thou not hear his coils rattle? dost thou not see the ramparts he has erected? Go thou, brave youth, and slay with thy strong arm the bane of Asgard that defies the holy gods. Wodan ensures thee victory. A life ended in glory is a life lived long enough."

The noble youth hearkened to her words in silent rapture, for she gave utterance to what he had long craved to accomplish. He looked up to the eagle as it hovered above his head on out-spread wings; but turning his eyes again to the vision of the fair woman, lo! she had vanished out of sight!

No longer did he doubt, Freya herself or one of her maidens had brought to him great Wodan's behest.

He forthwith sped through the wood to the Meeting of the Wise Men, and related all that he had heard and seen, and the task that had been set him. The men struck their shields in token of approval, and the quiet wood resounded again with the clash.

The crowd dispersed; each man returned to his native hamlet, and gathered together all the youths fit for war. In the third night they assembled, and, led by the youthful hero, fell upon the host of the Roman intruders, who were defeated in a bloody struggle that lasted three days.

Thus was the Roman dragon, the bane of Asgard, slain, and the people delivered by the hero, Arminius.

Such was the conception of Freya among the Teutonic tribes. She was the mighty goddess who sat by the side of Wodan on the high throne above the worlds, ruling over heaven and earth, guiding the fate of nations, allotting the issue of battles. Together with the Walkyries, or at their head, she hovered over the battlefield, and bestowed victory or a glorious death on the heroes. She shared the fallen warriors with her spouse, great Wodan, and led those of her portion to Folkwang (folk-meadow) and to her radiant hall, Sessrumnir (room of seats), where she dealt out to them the inspiring mead.

It seems also that she was more especially worshipped as Mother-Earth, being identical with Nerthus, the Jörd (Earth) of Scandinavia, who drove among the people in her sacred chariot, adorning the earth with fresh green, with blossoms and blades, making the seeds to thrive, and blessing the fruits of the field.

The Scandinavian myths made a decided distinction between Freya and Frigg. They held Frigg to be the highest amongst the goddesses, whilst to Freya the second place was given; nor was she looked upon as the wife of Odin. She was the daughter of the Wane-god, Niörder, and sister of loving Freyer, who each year marries fair Gerda. As goddess of beauty and love, she blesses all lovers who turn to her with prayers and sacrifices; but when marriage was solemnized it was great Frigg whom the husband and wife were bound to invoke.

The South German races knew of no such distinction between the goddesses; so they regarded Friday, the day dedicated to Freya, as the fittest for a wedding, and this custom was not given up until the Christian priests convinced the people that the day on which the Saviour was crucified must necessarily be an unlucky one. Yet they could not change the name of Friday, which still remains to this day.

At the time of King Hara'd lived Rerir, son of Thorkill the

P

Redbeard. In all his warlike strength he strove against the king; but the battle went against him, and he sought shelter on a lonely isle.

Helga was his love; but her father, the king's chief warrior and his faithful vassal, despised the poor houseless outcast.

Rerir, full of longing to behold once more his loved Helga, built a small, strong boat, and boldly landed near the castle where she dwelt with her father.

She stood upon the beach, wistfully looking over the bounding billows, which suddenly tossed at her feet a tiny craft; Rerir leapt upon the shore, and stood by her side.

Tearfully she told him how her cruel father was about to force her into a marriage with a noble of the court, yet vowed to him that none but he should ever have her love.

> " Helga !" he cried, "a lonely isle
>   There lies beyond the foaming sea—
> Bold rovers know the safe retreat—
>   O be thou mine, and fly with me !"

Trembling, yet half-willing, she refused to go with him. Rerir, full of grief and deadly pale, sank broken-hearted to her feet, entreating her again in passionate words.

No longer could she bear to look upon the anguish that she gave her loved one, no longer could she withstand his glowing words that spake of rapture shared by each :

> Down she steppeth with the hero
>   To the foaming wave-washed strand ;
> " Where thou wendest, my beloved,
>   Is alone my home, my land !"

> And the gaily-coloured vessel
>   Screens the youthful, loving pair ;
> Swelling sails and guiding rudder
>   Save the hero and his fair.

Hastening after them the vessels
    Of her father quick pursue ;
Far beyond them speed the lovers,
    And the land is lost to view.

＊　　＊　　＊　　＊　　＊

On the ocean's stormy bosom
    Cast about, they fain would die ;
And they wither like the blossom
    That has met the Evil Eye.

Suddenly the piercing sunbeams
    Burst the clouds, illuming all ;
Lo ! from out the heaving billows
    Rises Freya's blessed hall.

Peacefully, without a struggle,
    Enter the twain lovers in,
Quitting earth and life's hard battle ;
    Blessed they who Frey's hall win !

Freya always bears the radiant necklace Brisingamen, the
sparkling jewels of the heavens, the gaily-coloured flowers of
spring, when regarded as the goddess of nature and ruler of the
world, or as Mother Earth. When the skalds dethroned her from
her lofty height, humanizing her nature and her attributes, the
myth arose which told how the necklace was gained.

Four skilful dwarfs made it, according to the legend, in their
underground smithy, and worked into it the most costly jewels that
the earth produced, so that it glanced and glittered like the sun
herself. * But Freya chanced to see it, and her eyes were almost
blinded at its wondrous splendour. In exchange for it the dwarfs
asked nothing but her grace, which she extended to them, and
thus gained the necklace.

The goddess of beauty and love was described as a maiden in

---

* See note on page 24.

the Northern poems; yet there is a myth according to which she
was married to Odur, a scion of divine ancestry. She lived happily
with him, and several lovely daughters blessed their union.

But Freya was to learn that happiness is not eternal; for Odur
left her, and with him all joy and gladness passed out of her
life.

All Nature sorrowed with her; the flowers withered and faded,
the leaves fell from the trees, the earth looked waste and gloomy.
Freya moaned and wept day and night; her tears shone like
golden drops of dew in the Autumn sunshine. And so she spent
the long winter miserable and alone in her deserted hall.

Then she could bear it no longer; she set out in search of her
lost spouse, and wandered far and wide through distant lands and
amongst strange nations. She sought her lover diligently, and
found him at last in the evergreen fields where the golden fruit
ripens and the myrtle blooms. She clasped him lovingly in her
arms, and tears of joy, golden as the blaze of the new spring sun,
fell from her eyes when he returned her love with love.

On their arrival home again on their native earth, they were
received with the thousand-voiced song of birds; and the many-
coloured flowers and leafy trees whispered of love and of summer
time.

The beautiful goddess strove with all the force of love to keep
her husband by her side, that he should never leave her again;
but all in vain, for when Virgo sank after the autumnal equinox, he
once more left her and again wandered to the far country in the
unknown distance.

In the Fiölswinn Lay the same idea underlies the whole poem.

Menglada (jewel-gladness) awaits her bridegroom in her castle,
which is guarded by grim wolf-hounds and encircled by a wall
of fire.

A watchman, Fiölswider (much-knower), stands at the entrance, and sees a stranger coming in the distance. He approaches, and seeks admittance. The watchman cries—

"This is no place for beggars; seek thou the damp and foggy highway, and begone."

To which the wanderer makes answer—

"What monster art thou, that guards the entrance; of what race canst thou be, who refusest hospitality to the weary traveller?"

"Fiölswider is my name, in that I am wise in cautious counsel. Therefore canst thou not enter this castle."

The wanderer cast a longing look towards the castle-window, and replied—

"Unwillingly do I turn my eyes away, having once seen what I seek. Here, where a glowing belt girds golden halls, could I find peace."

Then the watchman demands of him his name and race, and hears that he is Windkald (wind-cold), son of Warkald (spring-cold). The stranger asks who is the owner of the castle, and is informed that it belongs to Menglada; he asks what is the girdle that surrounds the castle like a wall of flame, and whether there is no way to tame the grim wolf-dogs that sit on guard; he asks, too, of the mountain on which the castle stands, of the nine maidens who sit before Menglada's knee, and whether no man can enter the golden hall and go to her.

To all his questions he receives enigmatical replies, but to the last the watchman says that none can ever cross the threshold but young Swipdager, the expected bridegroom.

Thereupon he cries out—

"Throw open the gates, make way for the expected one! Swipdager has arrived, and seeks admittance!"

The watchman hastens to the hall of Menglada, and tells her that a man has come who calls himself Swipdager, whom the wolf dogs have joyfully greeted, before whom the castle gates have flung themselves wide open.

" May shining ravens tear out thine eyes if thou hast lied to me that my long awaited lover has at last returned ! " cries the maiden joyously, and hurries towards the entrance. As soon as her eyes alight upon the stranger, she knows him as her lover, and flings her arms around him.

" Whither hast thou been ? whence hast thou come ? what art thou called out there ? "

He tells her that he has come upon the wind-cold (Windkald) way, that the unalterable word of the Norns had taken him thither and borne him thence.

And she responded—

" Welcome art thou back again ! my wish is fulfilled. Long have I sat on the high hill, looking for thee by day, looking for thee by night. All that I longed for has at length come to pass, for thou art here again at my side."

WALKYRIES CONDUCTING THE FALLEN HEROES TO WALHALLA.

WALKYRIES LEADING THE
WARRIORS ON TO BATTLE.

PART SEVENTH.

THE old Greeks called the power which ruled over the deeds, the suffering, the life and struggles of man, Moira (Latin, *Fatum*), and were of opinion that the gods, if not actually dependent on it, were at least subordinate to it. Later, they held that there were three Fates —Future, Present and Past, and connected them with the birth, life and death of man. Their names and occupation are given in the well-known verse:

> " Klotho begins, Lachesis spins,
>   Atropos cuts the thread in two."

Tc these was added Nemesis, the avenger of human insolence and of every evil deed. At length, when the old religion faded away, they began to worship Tyche, blind chance or fortune, erected altars to her, and offered sacrifices to her.

The Teutonic ideas were curiously similar to those of the people of the south. Orlog or Urlak, Fate, the eternal law of the universe, ruled over gods and men. The latter were powerless in its hands, therefore the hero bore his fate with resignation after he had striven his best to turn it aside; the gods foresaw what was to befal them, but even their divinity could not avert their doom.

Orlog was neither created nor begotten, and was impersonal; he was of special significance in war, and even to this day a German war-ship of the first magnitude is called an Orlog-ship. This being, which ruled in secret, gained recognition and personality in Allfather, the Creator, Sustainer, Upholder and Ruler of the world, who existed undefined in the consciousness of the people. He was the unknown god who was to call the new world into being after the Last Battle and the destruction of the universe. He was the highest conception of Odin. Lastly, Orlog reappears in the Regin, the Powers who ruled the world, and who, seated on their judgment thrones by the Fountain of Urd, determined the fate of men, and judged their actions. Whenever they showed themselves individually, they were Ases, but not such Ases as those who ate, drank, slept, and had adventures like mortal men; they were mightier and nobler than those, although they were likewise possessed of passions and affections similar to the others.

The Regin come most prominently into view in the Starkad legend where they determine the fate of the mythical hero Starkad. This Wiking may with considerable resemblance be compared with the Grecian Herakles; just as Zeus and Hera decide the destiny of the latter, so do Odin and Freya of the other.

Starkad was of half-giant descent, and already when a child, like the Jotuns, of super-human stature, and furnished with eight arms. Under the training and by the magic of his master, Horse-hair Beard (Hroszharsgrani), he not only gained great learning and heroic valour, but was also endowed with human form and manly beauty.

When he grew up to be a youth, his master took a boat and sailed away with him to an unknown island. A great crowd was on the beach, and round the council-tree sat eleven grave men of noble appearance upon thrones; a twelfth and higher throne remained unoccupied. Horse-hair Beard mounted it, and was greeted by all as Great Odin.

Then the speaker arose—it was Asathor—and said, "Alfhild, Starkad's mother, chose not Asathor as father for her child, but a giant; therefore I decree that he be childless, the last of his race."

"Yet I," said Odin, "grant him a life three times the length of mortal man."

"Then," answered Asathor, "I destine him to do in each age a grievous outrage that shall be a work of shame and dishonour in the eyes of man."

Odin replied again, "And I bestow on him the stoutest armour and most precious garments."

"I forbid him," said Asathor, "both house and home, nor shall a piece of land be ever his."

"And I allot him gold and flocks in fullest plenty," answered Odin.

"Then I doom him to ever-growing thirst for gold and wealth, that he may never enjoy peace of mind."

Odin returned, "I confer on him valour and prowess, and victory in battle."

"Yet shall he from each combat bear a wound that reaches to the very bone," was Thor's reply.

"The noble lore of the skalds shall be his," continued his protector, "that he may sing; and each of his words shall be a song."

"His memory shall be cursed with forgetfulness of all that he has sung."

"The noblest and the best among men shall love and honour him," spake Odin.

"But all his tribe shall shun and hate him," was Thor's last curse.

The assembled Regin entered into council, and decreed that all should come to pass as Odin and Asathor had willed.

Thus ended the judgment, and Horse-hair Beard descended from his high throne, and went to the boat with his foster-son.

Starkad grew to be one of the most famous of the mythical heroes, and his name was handed down and celebrated even in historical times throughout the northern countries.

Once when on a Wiking raid with King Wikar of Norway, the fleet was overtaken by a tempest, and he had to seek shelter in a protected creek. He had hoped for a rich booty, but the hurricane continuing for many days prevented his starting. Vain were all prayers and sacrifices. Odin demanded a human life.

Then it was resolved to cast the fatal runes, and the lot fell to the king himself. Nobody dared to pronounce the dire decree, still less to put it into execution; when, all on a sudden, a man in a broad-brimmed hat appeared in the night before Starkad. He saw at once that it was Horse-hair Beard; he gave Starkad a thin willow branch and a reed.

Starkad at once understood the will of the god, and the next day presented himself before the king to show him these harmless objects, telling him that the gods would be satisfied with the mere show of a sacrifice: the king was to suffer the slender branch to be laid around his neck; they were then to tie him to the thin bough of a tree, and touch him with the reed. Thus the sacrifice would be accomplished, and Odin would again send them a propitious wind.

Wikar accepted this proposal; but the thin bough of the tree sprang upwards, the willow branch was changed into a rope, and the reed which Starkad flung at the king was turned into a spear, which pierced the victim to the heart.

Such was one of the shameful outrages that Starkad the Wiking perpetrated, as Asathor had doomed he should, although the myth does not point out that it was done with the aid of Odin.

The hero, reckless of his evil deed, went on his further adventures, and performed marvellous and valorous feats in Sweden, Denmark, Ireland and Esthonia among the various nations.

During the winter months, when at the courts of other kings, he sang of his far-famed Wiking raids and combats, and princes and Jarls listened to his lays in silent admiration of the mighty champion, while the people dreaded and hated him for his devastations.

Yet he received also many wounds, and once even fought with a split head, his helmet alone keeping his head together. Moreover, when an old man of a hundred years, he slew nine warriors, although his bowels hung from his wounded side. In the memorable Battle of Brawalla he had his body cut open from the shoulder to the chest, so that his very liver was laid bare. All these wounds miraculously healed, for according to Odin's sentence he had to live three ages.

Thus the Ases appear as Regin, forecasting the fate of man, which cannot fail to come to pass.

King Fridleif of Denmark was rich in treasures, which he had gathered together by bold deeds from the giants and the dragons that he had slain. Once when on his adventures he entered the cottage of a peasant, who received him hospitably. There he won the love of fair Juritha, the daughter of the honest cottager, and took her home with him. She bore him a son, who was called Olaf.

The ninth night after the birth of the child, Fridleif took him to the temple of the three sisters of Fate, to ask them about the future destiny of the boy. Before he entered the sacred grove, he read prayers to the godhead that the decree should be propitious, and made solemn pledges. Then he stepped into the temple, and saw three maidens upon thrones in the holy place, and they looked down upon him in silence as he approached.

The first goddess was grey with age, yet looked friendly and happy, even as the joyous days of past youth ; the second raised her hand aloft, like a Walkyrie, who, looking towards the enemy on the field of battle, points out the way the heroes should advance ; the third glanced darkly from under the veil which covered her temples.

"The noble youth shall be beautiful," said Urd of kindly heart, " and shall gain the love and service of men."

" I grant him untold valour in combat and generosity towards friends," continued Werdandi.

Thereto dark-frowning Skuld added, "Yet insatiable covetousness shall stain his soul."

We have frequently spoken of the Norns in preceding portions of the book. They are the Fatal Sisters who sit at the foot of the World-Ash Yggdrasil by the fountain of Urd. They can foresee the destiny of man, and make it known through the mouth of prophetesses and priests, or utter it themselves. At the same time they also *make* the fate of mortals to a certain extent, as is seen from the above story. They hover over armies as they are starting for the battle-field, and cast the deadly lots among the warriors. They follow the blood-stained track of the murderer, just as the Erinnyæ of the Greeks did, and fall upon him with their dire vengeance, no matter where or how he be hidden. They finally show upon the nails of man their runes, that is the white spots underneath the nail, which partly indicate good luck, partly misfortune ; formerly people understood their meaning and could read them, but in our days this art has been lost, because with man's averted faith in the Fates, all fear and respect for them also disappeared, so that they now manifest themselves in all sorts of more horrible ways.

The name Norn has quite disappeared from Germany, if indeed it was ever known there. The Anglo-Saxons called the Fatal Sisters Mettena, *i.e.,* the measurers, those who weighed in the balance. In the oldest conception of them, the sisters were held to be one, and were known as Wurd or Urd, in Anglo-Saxon Wyrd. But at the same time they were also known as a trinity.

In heathen times the three sisters were worshipped in a sacred grove. They were regarded as protectresses of the place, and in Christian times as saints who had erected chapels and shrines, but who nevertheless perished in the ruins of their castle. Another idea was that the three prophetesses lived on a hill surrounded by water. They span and wove linen, which they afterwards gave away to the people. They sang at christenings and marriages, which betokened good luck, and for this reason three ears of corn were offered up to them at the harvest. Thus the fear of the terrible Norns, who pursued the vile-doer and spun the irremediable thread of man's destiny, awarding life and death according to their pleasure, became softened in course of time ; while, on the contrary, the idea of Hel, the goddess of the under-world, grew ever more and more appalling.

We have already made the acquaintance of the goddess Hel as a monster horrible to look upon, and the daughter of Loki; but the original conception of her was far different from this. Death was not terrible in the oldest time. Mother Earth, who bore the living, and took the dead back to her bosom, appeared in no gruesome form to the ancients.

The patriarchs of Israel, after a long life of struggle, blessed their sons and made their will known to them, and then laid their heads down peacefully and quietly to take their eternal rest. Similar ideas may have prevailed amongst the Aryan races in their native land. The shepherd princes who watched their flocks and herds looked upon life and death calmly, and worshipped Mother Earth as the author of birth and dissolution, without fearing her.

But when the people began to distinguish spiritual life from the merely corporeal, Hel became the Ruler and Judge of souls. Meanwhile these conceptions of life after death were rather unsatisfactory in some respects. Homer made the spirits of the dead glide about like unconscious shadows moved by every breath of wind; in the poems of Ossian they whispered to the living in the waving of the reeds, the murmuring of the billows, and in the coming and going of the clouds, in which they appear to have had their dwelling.

Homer tells us of the punishment borne by those spirits who were condemned to Tartaros, and in the time of Tacitus the Teutons appear to have already had ideas respecting reward and punishment after death. They knew of Walhalla, where the storm and war-god, Wodan, received the souls of fallen heroes, But Hel was still the Earth-mother who dwelt in the depths, who made the plants grow and rise in the light of day; or she was Nerthus, who, under the guidance of the priests, went out to greet the people and wander through their land. The Edda only contains scattered allusions to the great goddess of former days, who decked the earth with flowers and fruits, who gave life and energy to man and beast, and who called her children back to her bosom. Odin is there said to have given her power over the nine worlds, or, according to another version, over the ninth world ; but certainly the great goddess of life and death may be described as having dominion over the nine worlds. She was represented as half corpse-like, half of an ordinary colour, which showed her power over life and death. The Brahmins described their goddess of nature after much the same fashion.

Holda was the bright side of the goddess of nature. In contra-distinction to her, the dark, black side of Hel came ever more strongly prominent, the greater the horrors of death and the grave appeared. The Edda teaches us that it took nine nights' ride through dark valleys to reach the river Giöl, which was spanned by a gold-covered bridge, on the other side of which was the high iron fence surrounding the dwelling of the goddess of the Under-world. No living creature, were he even a god, could bear to look upon that terrible face.

Her hall was called Misery, her dish Hunger, her knife Greed ; Idleness was the name of her man, Sloth of her maid, Ruin of her threshold, Sorrow of her bed, and Conflagration of her curtains. Within her realm, Corpse-strand, a hall was set apart for assassins and perjurers ; it was far from the sun and turned towards the north, and was roofed with serpents, whose heads hung down and spat their venom upon the floor, causing unspeakable torment to the wicked who were confined there. Still more horrible than this was Hwergelmir, the roaring cauldron, where the dragon Nidhögg devoured the corpses of the evil-doers. In front of Hel's dwelling was the Gnypa cavern. The monstrous dog Garm lived there, from whose jaws the blood constantly dripped as he gnashed his teeth and growled at the new arrivals of the pilgrims of earth.

Q

These and other terrible pictures show the Northern Hel as described in the later poems, but they were scarcely founded on the conceptions of the old Teutons regarding her. Still there are other places which prove that Hel also had a more kindly aspect, and that she received with a joyous welcome the good and worthy who might come to her.

When glorious Baldur was sent to her by insidious Loki's perfidy, he found the halls gorgeously decorated, the thrones all covered with spangles of gold, and goblets filled to the brim with sweet mead. For the goddess had also halls of joy for the good and brave who were not received in Walhalla.

In the Whispering Valley (Wisperthal), where lisping elf-maidens invite the wanderer to deceptive joys, there lies on a low cone-shaped hill the ruins of an ancient castle. In the underground caverns beneath, a black-and-white spirit-maiden is said to guard her hidden treasures. They say that many years ago she betrayed the treasures of the abbey to the enemy for gold, for which crime she was excommunicated by the Church at Rome ; her spirit will not find rest, it is said, until the enemy has been conquered and the stolen treasures restored. Formerly she was often seen by the light of the full moon, weeping and bewailing as she wandered among the ruins ; but of late years the spectre has not appeared. Perhaps the unknown enemy has been conquered, thus obtaining for her respite from her troubles.

The appearance of this black-and-white maiden reminds us of the wicked goddess Hel, and she may also be compared with Hilde, the Walkyrie who ever awakened up again the slain warriors in the strife between Högni and Hedin, that the fight might be continued.

THE WALKYRIES.

At Hledra, the proudest town in all the northern lands, sat King Hrolf Kraki one yule-tide with his twelve warriors, and together they emptied the goblets of sparkling wine. They vowed eternal companionship, that they would ever stand side by side in the fight, and if need be die together.

When summer came, they went out to battles and to wars, and many a Jarl and many a king was made tributary to them.

" Odin is with us," said Bodwar Biarki, one of the twelve.

" The Walkyries have protected us," said Hialti, another warrior.

" May they always grant us victory," added a third, " and guide us all in safety to Walhalla."

As they were thus speaking, Wogg, a young lad, came up to them, and asked to be allowed to take service under the king. Kraki gave him a golden ring.

As the boy fastened it on his left arm he said, " Now must my right arm be ashamed, lacking ornament."

Therefore the king, smiling, gave him a second ring.

Whereupon Wogg, laying his hand on Freyer's wild boar, vowed that he would be the King's avenger, if he were ever slain by the enemy.

King Hrolf Kraki once took his warriors to Upsala, where his father Helgi had been slain, to demand of the avaricious Adil, the spouse of Yrsa, his father's ring.

After a day's journey, he came to the peasant Hrany, who greeted him kindly, and advised him to send some of his people back as they would only be in the way during the fight.

The peasant wore a large hat, which completely shaded his face ; he had only one eye, but he spoke so wisely, that his advice was followed. The next evening they came to the same house, in front of which stood the same peasant.

Again they received the same advice, and King Hrolf now saw clearly that this was a man versed in magic lore, and he dismissed all the servants of his warriors.

The peasant looked pensively after the departing king; then he beckoned with his right hand, as though he were calling a servant, and through the clouds and evening mists appeared seven maidens, mounted on white steeds, armed with shields and clad in chain-mail. They stopped before him.

"Hrist (storm) and Mist (cloud-grey), Thrud (power) and Göll (herald), Gondul (she-wolf) and Skogul (carrier through), and thou, bold Hilde (war), use your art with King Hrolf, that he may be victorious."

Thus spoke the peasant, and the Walkyries hastened away to carry out his behest.

Then followed, through the treachery of the false Adil, fierce frays, in all of which the heroes conquered, and they returned in triumph to their home. They again sought lodging with Hrany, and they found him more hospitable than before. He showed Hrolf a shield, a sword, and a shirt of mail, saying,—

"Take the weapons, thou wilt have need of them."

But Hrolf refused to take such costly gifts from a peasant, whereupon Hrany waxed wroth, his face grew dark as night, and his eyes flashed fire.

"Then quit my house, rash sons of the Jotuns," he cried; "the Norn has beclouded your minds, she throws the thread north-wards."

The ground shook; the very house groaned and cracked, as though the building would fall. The heroes, terrified, mounted their stallions, and rode away. At last Biarki broke the silence.

"I think," he said, "that we have been foolish. The peasant is more than he seems."

"It is Odin himself, the one-eyed god," answered Hrolf; "let us return and seek him."

But it was in vain, for both Hrany and his house had disappeared.

For some time the king remained quietly at Hledra with his warriors; for he was afraid that the Father of Victory was displeased with him. The tributary princes and Jarls paid their taxes, without daring to raise the banner against their victorious lord.

At last, however, Skuld, Hrolf's sister, begged her husband, Hiorward, to take up arms against the king. She used cunning magic and baneful witchery in order to attain her end. Under the pretext of paying the tribute, they both arrived in the castle with many followers, leaving many mounted men concealed outside.

The king received them with great honour, and gave a festive drinking-bout. But when he and his followers, overcome by sleep and wine, lay resting in the halls, the troop of traitors silently crept in and slaughtered many a sleeping hero. Hialti, who was outside, came back just as the fighting had begun. He wakened Badwar Biarki. Both took their arms, and killing everybody who came in their way, they reached the king's sleeping hall, where the king armed himself amid his warriors.

Then Hrolf said, "Well, valiant comrades, drink with me the last cup to Odin, as we are going the way of Death."

They all drank with great zeal, and Biarki said: "Do you see the Walkyries above us, how they smile under their helmets and beckon to us? We come to you, powerful maidens; soon you will bear us to Walhalla, where Freya herself brings to the heroes foaming mead. But as long as life is granted to us, let us do our duty faithfully, that we may die an honourable death and show ourselves worthy of renown and skaldic song."

Thus spoke the undaunted hero, and the warriors following closely on the king, pressed forward against the foe, and their

swords clashed as if a whole army was fighting. The conspira-
tors fell under their blows and retreated from the halls and
castle, and the men of Hledra followed their brave lord as though
to victory.

In the meanwhile Hiorward brought fresh troops, and the pernicious Skuld stood in the midst of the battle, and by her magic
songs she revived the fallen warriors.

The heroes fell one after the other around their warlike king,
who towered in their midst.   Shots whizzed round him, sword-
blows clashed on helmet and shield; but the traitors fell before
his mighty strokes.   Only when his armour was utterly destroyed
did he fall pierced with lances on the bloody ground, profusely
strewed with armour and with broken weapons.   Hialti lay dying
at his feet.   Biarkı stood still, but his colour was pale, his
helmet and shield broken, his breast-plate and heart pierced by a
lance.

> The colour from his cheek is fled,
>   He speaks with quaking breath ;
> All power has left my weary limb,
>   That burns the wound of death
>
> Hialti lies upon the ground
>   Beside the dying king ;
> The Hero-King grants me to kiss
>   His lips ere life takes wing.
>
> At his head will I gladly sink,
>   Without fear, without dismay ;
> Walkyries above me beckoning
>   Bless'd shield-maidens gray.
>
> They call, inviting us above,
>   The heroes they bid speed
> To Odin's glorious halls,
>   Where they deal out ale and mead.

Hiorward, the victor, and Skuld sat together in the festive hall
at the drinking bout, laughing over their wicked cunning.

Then the enchantress said, "My brother has died with all his heroes as a Skioldung, a descendant of the noblest race of kings on the whole earth."

"Then is none of his brave men left?" asked the king. "I would honour him highly, and seat him as the first under my warriors."

Just as he had thus spoken a man covered with blood came up to him without weapons, but on each arm a golden ring. All knew him well, for he was Wogg, the same whom Hrolf had once received into his company. He said he would like to serve his new master faithfully; but he had no sword, as he had broken his in the fight. Then Hiorward handed him his own great sword; but Wogg said that Hrolf always held the sword at the point when he gave it to a man. This the king did also; but as soon as Wogg had the handle in his hand he dug the point deep into the king's breast with the words:

"Go thou to the kingdom of Hel, false traitor, where thou shalt walk through valleys of misery."

Then he received innumerable mortal wounds by Hiorward's warriors. With a dying struggle he dragged himself towards the yet living Hrolf, and said:

"Now have I fulfilled my promise, and have avenged my master. But I see them—the Walkyries. They have lifted the heroes on their horses; they wait for me. I follow ye; I come from blood and the pains of earth to share the joys of Asgard's glorious hall!"

The prophetesses who foretold victory to the people, or who even took part in the battle, holding up the banner in their strong hands, were either distinguished by their great and healthy old age or by their youth and beauty. When the warriors saw them standing amongst the chiefs and nobles filled with the enthusiastic certainty of victory, issuing their commands and uttering words of counsel which tended to ensure the victory they had prophesied, they may well have regarded them as supernatural beings worthy of all honour. It was the same with the Scandinavians. Many a warrior-maiden fought in the famous Brawalla battle; but yet these Amazons were, on that occasion, unable to change the fate of the day.

The existence of these Walas, or Amazons, formed the foundation of the belief in Walkyries, and poetic fancy imagined them to be heavenly beings, who gave victory to him that deserved it, and who took those mortals who had fallen bravely in the fight to Walhalla, that they might be with the Father of Battles and the blessed Einheriar. We have already met with them several times in the course of our history, riding on white horses and dressed in splendid armour, watching the fate of battles and of the heroes who took part in them. There were generally seven, nine, or even twelve choosers of the dead on such occasions, and Hilde (War) and the youngest Norn Skuld, were often comprised in their ranks. They rode on air and water, for their horses were the clouds that floated over the world of mortal men. They were possessed of swan garments, wrapped in which they could fly in the guise of swans to the place where heroes were contending for death or victory.

The celebrated Brynhilde was a Walkyrie. She said on her Hel ride that Agnar had stolen the swan garments belonging to her and her sisters, and had thus forced her to give him the victory over Hialmgunnar against the will of Odin, for which reason the god had cast her into a magic sleep. Swawa and Sigrun, like Brynhilde, were of human extraction, and they used to hover protectingly round their favourite heroes during the fight; but they lost their Walkyrie power as soon as they married them. Maidens alone could receive the divine nature, which they lost again if ever they married a mortal hero.

The Walkyries, Norns, and divine women reappear under the name of Dises. This appellation connects them with the war and sword-god Tius (Tyr, Zio). They were not his servants, however, but were quite independent of him. Idises, or Dises, were known and reverenced by the Teutons before the time of Tacitus. It seems that inspired prophetesses and seers like Weleda were looked upon as Idises. We have already shown what influence they possessed in time of war; but they used also to go about the land, enter houses, and bring help in sickness, for they knew of remedies which were of much avail to whomsover believed in their efficacy.

It is said in Latin accounts that one of these women went to meet Drusus when he had advanced as far as the Elbe. She wore the Teutonic costume, was of superhuman height, and commanded the conqueror to withdraw from the sacred soil of the fatherland, for death was approaching him. He was so terrified that he was induced to retreat, and it is well known that he soon afterwards died of a fall from his horse. This tale probably had its rise in Teutonic tradition, but it shows what faith the ancients placed in the greatness and power of these prophetesses, who were also called Wise-Women. It was beautiful to see how these seers kept the desire for the weal of their people in their hearts, incited them to warlike deeds, carried their banner into the fray, bore the wounded out of the fight, bound up their hurts, and nursed them or brought help and healing to the sick. Very different was the reverse side of this picture, when they accompanied wandering hordes in their raids. Wild-looking figures with loosened hair, they there mixed with the fighting men, joined in the fierce battle-cry, and after victory had been attained they stood by the sacrificial altar, slew the prisoners, and foretold future events by their witch-like incantations over the bodies of their victims.

Old authors tell us of other women whom the people held to be Idises. One of these appeared to Attila by the Lech, and made

him afraid to cross the river. Some writers are of opinion that
they were called Alioruna, and prove their assertion by comparison
with Jornandes, who maintained that the mis-shapen Huns were
descended from the Aliorumnes. These beings were afterwards
called Alrunes or Alrauns.

It was said that the Alraun was cut out of a root with a distant
resemblance to the human form. For a long time the well-known
climbing plant, bryony, was regarded in Germany as an Alraun.
But when the Germans invaded Italy in the tenth and eleventh
centuries, they found the mandrake which resembled what they
imagined much more nearly than the bryony.

According to tradition this plant only grew under the gallows
upon which some one had been hung. A wise woman dug there
at midnight while using horrible incantations. The moment to
enter on the search was at the time of the solstice, when the moon
in its last quarter was throwing its pale light around. The root
was disinterred with a low cry of pain. The woman, a look of
madness on her face, hastened away with her prize, which writhed
like a living thing in her arms. She took it home and laid it on
her soft bed. There the misshapen creature lay before her, pale as
death, without eyes, and on its thick skull a few bristly hairs were
visible. She felt bound to it with an overflowing love like a
mother to her child. She pressed two juniper berries into the
holes where its eyes should have been, and a third one into the
back of its head. These berries became real eyes, but were round,
not oval, like human eyes.

The earth-born creature grew rapidly under her care, but only
reached the height of a three-years child. He climbed roofs and
trees like a monkey, and laughed at his foster-mother's anxiety for
him. He found and dug for her treasures of silver and gold that
had lain hidden under the earth.

Thus the family grew rich and respected, but the woman was not happy. Her father, trusting in his riches, strove to gain princely power and was executed for high treason; her lover and her brother killed each other for the sake of her wealth. The Alraun laughed at her tears; he had a diabolical delight in plaguing her until at last she died insane under the same gallows from beneath which she had dug him up.

This story reminds us of Wodan, the hanging god, and of the degrading influence of wealth on the human mind. It also leads our thoughts on to the witches, who originally had no resemblance to the barbarous women we mentioned before.

FINGAL'S CAVE.

PART EIGHTH.

ÖGIR AND HIS FOLLOWERS.

IN the Black Forest, a few miles from Lake Mummel, whither we have once already led our reader, lay a village; the inhabitants were wont to delight themselves on the merry Maydays with joyous game and dance.

To these festivities there often came a strange maiden, who joined in the gay country dance. A string of pearls bound up her hair, and another hung round her neck; a green silken robe draped her graceful figure. Her features were so exquisitely lovely, that the hearts of the young fellows beat higher in their breasts as they led the maiden to the dance.

She seemed to favour one Michael Stauf more than all the rest. He was the strongest lad in wrestling and in boxing, and the most expert dancer. The old folk, who watched the games of the young people, said they had never seen a more comely pair upon the dancing green; however, when the clock struck eleven, the young girl always left the dancers, and although many a lad followed her eagerly, she had disappeared into the darkness of the forest before he could come up with her.

Yet once, as Michael followed her, he discovered traces of her footsteps; he hastened after her, and overtook her. They walked on together side by side, until she led him by a path which he had never seen before, although the wood was fully known to him, since he had been born in it.

After a while, they reached the lake. He asked her, if she would return with him to his farm, and be his wife. She answered, she would ask her father, who was a strict and severe man, but she feared he would not allow such a union.

With these words she sprang into the water and disappeared from his sight.

Michael now saw that she was a water-nixie; but his heart still clung to her, and all his thoughts were how he should make her his own.

The merry day of festivity was over; work in the fields began, and left Michael little time for pondering on marriage. But when winter came, and his leisure hours were many, his imagination was constantly engaged in picturing to himself how happy he would be if he could only make the lovely maid in the green robe the mistress of his farm. Day and night he dreamed of her, and all the pleasure that he once had taken in games of cards and dice forsook him, and he never now visited the noisy company in the village inn, where formerly he had rarely failed. And in the spinning room he was never seen, and the spinsters were greatly troubled in their minds why the rich Michael no more visited them.

Anxiously, full of longing, he awaited the month of May, and when at last it came round he was the first upon the dancing-green. His hopes were not deceived, the maiden of the lake appeared as before, and danced and chatted with him ; when the hour of eleven sounded from the bell, she accepted his company on the homeward road. Yet when he spoke of his marriage plans she became sad.

" My father," she said, " will allow of no union with mortals, and he is very strict ; he allows no disobedience."

" A woman shall leave father or mother, and cleave unto her husband," he cried ; " if thou wilt, we will at once return, get married, and when thou art in my home, we will see who can take thee away against both our wills."

" Hush," she said, frightened, " lest my father hear thy words. Dost thou not see the springs and brooks around us ? They are all in his service ; they would swell up to furious torrents, and overwhelm us, if he bade them. Do not arouse his anger. He will have no connection with mortal men, for they have nicknamed him Duck-bill, because he has a nose of horn, like all men with us. Yet he is friendlily disposed towards thee, and sends thee this ring, with a great carbuncle in it, which will indicate to thee where all the treasures of the earth lie hid."

With these words she put the jewel on his finger. The stone flashed like the rays of the sun, and when he turned it towards the ground, he saw in the depths below his feet veins of gold and silver, which ran through the earth like frozen brooks.

" A wonderful sight," he said, " but I desire no other treasure

than thee ; I am rich enough already for us two to live in peace
and plenty."

They had come to the shore of the lake, and after a hurried farewell, she disappeared into the flood.

Michael was a bold and fearless lad. If he got an idea into his
head, nothing could get it out again. He would have liked to have
had the water-king before him, that he might fell him to the
ground. As this was not possible, however, he had to content
himself with brooding on his way home over a plan by which he
might bring the beautiful girl to fall in with his ideas.

On the following day she came at the usual time, and was more
beautiful and more friendly to him than ever. Towards evening
he slunk away from the dancing-green and climbed up the church
spire, and there put the hands of the clock a whole hour back.
When he returned he hurled a young fellow away who was leading
the lake-damsel to the dance, and carried her off himself, as though
he would dance his life away. He did not become tired, and she
too seemed of like mood ; the pipers grew blue in the face, the
fiddlers' arms grew weary, but they dared not cease : he threatened as he rushed past them, he promised a threefold reward.

At last the clock struck eleven. Then the maiden escaped from
his arms, and started off for the wood. He followed her, and they
had hardly gone a few paces when they heard the clock in a
neighbouring village strike twelve.

The maiden was horrified, and trembled in all her limbs. He
told her what he had done, and vowed that she should be his that
very night. Yet all his pressure, all his arguing, was in vain ; she
only hurried her steps, weeping and lamenting.

At length they stood on the bank of the watery mirror, over
which the full moon played. It was in vain that he sought to
hold her back ; she whispered only softly,—

" Take heed what happeneth ; if a milk-white flood ariseth from the lake, I am saved, and will be thine; but if a blood-stained one, then I am lost."

Scarcely had she said these words than she sprang forward, and sank beneath the waters. Where she had disappeared a funnel-shaped cavity remained, from the edge of which wave-rings extended over the whole lake.

Michael looked upon the surface of the water in breathless expectation, and now, now there rises up from the cavity not milk-white but a blood-red stream, and a cry strikes his ear, entering his heart like the thrust of a dagger.

"Fiendish Neck!" he cried. "Murderer of thy child! take back thy magic ring, thou wicked Duck-bill!"

And he threw the jewel against a rock in the lake, so that it flew into a thousand pieces.

As soon as the fragments touched the water it began to foam and bubble, as if a subterranean fire were causing it to seethe. It swelled and swelled, higher and higher, and in the middle a monstrous crested wave rose frothing up. The lake heaved, and its depths raged fiercely. It overflowed its banks; the monster wave bore the struggling youth along with it, in spite of his frantic efforts. Far and wide did the growing waters work devastation, and never were either the rich Michael or the Maiden of the Lake seen again.

Like this story, there are very numerous others, whose scenes are laid by springs, brooks, rivers, and lakes. They are told in England, Germany, in the Sclavonic, and in the Romance lands. Also from classic antiquity we have received the Naiads, River-gods, Sirens, etc.

Another legend, very popular in Germany, we give, translated into verse. Every one who has travelled up the Rhine has been shown the Loreley Rock, and been told the superstitions connected with it.

LEGEND OF THE LORELEY.

Unearthly music floats upon the air,
  The setting sun illumes th' impending crag,
The silent fishers watch their lurking nets,
  Or from the deep their finny booty drag.

That is the siren-song of Loreley;
  In jewelled sheen she sits upon the height;
Swift o'er the lyre her magic fingers flit,
  Her golden hair gleams in a flood of light.

See yonder bark by nervous arm impelled,
  So swiftly shooting down the glassy stream!
Anon it creeps, borne onwards by the tide,
  The youthful boatman rapt as in a dream.

That strange, weird melody enchains his soul,
  Upon the oars his listless arms repose,
Spell-bound he gazes on the dizzy height,
  With longings new and wild his bosom glows.

More swiftly glides the bark, the rock is near,
  He sees the siren beckon from the height,
Her song more thrilling, and more sweet her lyre,
  Her locks more golden in the golden light.

The reef-rocks rise, alas! he sees them not,
  Heeds not the warning shout from yonder shore,
The startled echoes sound from crag to crag,
  But by that boatman they are ne'er heard more.

The story of the "Old Man of the Sea" is perhaps a recollection of the Northern Ögir, who, if not the king was at least the highest and greatest of the water spirits.

Ögir, *i.e.* the Terrible, like his brothers Kari, ruler of the air, and Logi, ruler of fire, was a son of the old giant Forniot. Judging from the etymology of the word, he seems to be identical with the Grecian Okeanos, but possessing a more distinct personality, for the Greeks probably only knew the ocean from the stories of Phœnician sailors, while the Northern skippers boldly faced the

R

mighty sea and its terrors in their weak vessels, which they called dragons or snakes. Dreadful Ögir was married to Ran, who, like her husband, used to drag men down into the deep and bury them in the sand, or who, according to other accounts, received the souls of those who died at sea, as Hel did of those who died a "straw death" on land. They had nine daughters who afterwards became the mothers of Heimdal. The name of the Ögishelm, *i.e.* Helmet of Terror, comes from the King of the ocean. It was believed that the very sight of it filled the beholder with such terror that he would let his weapons fall as though he were paralyzed by magic art. The front of this helmet was adorned with a boar's head which yawned open-mouthed at the enemy. The Anglo-Saxons and Esthonians of the Baltic wore helmets of this sort, and the latter people believed that these head-pieces made the wearer either invisible or impervious to wounds. This reminds us of the dusk-cap in the Nibelungen Lay, whilst the boar's head puts us in mind of Freyer's Gullinbursti. The Ögishelm, judging from the formation of the word and from its meaning, seems to have been identical with the Ögis shield of Zeus, for this was by no means a goat's skin as people said later on, but was a weapon arousing feelings of terror. Zeus sometimes lent it to his son Apollo, who showed it to the enemy and made them fly in fear. The shield of Pallas Athene with the Medusa's head had much the same effect.

Ögir, the terrible king of the ocean, did not appear armed with the boar's helmet in the northern poems, but he must have worn it in the old days, the records of which are lost. He was milder of aspect than of yore, and although of giant race, he lived in friendship with the Ases. He was also represented as sitting on a rock, playing on a harp or a shell. No sooner was Ögir's music heard than the waves piled themselves mountain high, and flung themselves against each other with a wild roar, so that the earth trembled and the heavens threatened to split

ÖGIR AND RAN.

in twain. The vassals of Ögir were numerous, mermaids and sprits of all kinds were subject to him, and there are a great many interesting tales regarding them in every land. The stories of the magical music of the Necks are probably founded on the melodious sounds made by the water when falling over rocks or by the waves of the sea when confined within some cavern, such as Fingal's cave, etc. Nixies also sought the love of man, for thus and thus alone could they obtain the object of their desire, a loving immortal soul. The tragic turn which these stories generally take, almost seems to show that the possession of a soul was not happiness. Fouqué's "Undine" is one of the most beautiful of these tales.

Although the water spirits had no souls, they yet were filled with a longing for redemption and resurrection. There is a Christian tale which is a good illustration of this idea. Two children were once playing upon the sea-shore. A merry Neck was seated on a rock in front of them surrounded by water, and as he sat, he played on his harp so cheerily that it seemed to the children as if the very waves were dancing to his tune.

Then the elder boy called out to him jestingly: "Play on, merry sprite, play on; thou hast no hope of redemption or of resurrection."

"No hope!" wailed the Neck, beginning to play such sad music out of his sorrowful heart that the waves ceased to dance and the children felt quite miserable.

They went home and told their father, who was a Christian priest, what had happened. He chid them for their forwardness, bade them at once return to the Neck and tell him that there was hope of redemption and resurrection for him, for the Saviour had said: "I am not come into the world to judge the world, but that the world through me might be saved."

The boys did as their father told them. They found the Neck

still weeping bitterly. But when he heard the message of glad tidings, he smiled through his tears and touched the strings of his harp making them play mighty chords, and it seemed as though the heavenly hosts were singing to the music.

"The Saviour did not come to judge the world, but that the world through Him might be saved."

In this simple legend we see the triumph of Christianity over heathenism. It is sad that this aspect of Christianity is not always recognised by those who are called upon to teach its principles. But Charlemagne's Saxon war, the Inquisition, and other more recent events show how much the fundamental idea of its teaching has been misunderstood.

PART NINTH.

LOKI AND HIS RACE.

HE stood with his peasant wife and his two sons on the household hearth, and prayed to Odin that he would take under his protection their eldest boy, whom the monster had demanded.

Hardly had the prayer been offered up, when the king of the Ases stood in the hall, and promised to hide the boy securely, and to bring him back to them unharmed.

At his command the corn grew up in the night over many a wide acre, so quickly that it was ready for harvesting. In the middle of the field, he hid the boy, in a grain of an ear of corn. But in the morning the giant stood in the field, and with his sharp sword mowed down the corn. He shook with all his force the ears, and lo! there fell at last into his hand the very grain which hid the boy. In his need, he called to Odin, and the mighty god removed him from all danger, and took him back to his parents, who were in great care about him.

"I have fulfilled my promise," he said, "more ye must not demand of me."

With these words he disappeared; but the peasant and his

wife were not yet free from care, for the giant stood threatening in a neighbouring field, and was now coming towards the house, where he scented his victim.

They prayed Hönir that he might guard their darling from the monster; the beneficent god did not tarry; he took the boy with him into the greenwood, where immediately two silvery swans settled down before him, and he hid his little charge in the form of a feather of down in the neck of one of them.

However, the giant, who was called Skrymsli, strode onwards to the greenwood; he was powerful in magic, and enchanted the right swan to him, and bit his neck off. Yet the feather of down was wafted from his mouth, and Hönir caught it up, and carried the terrified boy back to his anxious parents.

The peasant and his wife now called to Loki for his help in their need; for they saw the giant coming with angry strides out of the wood. The god appeared at once, took the boy to the strand, and rowed with him far out to sea. And he angled and caught three large flounders.

After he had hidden the boy as the tinest egg in the roe of one of them, he threw the fishes overboard, and turned again towards land. Here he saw with astonishment, that Skrymsli had prepared his boat to go out fishing; he got into it with the giant, and sought, but all in vain, to put a stop to the voyage; the vessel flew on, driven by the powerful strokes of the giant, hurrying over the sound into the open sea, where the boatman sank his angle and stone into the water. He caught at once three flounders, and amongst them the desired Rogner.

" Give me that poor little fish," asked Loki insinuatingly.

" Hast thou an appetite then, Gaffer, hey? " snarled the giant; " thou wilt have to wait a long time I fancy! "

Thereupon he took the flounder between his knees, and counted every egg in the roe, until he found the one he wanted. But with a dexterous finger Loki snatched it up, and told the boy, when they reached the land, to spring with a light foot over the sand towards home.

Skrymsli saw the boy running, and hastened after him, but with every step he sank knee-deep into the sand. He found the door of the house shut; when he threw himself against it with great force, it broke in two; but, springing forwards, he ran his head into an iron pole. Loki was at once at hand, and cut off one of his legs, and then the other; and so the monster died; and his body covered the field.

The peasant and his wife brought thank-offerings to the god Loki, for their darling, whom the other gods had only hidden a short time, and who now rested safely in their arms.

The above story is still told on the Faroe Islands, and in fuller detail than we have been enabled to give it. It shows us an important fact, that Loki was not always looked upon as the principle of evil, as the enemy of gods and men.

Originally he was the god of the indispensable household fire, the god of the beneficent, kindly hearth; therefore he regularly appears in the trinity: thus the sons of the primeval giant Ymir were called Kari (air), Ögir or Hler (water), and Logi (fire); and similarly on the creation of mankind the trinity appears, Odin, Hönir and Lodur. Loki also accompanied Odin and Hönir on their travels to the giant Thiassi.

The father of Loki was Farbauti and his mother was Laufey (leafy isle). The former was probably the same as Bergelmir, the giant who escaped drowning in the Deluge by taking refuge in a boat, as another name for his mother was Nal, ship. Logi, the element of fire, was distinctly separated from Loki, for we saw that when in the halls of Skyrnir or Utgard-

Loki, the two were rivals in a wager as to which could consume the greater quantity of food in a given time. At first Loki was held in high honour as the giver of warmth and god of the domestic hearth, and was looked upon as the brother of Odin and Hönir, for the elements air, water and fire are intimately connected. He therefore belonged to the Ases, sat in their council, and often helped them out of difficulties by means of his cunning. As fire is not always the friend of man, but is also the element of destruction, the Loki of the myth developed ever more and more the dark side of his character. He showed himself as a cunning adviser, a false, traitorous comrade, and lastly as the murderer of all that was pure and holy. He destroyed innocence and righteousness, became the blasphemer of the Ases or their evil conscience ; and although he received immediate punishment for his wickedness, he yet succeeded in bringing about the universal destruction.

The name Loki has been derived from the old word "liuhan," to enlighten. It therefore has the same origin as the Latin *lux*, light. Thus he was also related to Lucifer (light-bringer), a title of honour which was given to the Prince of Darkness. In like manner as the northern tempter was chained to a sharp rock, Lucifer was believed in the middle ages to be chained down in hell. Saxo Grammaticus describes his Utgarthlocus (Utgard-Loki) as laden with chains in Helheim, which proves that the myth of Loki and his punishment was believed long after the Christian era.

As has been said before, Loki had three wicked children by the giantess Angurboda (bringer of anguish), Fenris, Hel and Jörmungander. But he also had a lawful wife, the faithful Sigyn, who brought him two sons, Wali and Narwi, and who remained with him during all the misery his punishment brought upon him. He had no servants or subjects, for the Salamanders or Fire-spirits which played a part in Roman and Oriental mythology were unknown in the north. But he had other mighty relations, namely Surtur of the Flaming Sword and the sons of Muspel, who helped him in the Last Battle when he had got rid of his bonds. The Dwarfs and Black-Elves that needed fire for their labours were in alliance with him, but were not subservient to him ; indeed, as we have already seen, they were often his enemies.

PART TENTH.

THE OTHER ASES.

WIDAR.

THE duel was over, Ases and Einheriar were seated in Walhalla emptying horns of foaming mead. Steps were heard approaching, and Widar came in, receiving a joyful greeting from all.

"Hail, Widar," said Bragi, the divine singer, and Hermodur, the bright herald of the gods, "hail, Widar, thou strong protection, thou help in every time of danger! Receive with this greeting the golden drink which beseems thee."

He thanked them and drank. He looked very grave, and spoke but little. Then Odin made him a sign to approach, and as he walked up the hall, he looked great and noble in their eyes ; his broad sword clanked at his side, and the sound made by the iron shoe on his right foot rang musically through the immeasurable hall.

"Widar, my silent son," said the Father of the gods, "in the time to come thou shalt be Avenger, Victor and Restorer. Come, follow me to the well of Mimir, that we may look into its depths and see what is hidden from gods and men."

And now the god of armies rose and went away followed by

Widar the Silent. They crossed the Homes to Mimir's Well. There sat the three Fatal Sisters, and there the swans floated noiselessly on their circling course.

Odin demanded a word of wisdom from the Norns.

Then they answered one after the other:

"Early begun!"

"Further spun."

"One day done!"

And Wurd said in conclusion:

"With joy once more won!"

After that the sisters rose and spoke together: "The circling ages roll on and change. Past and Future, passing and beginning again, thus the ends of existence meet. If the Father falls on the field of Wigrid, he reappears in Widar, the Avenger, the Victor, new-born in the halls of blessedness."

When the Norns had finished, the leaves of the World-Tree rustled melodiously, the eagle on its topmost bough sang aloud some song of storm or of victory, flapping its wings the while, and the dragon Nidhögg looked up, and forgot to gnaw the roots of the tree.

Meantime another witness had approached: it was Grid, the Giantess, the mother of Widar, who had lent Thor her girdle, gloves and staff of strength when he was about to find the river Wimur on his way to Geiröd's-Gard.

"Happy mother!" said Odin solemnly, "who was once wedded to me, thou also shalt rise again in thy son when the battle has been fought out on the field of Wigrid and Surtur's flames have been extinguished."

All three, their hearts filled with gladness, looked up at Yggdrasil, the holy ash-tree, the leaves of which rustled melodiously, while all creatures around were silent, as though they were listening to some wondrous music which told, not of death, but of eternal change.

Widar went home through the long green grass and bushes that never faded. He soon reached Landwidi, the house hidden in the wood. He ascended his throne, twined with green garlands, and sat there, silent as ever, thinking over the riddle of life. When and how did the immeasurable come into being? Why does it go on? How and when will it end? These are questions which the wise of all ages have puzzled over, and which they have tried to solve in divers ways, but without satisfying themselves, because there are limits set here to the inquiring mind. They only find words which they cannot explain, cannot understand: Eternal, Everlasting, Immeasurable. How grand and glorious it sounds, and yet the finite mind can have no conception of that yawning gulf without beginning and without end! The childlike faith alone, that had its rise with the star of Bethlehem, like the beautiful dawn of a new day, gives peace to the soul that thirsts after truth. For "although everything circles in eternal change, yet even in that change is preserved a quiet mind."

The myth does not inform us whether the silent Ase found a solution to the riddle, for, as we have seen, he was silent as the the grave; but he went forth boldly to the battle on the field of Wigrid, trusting to what the Norns and his father had told him. In this god we see an emblem of the inexhaustible power of Nature in making ever new shoots and flowers spring from what had grown old and faded.

HERMODUR THE SWIFT.

Odin, king of the Ases, was sitting on Hlidskialf weighing all past and future events. He saw blood flowing, noble blood; but all that was to come to pass looked indistinct and misty, like the sea in a fog, and the Norns had been silent when he questioned them.

His son, Hermodur, the bright herald of the gods, was standing before him, ready to be sent to make known his decrees to the people. The king signed to the Walkyries, who at once brought helmet and coat of mail, spear and shield, and armed the brave warrior for the battle.

"Up, my son," said the king, "saddle the good horse Sleipnir, and ride along the wind-cold roads, over frozen lakes and rivers and mountains, till thou comest to the land of the wild Finns. There in a gloomy dwelling amongst the fens shalt thou find the robber Rosstioph (horse thief), who entices travellers to come to him by magic art, binds them with enchanted bonds, murders them, and, after having robbed them, casts them] into the sea. He knows what will happen in future times ; force him with the Runic staff to tell thee what will come to pass."

Then Hermodur laid aside his spear and seized Gambantrin, the magic staff, instead. He saddled good Sleipnir, and hastened away to the land of the Finns, where Rosstioph lived in a gloomy dwelling amongst the fens.

The robber saw the storm-compelling rider at a distance. He used his magic arts to induce him to approach, and laid invisible snares for him. Hermodur saw ghost-like airy monsters trying to clutch at him with teeth and claws, but he beat them back with his staff, and Sleipnir leapt over all the magic traps. When the robber attacked him in giant form, Hermodur felled him with his club, and bound him hand and foot with his own cords, tying his throat so tight that he groaned out his readiness to tell what Hermodur wished to know.

So the Ase let him go, and he immediately began his terrible incantations. The sun lost its brightness and hid her face behind dark clouds ; the earth shook to her foundations ; the storm-wind shrieked, calling to mind now the howling of wolves, and now of the moans and groans of dying men.

"See there," cried the Finn, pointing over at the fen, "the answer to thy question is rising even at this very moment."

The Ase saw a stream of blood flowing that reddened the whole ground. Then a beautiful woman appeared, and afterwards a little boy rose close beside her; he grew in one night, and was armed with a bow and arrows.

"The king of the Ases shall offer his love to Rinda in the land of the Ruthenes, and she shall bear him a son who will avenge his brother's death."

Rosstioph ceased, and Hermodur returned to Allfather and told him all that he had heard and seen.

Hermodur went on many other errands for Odin, and as these errands were often of a warlike nature, he was perhaps regarded as a sword-god; indeed, he was supposed to be connected with the universal god Irmin, or Hermon. Amongst the Anglo-Saxons, on the other hand, he was looked upon as identical with dark Hödur, the Ase who brought the greatest misery upon Asgard.

WALI OR ALI, SKEAF.

Wali or Ali was the son of Odin and Rinda, who, as Rosstioph prophesied, should one day avenge the death of Baldur. We shall meet with this god again when we treat of the beautiful poem of Baldur's death, and will therefore merely remark in this place that Rinda means the rind, the hard-frozen crust of the earth, whose favour the god of heaven long woos in vain, in like manner as the cold of winter takes a long time ere it gives way before the warmth of spring, and it is only when summer's magic wand is brought in requisition that the victory is complete. Thus the god tries in vain to teach her that mild weather is the time for warlike deeds. He offers her shining garlands of flowers and golden ears of corn, but all to no purpose. He is at length obliged to use his divine power before he can force her to marry him. Her son is called Wali or Ali in the Edda ; according to Saxo, the Danish historian, he is Bous, or Bui, also Beav, *i.e.* the peasant, who, after the victory of the god of heaven, comes out of his dark hut and resumes his labour of tilling the earth.

The myth of Wali has, to a considerable extent, passed into the Hero-lays. We will now give one of the tales which owed their origin to this source.

Once upon a time many people were assembled on the sea-shore in the land of the Angles and not far from Schleswig. They were watching a small vessel sailing over the crested waves towards them. A gentle breeze filled out the white sails, but neither helm nor helmsman, nor yet sailors were to be seen. Bound to the mast-head was a shield, bright as the sun, though not blood-red, which would have betokened the arrival of an enemy.

The little vessel rounded the promontory at the mouth of the harbour as cleverly as though a good pilot had been on board, and made straight for the land. The people now saw a little new-born child lying on a sheaf of corn (Schof, Skeaf) on the deck, with ornaments of gold, silver and precious stones scattered about it. The boy sat up and looked at the surrounding people so lovingly that all with one voice exclaimed :

" He is the child of some god ; we will take him and bring him up, and he shall be our king."

They did so, and the boy grew strong and active, soon got the better of his comrades in the lists, learnt to honour the laws and ordinances of the free people who had adopted him, and gained the hearts of all by his wisdom.

When he had grown to be a man, the free people of the land raised him on a war-shield, and said :

S

"Thou shalt be our king, for we shall be better off under thy rule than were we to remain a republic, and thou shalt be called Skeaf, because thou didst come to us lying upon a sheaf."

The new king governed the land wisely and justly, and the favour of the gods was with him, so that the harvests were plenteous and the country visibly prospered. His judgments filled the people with admiration, whether given in the law-courts or in the assembly; therefore he was loved and honoured as a father. His fame spread over every land, and kings of foreign nations made him umpire in their disputes. No neighbouring people ventured to declare war upon him, nor was any Wiking-raid made upon his coasts. His subjects enjoyed peace and security of life and property.

At length the time came for him to leave the world, and he desired his faithful friends to lay him once more on the sheaf of corn in the little vessel and scatter about him the jewels he had brought with him, that he might return to the place whence he came.

The corpse of the king, its head crowned with flowers, was placed on a sheaf in the little vessel, and all the ornaments he had brought with him were placed about him as before. Then a gentle breeze arose and wafted the ship far away to the Home of the Light-Elves, the land of spirits, from which Skeaf had been sent when a child. Meanwhile his faithful friends stood on the shore for a long time weeping for the loss of their good king, as men always weep when a dear friend leaves them.

Before his departure Skeaf had promised his sorrowing people that he would send his son from the happy home to rule over this kingdom, and, as we learn from Danish and Anglo-Saxon traditions, he kept his word. His son, however, did not come to the Angles, but to the warlike Danes.

BALDUR AND HÖDUR.

Baldur was bright and beautiful, and a radiance like that of the sun proceeded from him.   The camomile flower was called Baldur's eye-brow, because of its bright purity.   Kindness, innocence and righteousness were the qualities by which he was known, and he could win every heart by the eloquence of his words.   In his palace, Breidablick, nothing impure, nothing evil could ever take place, nor could any injustice be done.   It was a holy house.

The wife of Baldur the Beloved was Nanna, daughter of Nep, according to Uhland, Blossom, daughter of the Bud.   She also was the joy of gods and men, and loved her husband ever after his death.

In one tale Nanna was the daughter of King Gewar of Norway, and Hödur was her foster-brother.   They were brought up together by Gewar.   Once, when returning home from the marriage of his friend King Helgi of Heligoland to Princess Thora of Finnland, Hödur lost his way in a fog, and while trying to find it again, came to the dwelling of three wood-spirits, who greeted him by his name, and gave him a suit of armour, adding that he must beware of Baldur, son of Odin, and that he should first have victory, but should afterwards be defeated.

When he got home he found that Baldur had seen Nanna, had fallen in love with her, and had asked her hand in marriage.   The king had then replied that there could be no real bond between Ases and mortals, and Baldur had gone away threatening vengeance.

On hearing this, Hödur said that he was not afraid of the Ase, and entreated Gewar to give him Nanna to wife.   The king answered that he loved his foster-son, but that Baldur was invincible ; if, however, Hödur could manage to gain possession of

the magic sword of Mimring, the wood-demon, he might marry
Nanna, as the odds would not be then so great in the Ase's favour.

After infinite trouble and danger, Hödur succeeded in conquer-
ing the Hrimthurse and in carrying off his sword and a wonderful
bracelet, the thickness of whose gold increased every night.

The fame of this deed, and of the magic sword and bracelet,
spread through every land.   Geldar, Duke of Saxony, heard of
it, and trusting in his men and ships, set out to try and gain possession of the treasures.   Hödur sailed out to sea to meet him in battle
array.   Before any mischief was done, Geldar hoisted the white shield
of peace, as a sign that he wished to treat with the Norwegians.
After a short parley, Geldar and Hödur concluded terms of peace,
and entered into alliance with each other.   While they were feasting together, news came that Baldur was sailing up to give them
battle and carry away beautiful Nanna.   They hastened to her
defence, and on the way were joined by Helgi.

There was a terrible battle, and Mimring's sword flashed like
lightning in Hödur's hand.   Hödur threw himself into the thick of
the fight, and his coat of mail, which had been given him by
the wood-spirits, kept him safe and sound.   Man after man fell
dead under his blows.   But the Ases, with strong Thor, were
amongst his opponents, and Geldar and many more were slain
by them.   After a desperate struggle, Hödur succeeded in disarm-
ing Thor.   No sooner was this the case than terror seized the
enemy, and Ases and warriors fled pell-mell.   Even Baldur forsook the field in cowardly fashion.   Hödur then commanded that
a great funeral pile should be erected for friend and foe, but chief
of all, he placed the corpse of his faithful brother-in-arms, Geldar,
the Duke of Saxony, to whom a grave mound was built.   Hödur
now pursued his victory and conquered Denmark and Sweden.

According to other versions, Hödur was already King of Denmark,
and the battle took place near Roesfild in Zealand, whe˙˙

Baldur's well, Baldur's haven, and Baldur's sound (the Baltic Sea), still remind us of the circumstance. The Danish rhymed chronicle indeed informs us that Baldur was killed here and was buried in the Sound.

We see from this how the myths of Baldur and Hödur have been formed by story-tellers and poets, and if these now given are much more modern in their origin, they still give the battle between summer and winter, in which the god of winter has the victory at the end of autumn.

After this battle Hödur married Nanna, and they spent a happy winter together.

When spring returned, Baldur once more raised his head, and was filled with new courage. He again prepared to fight for the lovely Nanna.

The battle raged night and day, and Hödur got the worst of it, in spite of Mimring's magic sword. He had at length to fly to Jutland and wait there till he had collected a new army.

One day, as he was wandering in a wood, he saw the three wood-spirits who had given him the coat of mail. He now recognised them to be Walkyries by their white horses and armour. He reproached them for having prophesied good fortune when he had had evil fortune. But they replied : " First victory, then defeat, was what we promised. But now the time of good fortune is returning to thee. If thou canst only get hold of some of the food which increases thine enemy's Ase strength, thou mayest yet wound his sacred body with. Mimring's sword. Three women wrapped in the garments of night, their heads hidden under dark veils, prepare and bring him this strengthening food."

No sooner had they spoken these words than they and their dwelling vanished from before his eyes.

The hero stood alone in the dark pine-wood ; his heart filled with new hope. He went down into the valley and called upon his faithful followers to rally around him, and they came in crowds. He soon found himself at the head of a large army, and when he went to seek out his foe, he found him ready to receive him. Baldur was still dissatisfied in spite of his victory, for he had not gained the lovely Nanna, he had not been able to carry her away, to her natural home the sunny south.

The battle lasted, as before, all day, and only ceased when it was too dark to see to fight. Hödur could not sleep, so he got up in the third night-watch and set out to see what was going on in the enemy's camp. All at once he saw three women dressed in garments of night, and with their faces hidden under dark veils, walking rapidly through the wood. He followed them and entered their house after them. He pretended to be a great skald. A harp was given him and he played marvellous airs. While doing this he watched the women preparing some gruel, and saw how they held snakes over it, making them breathe into it after it was finished.

"That must be the food that increases Baldur's Ase strength," he thought, so he asked for some as payment for his music. The women consulted together; one refused, but the others were of opinion that it could do no harm to give the stranger what he asked, maintaining that it would only make him a better skald than before. They therefore granted his request.

He swallowed the plateful given him as rapidly as possible, and immediately he felt an unusual strength in all his limbs; he felt as if he could have challenged all the Ases to battle, he was so strong.

The women sought vainly to prevent the skald leaving them. He rushed out into the open air and found that a bitterly cold north-wind was blowing. As he was hastening along in the dim grey morning light, he unexpectedly met his deadly enemy. They at once prepared to fight. Each thought only of attack

neither of defence; the one was protected by his coat of mail
the other by his divinity; but at length Baldur received a
terrible blow on his hip, and Mimring's sword passed through
his body. Hödur hastened to the camp, told his people what
had happened, and led them on to battle.

Meanwhile, Baldur was only wounded, and not dead as Hödur
had supposed. He had himself laid upon a stretcher and carried
into the dreadful battle, which raged undecided until night-fall.
In the night dark Hel approached his couch. She told him
that he should enter her realm on the following day, and that
she had a feast ready to greet his arrival. Her prophecy was
fulfilled.

Baldur's sorrowing followers buried him with royal honours
under a mighty mound, which the gods consecrated and protected by miraculous signs.

Hödur regained possession of his kingdom, but he never returned to his beloved Nanna, for Bous (Bui = peasant), son of Odin
and Rinda, took the field against him in the following spring
and slew him in the fight, for he had lost the coat of mail
given him by the wood-spirits and had vainly sought for the
women in the garments of night, to beg them to give him some
of their magic food.

We recognise the natural myth of the struggle between light
and darkness, summer and winter, in this story. Moreover,
Gewar means spring (from war, Latin, *ver*), and he was the father
of Nanna, blossom. In this tale the original signification of the
myth had been forgotten. The songs of the Edda regarding
Baldur were almost entirely concerned about the death of the
god of light and the love his wife bore him, about the changes
of the seasons and the coming of Ragnarök.

FORSETI.

In the land of the Friesians twelve men, well known for their wisdom and righteousness, were chosen as judges in the olden time. These men, who were called Asegen, *i.e.* Elders, went about from one district to another throughout the country deciding difficult questions and settling disputes according to the ancient laws and privileges. It was always said that it was from Fosite, Baldur's son, that the Friesians and their first Elders had learnt the laws by which the country was governed. The place where he had taught them these righteous ordinances was an island, which is now known as Heligoland or holy land, whose skippers even yet show their Friesian descent in their muscular and active forms.

According to the northern myth, Forseti was the son of Baldur and Nanna; for righteousness, whose representative Forseti was, proceeds from clearness of judgment and immaculate purity. He used to sit all day long in his hall Glitnir, whose silver roof rests upon golden pillars, and settle all disputes and differences of opinion. As he was only, as it were, an attribute of his father personified, he seems to have vanished with him from the worlds of Ases and men, after which the Wolf's time of power began, and immoral, evil forces gain'd ever more and more the upper hand, until at length Ragnarök, the Judgment of the gods, began and the drama of the northern faith came to a close.

FREYA AMONG THE DWARFS.
(*See page* 211.)

PART ELEVENTH.

SIGNS OF THE APPROACHING DESTRUCTION OF THE WORLD.

THE GOLDEN AGE.

THE poems of the skalds tell us of the Golden Age, that happy time of child-like innocence. No human being lived then on the green earth, which was inhabited by the Ases, who dwelt there without restrictions of any kind, or any longing after the unattainable. They had no past dimmed with tears, no difficulties in the present, nor did the future threaten them with a grievous doom. They lived for days and years in untroubled joy. They laid up stores of food, made hammers, tongs, anvils and tools of all kinds for themselves. They forged metals and carved wood, and whatever they did was beautiful to look upon. They had so much gold that they used it for making their household utensils. Still they did not know the value of the metal, and only liked it because it was bright and pleasant to look upon. They called this happy time the Golden Age, because life was then without care or sorrow, and not because of their wealth. They built houses and holy-places for themselves; they played merry games with golden disks in the court-yard and on the Field of Ida. They felt neither love of money nor desire of gain, nor yet did they ever wish to do themselves good to the injury of others.

Then they jestingly created the numerous race of Dwarfs, who burrowed in the earth and brought its hidden treasures forth to the light of day. The Ases looked covetously at the glittering hoard, and then the Golden Age, the time of innocence, passed away.

After that Gullweig (golden step), the wicked enchantress, was born. Three times the Ases thrust her into the smelting-pot, and each time she rose again more wondrously entrancing than before, so that their whole souls were filled with covetousness and other evil desires.

SIN.

Gullweig was probably the cause of the first war, the war between the Ases and Wanes. She glided about from one camp to the other stirring up dissension. But fortunately peace was soon concluded. The eyes of the gods were now opened, so that they perceived the danger that threatened them. They saw the Moun-

tain-Giants and Hrimthurses far away over in Jotunheim, saw how
they had increased in numbers, how they had already made good
their entrance into Midgard, and were looking threateningly up at
beautiful Asgard, with its palaces, perfumed groves and flowery
meads.

Heimdal was a faithful watchman, but still the Ases feared lest
he should be taken unawares. So they assembled in their hall of
judgment, and took counsel together how best they might ensure
their safety. It seemed to them that their surest plan would be
to build a wall round Asgard, reaching to the skies, in which strong
doors should be placed.

While they were consulting as to the best way of carrying out
their plan, a tall, stately man, with a disagreeable expression of
countenance, came up and offered to complete the wall, without
help from any one, in three winters. He said that he was a smith,
a very skilful man, and that he thoroughly understood the art of
building. In payment for his work he demanded that divine
Freya should be given him to wife, and that he should also have
the sun and moon awarded him, as they would make such good
lights for him to work by. The Ases were undetermined ; but
Loki, the arch-scoundrel, whispered in their ears that they should
promise to grant the builder's request on condition that he finished
the work in the course of one winter. The man consented to these
terms, saying that he would wager his head he could finish the
work within the appointed time, if he were allowed to have the
help of his horse Swadilfari. Again the Ases hesitated, but Loki
strongly urged that they should consent, as an unreasoning animal
could not be of much use.

So the bargain was concluded, and each party swore holy oaths
by dark Hel, by the Leipter Flood and the primæval icebergs, that
the conditions made on either side should be fulfilled faithfully and
truly.

The work was begun on the first day of winter. The Ases saw what monstrous loads of rocks and stones the builder's horse carried, swift as the wind, wherever his master desired. The wall grew apace, and was strong and solid as an iceberg. It was as smooth and shining as polished steel, and at the end of winter it was nearly finished.

The great gate of the fortress was now alone to be made, and that could be easily done in the three days that were still to elapse before the beginning of summer.

The Ases consulted together in their distress, for if the smith were to carry Freya and the sun and moon away with him in payment for his work, beauty and sweetness would vanish from Asgard, and eternal night would overwhelm the world.

Many of the gods longed for the presence of strong Thor, who had been far away waging war on monsters of all kinds when the contract was made with the smith, and who had not yet returned. They seated themselves on their thrones of judgment, and tried to find a way out of their difficulty. They asked each other who it was that had advised them to conclude the bargain with the smith. Every one knew that it was the author of all evil—false, treacherous Loki. Then they all crowded round him accusing and threatening him.

"Let him die a shameful death," they cried, "if he does not help us out of our difficulty."

Loki tremblingly promised, with a holy oath, that he would prevent the builder finishing the wall, and would thus deprive him of his reward.

The next day, when the smith went to the mountains with Swadilfari, to fetch stones and wood for his work, a mare galloped towards them whinnying. Immediately the horse rushed to meet her, kicking the cart and harness in pieces. He followed the flying mare through wood and meadow, pursued by the breathless smith.

The pursuit lasted the whole day and night, and when the builder at length succeeded in catching his horse they were both so exhausted that they could do nothing next day.

That evening, as the man stood looking at the wall which he knew he could not now finish in time, a giant's rage came over him. He accused the Ases of being false perjured gods, who had deprived him of his just reward by cunning and by treachery. He threatened to make himself master of Asgard by force, and lifted huge rocks and trunks of trees with which to destroy the place and its inhabitants. And now the Ases perceived that he was a giant, and that they had allowed one of their deadly enemies to enter their holy city. They cried aloud for strong Thor to come and defend them against the giant.

A thunder clap was heard, a flash of lightning lit up the darkness, the earth trembled, and Thor was standing between the Ases and the enraged giant. He at once recognised the Hrimthurse, flung Miölnir and broke the giant's skull, which was as hard as a stone, and bits of it went flying in all directions. The black soul of the monster sank into Nifelhel, which was its proper habitation.

In course of time the mare that had enticed Swadilfari from his work had an eight-legged foal, and this foal was Sleipnir, which when it was grown became Odin's horse, and used to bear the Father of the gods swift as the wind through the air and over the waves of the sea. But the Ases had sinned, they had broken their oath ; for they had sworn to fulfil the contract they had made with the smith without trickery of any kind, and the Jotun had justly charged them with perjury. Their tempter was Loki, and he it was who in the form of the mare had enticed Swadilfari away from his work, and had thus prevented the completion of the wall.

IDUNA'S DEPARTURE.

Fair Iduna had made herself an airy dwelling amongst the green branches of the world-tree Yggdrasil. There she received her beloved husband, Bragi, every evening, and he rejoiced her heart with his songs. The woodland birds joined their singing to his, and the music they made was so sweet that even the grave Norns were touched by it.

When all living things were sunk in sleep, the goddess sprinkled the ash from the well into which the divine mead had flowed that had been brought there by Odin, and so the World-tree remained fresh and green. The well, like the mead, was called Odrörir, and was that draught of inspiration which Gunlöd had once kept hidden in a mountain, but which Odin had rescued for the needs of gods and men. Like Iduna's apples, it had the power of making all who tasted it younger and more beautiful, and was identical with the fountain of Urd, with the water of which the Norns sprinkled Yggdrasil. Unnumbered years passed away; the World-tree flourished and remained young and strong as ever, thanks to the care of the Norns and Iduna; Bragi sang to his wife and to the world; but sin had defiled Ases and men, holy oaths were broken, truth, faith and the fear of God had disappeared, murder and war were everywhere to be seen; then it was that the Destruction of the Universe came nearer, and the Wolf rattled his chains preparatory to breaking them.

Now it happened about this time that one evening neither the songs of Bragi nor of the birds were to be heard, that the branches of Yggdrasil hung down sapless and withered, and that Odrörir seemed to have dried up. Next morning, when the Ases, terrified by these signs, asked for Iduna, they found that she had fallen from the tree down into the deep valleys below to the daughter of

Norwi (night). The well was really dried up, and every green thing threatened to fade and wither.

So Odin sent his raven, Hugin, away to find out the meaning of these portents of evil. Quick as thought the messenger flew through the wide heavens, and then sank down into the realm of the Dwarfs, Dain (dead) and Thrain (stiff), both of whom knew what should come to pass. But they were lying sunk in a heavy trance-like sleep, and in their sleep they moaned indistinctly some few words about coming horrors and flames. The Ases, therefore, knew not what to do, and watched all nature and Yggdrasil slowly fading and dying. They stretched a wolf-skin, white and soft as the winter's snow, over the abyss where Iduna lay sorrowing, that she might no more see her happy home amongst the ash-boughs. The Father of the Gods sent Heimdal, the faithful watchman, cunning Loki, and sorrowful Bragi to question the fair goddess as to the future. The messengers, after passing innumerable were-wolves on their way, at last came to the place where Iduna was lying, pale and sad. They asked her eagerly what she could tell them of future events, but she only answered them with tears.

Heimdal and Loki returned full of sorrow, but Bragi stayed with his wife, that she might not die of grief. After the return of the messenger, the Ases consulted together as to what was to be done next. But they were all weary and much in need of rest, so the Father of the Ases dismissed the assembly until the morrow.

Next morning, when Odin awoke, he found Frigga standing weeping by his bed. Her lips trembled as she told him that her son Baldur, the well-beloved, had dreamt that pale Hel had come to him and had signed to him to follow her. Then the mighty god arose in his strength. He had made up his mind what to do : he would seek intelligence of the realm of the dead ; he must know what was coming upon the world and the Ases.

This is what we learn from the lay called "Odin's Magic Raven"

(Hrafnagalder), which is a description of the beginning of autumn or early winter. Would the goddess Iduna rise again in spring and bring new life to the dead leaves and flowers, or was her departure a sign that the Last Battle was about to be fought, and that the flames of Surtur would soon begin their devastating work? These questions filled the minds of the Ases.

One writer states that in his opinion the events mentioned in this poem refer to an unusual drought in Osning, and to the long cessation of the flow of the intermittent spring which, with other brooks, forms the Bullerborn, and which has never once dried up since 1630. Still, it must be remembered, while considering this interesting hypothesis, that a northern skald translated the original Saxon poem, or rather worked the idea of it out anew, and that as he did so he was filled with the thought that Iduna's departure, and the fading and dying of all nature, portended the approach of the Last Battle.

PART TWELFTH.

BALDUR'S DEATH.

HOW WALA WAS CONJURED UP.

THE myth tells us that when Mother Night sank as usual into Nifelhel, Day followed her looking bright and glorious. His golden-maned horse bore his glittering chariot across the heavens. But soon a grey mist rose and hid the shining equipage. The sun looked down sadly upon Midgard and upon Asgard, as though through a thick veil, and seemed as if mourning some dreadful catastrophe. A dense fog rested upon Breidablick, so that its golden roofs and battlements were invisible. The gods and goddesses hastened to the assembly full of dismay about the departure of Iduna and Baldur's dreams. They shook and cast the runes, and those of death lay uppermost. Terror seized the Ases, but Odin rose in all his majesty and said :

"I foresee only too clearly what is about to happen ; yet will I call up Wala from the realm of the dead, and she shall give me a sure answer to my questions as to what will come to pass."

Then he saddled Sleipnir and rode off swift as an eagle, to the north towards Nifelheim.

Meanwhile, the gods consulted together and proposed various

T

plans. At last it seemed to them that the best thing they could do would be to make all living creatures, and even by means of magic power force every inanimate object, to swear to do no hurt to Baldur's holy body.

Frigg, the anxious mother of the god of light, herself undertook the task. She went through every country as quickly as the sun passes over the sky. And all mortal men, the Hrimthurses, the Light-Elves, the Water-sprites, and even the Black-Elves, that race which shuns the light, swore a solemn oath not to harm the Well-beloved. Trees and plants, stones and metals were also bound over to spare Baldur.

Meanwhile, Odin rode through dark glens down to Nifelheim. A dog with gaping jaws came out to meet him from the kingdom of Hel, and as he came drops of blood fell from his jaws upon his neck and chest. He stood still and howled as the god rode past. Odin hastened to the eastern gate of the dark abode. There he found the mound of Wala who had long been dead. The Father of the Gods dismounted. He stood on the grave mound that was surmounted by a memorial stone, and began his incantation, the song that awakened the dead.

"Awake, Wala, awake from thy death-sleep! Arise from out the grave wherein thou hast rested so long! Three times do I strike thy dwelling-place with my runic staff that thou mayst know no more peace on thy bed of mould, until thou hast given me a true answer to my questions."

He then struck the grave thrice with his mighty staff, and the ground shook, the stone sank down, the earth opened, and pale Wala arose wrapped in her shroud.

"Who is it?" she asked in a hollow voice, "that troubles my repose? Snow has covered my bed, and the rains and dews have watered it for many years. I have long been dead."

Odin replied : "Wegtam (knower of the road) is my name, and

I am the son of Waltam (knower of battles). Speak, for whom has Hel prepared the benches with rings and the golden beds ?"

She answered : "A shining goblet is standing ready for Baldur the good, which he must drink with Hel to the woe of the Ases. If I am forced to speak I must make known the coming evil ; grant me therefore silence."

"Thou shalt not be silent !" cried the god, "until I know all that I dimly foresee. Who is it that is to send the glorious son of the Father of Battles down to Hel's dismal abode ? "

Then the prophetess said dejectedly: "The brother will send his brother there, the god of darkness will send the god of light, Hödur will send the son of the Father of Battles down to the realm of Hel. Forced to speak, I have to make known the misfortune that was coming ; grant me now silence."

The King of the Gods, who was accustomed to look future events in the face without fear, stood there drawn to his full height, and went on questioning Wala. He asked who was to avenge Baldur, and bring death upon the murderer. She told him that Odin would have a son by Rinda who would grow up in one night, who would not wash his hands nor comb his hair until he had brought the murderer to the funeral pyre. Then he asked the name of the woman who alone of all creatures would not weep for Baldur the well-beloved.

"Thou art not Wegtam," she cried, "thou art Odin and knowest all things. Go home now to Asgard. Thou hast awakened the dead with thy mighty runes, and made her speak with thee. None other will disturb my slumber until Loki is free again and the gods are about to pass away."

We have given this ghastly but beautiful poem almost in its entirety, and have only endeavoured to make some vague expressions somewhat clearer, and to smooth away a few discrepancies.

The poet probably saw that the days were growing shorter, and that the sun scarcely showed above the horizon in the far North, while a cold frosty mist covered land and sea ; these were to him the signs of the approach of winter, of the death of the god of light. Odin had a foreboding of what was about to happen, but could only gain certain intelligence in the realm of the dead. So the poet let him descend there and question Wala who had long been dead.

Joy had returned to the green home of the gods. Baldur's life seemed to be secure now that all animate and inanimate things had been bound by an oath to do him no harm. Who would hurt the darling, the light of the world ? The Ases laughed and jested, played with golden balls, shot arrows, flung spears and aimed blunt weapons at Baldur for fun, and not one of these missiles struck his holy body. It was as though an invisible power turned them aside as they approached him, for all, wood, metal and stones were sworn over to spare him.

The Ases then tried sharp weapons, and to their delight found the result the same. Loud was the laughter when it was discovered that the best aimed blow of a sword did not touch him, that spears, stones and arrows missed him.

Frigg heard the shouts and cheers as she sat in her golden halls of Fensaler, and longed to know what was the matter. At this moment an old woman limped past leaning on her crutch. The queen signed to her to enter, and asked her what was going on. The old woman immediately gave her a long description of what she had seen, ending by saying that Baldur was standing smiling in the midst of the hail of weapons looking as if they were only flowers with which he was being pelted. And Frigg's heart rejoiced within her as she thought of the strength of the Ases, and of how she had conquered the evil fate that was to have come upon her son.

" Yes," she said, " everything that is in heaven and earth and under the earth swore willingly to do no hurt to the giver of light and joy, of growth and bloom."

"Thou must have had hard work," said the old woman, "but of course thou didst not think it necessary to bind the grass and flowers and other harmless things with an oath?"

"No trouble was too great to take for our darling," answered the goddess, "and the only thing I passed over was the little plant of mistletoe growing on the great oak at the gate of Walhalla, and that really does not matter, it is so soft and so weak a thing that it could do no harm."

"Thou art a careful mother," said the old woman; "it would have been very unwise to have passed over the flowers, for in their perfume a deadly poison is often hid. But as for the mistletoe, that only grows and bears seed in the cold winter time, it could not hurt the god of light."

With these words the old woman took leave of the queen, and continued her walk down the lonely road that led to Walhalla. When she reached the great oak at the gate on which the tiny plant of mistletoe grew, she threw off the woman's dress, and behold it was Loki, looking more diabolical than ever! Until now he had only rejoiced in the misfortunes of the Ases, and had done them injury now and then by his cunning, but had always been forced by their threats to help them out of the scrapes he had got them into; now, however, envy and jealousy were driving him to commit a horrible crime.

He drew circles, muttered many a magic spell, and touched the tiny mistletoe twig with the end of his crooked stick, and immediately it grew as long as the shaft of a spear. Then he tore it down from the tree, cut away the side branches and knots, and made it resemble a spear in every respect.

"Thou seemest so young and weak," he said, with a scornful laugh, "let us see whether thou art not stronger than all the weapons of these foolish jesting Ases, stronger than that much be-praised and famous Baldur."

He went to join the Ases, and found them still amusing themselves as before. Strong Hödur was standing outside the circle, taking no part in the games.

"Why art thou so lazy?" asked Loki, "thou art the strongest of all the Ases, so why dost thou not fling a spear in Baldur's honour?"

"I have no weapon, and I am blind," answered Hödur; "night is all around me, before me and behind me."

"Here is a spear for thee," said the tempter, putting the mistletoe bough in his hand; "I will direct it for thee; now fling it with all thy might."

Hödur did so, and—the sun lost its light, the earth quaked—the murder, the patricide was committed—Baldur lay stabbed to death on the ground, the blood flowing from his side on to the darkening earth. Breathless and silent the gods stood around; they could not take in the monstrous, the terrible fact; it almost seemed as if they themselves had received a death-wound. When they were able to move, some of them crowded round the corpse and watered it with their tears, while others asked eagerly who it was that had done the evil deed.

"Dark Hödur threw the spear," was shouted on every side. Friendless Hödur stood alone as ever in the midst of the excited Ases; Loki had deserted him at once, as the tempter always does, leaving his victim to bear his misery alone.

Darkness surrounded the luckless Ase, and darkness reigned in his soul. He heard the curses and threats that echoed on every side, and the clash of the swords and spears that were turned against him. Suddenly Allfather appeared in the midst of the Ases, grave and calm, and in all his divine majesty. His own forebodings, and Wala's prophecy, had prepared him for what had happened. It was Orlog's will and neither gods nor men could do aught to hinder it. So he, the Father of Heroes, bore his sorrow without cowardly complaint; in spirit he saw the approach of Ragnarök and was determined to fight the hopeless battle to the end, for even mortal heroes do not let the sword fall from their dying hands until their last strength is exhausted. He commanded his people to cease their clamorous woe, to raise the corpse of the Well-beloved, to dress it in clean garments, and prepare the funeral pyre.

Then came Frigg, Odin's faithful wife, her eyes red with weeping. But now she checked her tears, for she thought she had found a way to regain her darling.

"Which," she asked, "which of you brave sons of the Ases will ride down to Helheim and will dare to entreat the goddess of the Under-world to restore Baldur, the light of the world, to Ase-heim? He who does this shall be held highest in my esteem and in that of Allfather."

Hermodur, the swift, immediately offered to be her messenger to the realm of shades. He at once saddled Sleipnir and set out on his journey.

The myth of the sun-god Baldur and of his death and resurrection is very old. The Teutonic races brought it from their original home, and formulated it in the northern lands to which they emigrated in accordance with the rude climate and the mode of life to which they had there grown accustomed. The sun-god was worshipped by all the Aryan nations, had costly sacrifices offered to him, and prayers and songs made for him. The Semitic peoples also, the Babylonians, Phœnicians, etc., regarded him as the god who blessed arts and manufactures, trade and ships. The festival of Adonis and the mysteries of Mithras, which the Romans brought into Europe from the East, clearly have reference to the death of the sun-god after the summer solstice, and to his resurrection after the winter solstice, and traces are still to be found of the Mysteries of Mithras in such parts of Germany as the Romans settled in.

The Ases were still standing about the corpse of Baldur. The body was dressed in its grave-clothes and laid upon Baldur's own ship Hringhorn. By Odin's command the wood for the funeral pyre was heaped high on the deck of the vessel, so that the flames might be seen in every land.

Nanna was standing beside her dead husband. She had no tears with which to weep for him, her low shuddering sobs alone showed the intensity of her grief. When the torch was lighted with which the wood was to be set on fire, her heart burst with sorrow and she sank down beside the corpse pale and lifeless, like a broken flower.

So the sorrowing Ases laid her on the pyre by her husband, and beside them they placed the horse of the god, which had to die with its master. Then Odin added the golden ring Draupnir, from which eight other rings dropped every ninth night. He also whispered a word in the ear of his son, so low that none of the bystanders could hear. Perhaps it was the comforting assurance of resurrection to a new and better life.

Crowds had assembled to gaze upon the sad spectacle and join the Ases in showing their respect for the darling and benefactor of the world. The Walkyries were there leaning on their spears, and the Dises wrapped in their dark veils ; the Light-Elves and the Wood and Water-sprites were also there. Besides these came the Mountain and Frost-giants, and even the Black-Elves.

Odin's ravens fluttered sadly round the ship; they knew well what the gods and heaven and earth had lost. The ship had been drawn up on the shore and placed upon rollers, that it might be pushed down into the water before being set on fire. But it was so heavy, because of the quantity of wood and costly gifts piled upon it, that it was impossible to move it. Then the

Mountain-giants said that a woman named Hyrrockin, who lived in Jotunheim and who could move mountains unaided, would soon shove the ship into the water if some one would go and fetch her. So a Storm-giant started at once in search of her. She soon came, but not borne on the wings of the messenger as they had expected ; she was riding a monstrous wolf, whose bridle was a horrible snake.

She dismounted and looked round her scornfully, as though she regarded all present as a set of weaklings, after which she gave her strange steed into the charge of four Berserkers whom Odin sent to hold it. Whilst these managed to hold the wolf with infinite difficulty, the woman went up to the ship and pushed it into the water with the first shove ; but the friction was so great that the rollers caught fire. This enraged Thor so much that he swung Miölnir preparatory to throwing it at the woman's head ; but all the Ases entreated him to be calm, and to remember that Hyrrockin had come under their safe conduct, and that she had been of service to them. He allowed himself to be appeased, and got into the ship to bless it with his hammer. While doing this the little dwarf Lit got into his way, and he kicked him into the fire, so that he was burnt with the corpse. The flames mounted high into the air and sky ; earth and sea were reddened with them. They made known to the whole world that the god of innocence, love and righteousness was dead, and that his blessings were lost to them henceforth.

It was not at all uncommon for the dwellers on the sea-coast to bury their dead on board their ships. It was a very ancient custom, and still existed after grave-mounds and the burning of the dead had been introduced. Even amongst the Allemannes by the Rhine and Danube we find coffins carved like boats. There are many stories about this mode of burial, amongst others that regarding St. Emmeran.

Frigg alone of all the Ases still nourished hope of her son's restoration. She believed that Hel would allow herself to be moved by Hermodur's intercession, and would permit Baldur to return to the Upper-world. The divine messenger set out on his journey to the Under-world. Sleipnir bore him for nine nights through dark valleys and glens into which no ray of light pene trated. The silence of death was all around, and the only sound to be heard was that made by the horse's feet. At length Hermodur reached the banks of the river Giöll, which divides the kingdom of the dead from that of the living.

He was about to ride over the gold-covered bridge that spans the Giöll, but the gigantic porteress Mödgud (spiritual conflict) came forward and asked him what he was doing there.

"Yesterday," she said, "crowds of dead rode over the bridge, and yet they did not make as much noise as thou alone; and besides that, thou hast not the colour of death. Speak, what dost thou, a living man, want with the dead?"

"I seek for Baldur, my dear brother, who was slain. For his sake I have ridden down the Hel road that I may entreat the goddess to let him go free. If thou hast seen him, show me where I may find him."

Hermodur ceased, and the porteress pointed to the north, as she said that she had seen Baldur ride over the bridge, and he was even now with Hel.

Then Hermodur continued his journey fearlessly, until at length he reached the fence round Hel's abode, and there he could find no mode of entrance.

It was a question of his brother's restoration, so he did not hesitate. He dismounted, drew the girths tighter, and then remounting set spurs to Sleipnir, and Odin's horse leapt high over the fence and landed safely on the other side.

Hermodur was now in the realm of shades, and surrounded on

every side by grey rocks which seemed to stare at him with hollow eyes.

He felt as though in a dream, as he made his way to a house he saw before him. He entered, and there he saw the queen of the land, stern of aspect and adorned with gold and diamonds. She was pale as death, and her eyes were fixed upon the ground. She knew no mercy, for the golden light of the sun had never shone on her. Near her was Baldur, seated on a throne, and looking wan as the withered wreath of flowers on his head ; by his side was Nanna, who had died for love of him. A golden goblet filled with sweet mead stood before him untouched.

Hermodur approached him, and spoke to him of his return to Ase-heim, which Hel would certainly permit, as every creature longed for it. But Baldur shook his head and pointed at Nanna, as if he wished to say, " Take her with thee, she is too young for the world of shades." And she crept closer to him, whispering, so low as to be almost inaudible, " Death and the grave cannot destroy true love ; Nanna (blossom) remains with him who gave her life and being. I will stay with thee for ever." So the three talked together for a whole night. Next morning Hermodur asked Hel to restore Baldur to the Ases, for not only the gods, but also every one in heaven and on earth, mourned for him.

The goddess rose from her dark throne, the gold and diamonds on her breast shone with an unearthly lustre, and the abyss trembled.

She answered in a monotonous voice : " If all creatures mourn for him, if everything that has life weeps for him, then, in accordance with the eternal decree, Baldur may once more return to the light of day ; but if one eye refuses to weep for him, he must remain in Helheim. There is no other choice."

Hermodur knew that what the goddess had said was unalterable. He took leave of his brother and Nanna. Both went with him to the door, Baldur gave him the ring Draupnir to return to Odin, as that symbol of plenty was worthless in the kingdom of the dead. Nanna sent Frigg a veil and other gifts, while to Fulla she sent a golden ring with which one day to adorn the blooming bride.

The divine messenger now set out on his return to the Upperworld and Asgard, and when he got there he told all that he had seen and heard. The Ases looked upon his news as good news, and at once sent servants into all parts of the universe to call upon every creature and every inanimate object that had life to weep for Baldur.

Tears hung like pearls from every flower and plant, they dropped like dew from the leaves and branches of the trees, and the very metals and stones exuded moisture. On their road home the messengers passed by a dark cave, in which they found the giantess Thöck (darkness), who was as terrible to look upon as Hel herself. They asked the woman to shed a tear, so that Baldur, the god of light, might return ; but the giantess answered :

"Thöck can only weep with dry eyes for Baldur's death. He was of no use to her living or dead, so Hel may keep what she has got."

The messengers vainly strove to soften the hard heart of the giantess ; but she vanished from their eyes into the black depths of the cavern, and they could see her no more.

So they continued their journey sadly ; but one of them said that he had recognised Loki in the woman's dress. And then at once their eyes were opened and they said that he was right. When they brought the sorrowful tidings to Asgard, loud was the lamentation of the gods, for they knew that Baldur's return was hopeless.

Days passed, and every day made their loss appear greater. Whenever the Ases assembled under the holy oak, the word vengeance was on their lips. It was the first law, the highest duty, the oldest justice, and had been exercised from the earliest times. But it was difficult to carry out, for Hödur avoided the light of day; he only went out at night, and his Ase strength grew in the darkness. He was blind and could use neither spear nor bow. It was known, however, that the Wood-demons had given him a magic shield to protect him and also a terrible magic sword, and every one feared to meet him in the dark night. So Hödur used to glide about through the lonely forest like a ghost at midnight without fearing the avenger of blood, whose duty it was to punish him for the crime of patricide.

One day, a lad with a child-like face and a strong, well-knit figure walked in at the gate of Asgard. He pursued his way as if he knew where he was going, and when he reached Walhalla, he tried to enter, but the door-keeper stopped him, saying:

"No youth with uncombed hair and unwashed hands is allowed to enter here."

The lad pushed him aside and went into the hall unannounced. The Ases and Einheriar gazed with pleased surprise at the youthful stranger, and Odin called to him to approach, adding in a loud voice:

"This is Wali, my son by the lady Rinda,—this is he who is called to the holy work of the avenger."

Then the Ases said amongst themselves: "How is it possible for a youth like this to conquer strong Hödur?"

"It is true that I am young, that I am only one night old," cried the lad, "but still I shall conquer Hödur, in like manner as young May conquers strong Winter."

Night came; Hödur walked as usual along the dark paths he knew so well. Suddenly he heard a voice exclaim:

"Murderer of Baldur, beware, the avenger is nigh."

The god of darkness girded his magic shirt closer round him, and advanced with his drawn sword towards the place from which the voice had come. Then an arrow hissed through the air, a second and a third followed, and the last struck the blind god to the heart. The bowman's shout of triumph was so loud that it echoed throughout Asgard, and all the gods and goddesses hastened to the spot.

There is no doubt that this is the description of the victory of Spring over Winter. As we learn from Saxo, it was originally Baldur himself who conquered Hödur, the god of the long night of winter; but when the myth of Baldur became part of the great universal year, the story of Wali, the god of spring, was added, and he it was who avenged his brother's murder.

PART THIRTEENTH.

LOKI'S CONDEMNATION.

THE time of the flax harvest had come. The Ases were about to celebrate the festival in Ögir's crystal halls. They were still sorrowing for the loss of Baldur, and hoped to forget their grief for a time in the flowing bowls of mead offered them by the god of the ocean.

Odin was there with his golden helmet on his head, and Frigg, the Queen of Heaven, with her circlet of stars, Freya wearing the beautiful necklace Brisingamen, golden-haired Sif, Bragi, Niörder and Skadi, Freyer, Heimdal, Widar and other Ases. Strong Thor alone was absent; he had gone to help his peasants till the ground and slay any giants or other monsters who made themselves obnoxious.

Sly Loki glided into the hall with his soft, cat-like step, hoping to enjoy the golden mead that Ögir had provided for his guests. As he was advancing, however, he was stopped by Funafeng, who had been stationed at the door to guard the entrance.

"No seat is prepared for thee in Ögir's halls," he said; "go, seek a place for thyself in the house of Angurboda, Fenris's mother."

Loki was very angry when he heard these words, more especially as the Ases all joined in praising Funafeng for what he had said. He struck the man so that he fell down dead on the spot. A great uproar ensued, for murder had been committed in a sacred place. The Ases seized their weapons and would have rushed upon Loki, but he had hidden himself in a wood that was close to the palace.

Quiet was at last re-established. Beyggwir, and Beyla, the house-keeper, served the guests. This task was made much easier for them because the cans from which they poured the mead were so cunningly devised that they refilled themselves as fast as they were emptied.

Meanwhile Loki returned. He found Eldir guarding the door, and spoke to him as if nothing had happened. He asked what the gods of victory were talking about.

"Of arms and brave deeds," replied Eldir, "but they have not a single good word for thee."

"Very well then, I will go and join them," said the villain; "I will so cover them with shame and guilt that none of them will have a word to say in answer."

With these words he thrust Eldir aside and entered the hall. Suddenly all conversation ceased and was succeeded by a death-like silence. Every eye was fixed on him who had sullied the sanctuary with murder. But Loki asked boldly if they were going to refuse him, an Ase and their equal, a seat at the banquet and a cup of mead. And Bragi answered that they would never again consent to receive such a villain as one of themselves.

Then Loki turned to Odin, and thus addressed him:

"Hast thou forgotten how we in the olden time mixed our blood, swore brotherhood, and promised never to drink a refreshing draught that was not offered to the other?"

He did not speak in vain; Allfather remembered how he had long ago entered into the bond of brotherhood with Loki. So although his former friend was perjured and forsworn, he desired Widar to make room for him and give him a bowl of mead. This was done, and Loki emptied the goblet, saying:

"All hail, holy gods and noble goddesses, but confusion to Bragi, who denied me drink when I was thirsty."

The Prince of Song was silent for a few minutes, and then he said that he would give his sword, horse and ring to ensure that Loki did no more harm. And Loki answered that Bragi was not rich in treasures, and that his sword was of little use to him, and that he only required his horse to escape from danger. Bragi challenged the blasphemer to instant combat; but Loki went on quietly with his accusations, overwhelming all, gods and goddesses alike, with his aspersions. Even Odin and Frigg did not escape, and the latter exclaimed:

"Oh that my son Baldur were here, he would soon have silenced thy slanderous tongue."

"Ah well, great goddess," Loki went on, with a malicious sneer, "shall I tell thee yet more of my misdeeds? Dost thou know that it was I who gave the mistletoe bough to blind Hödur, that he might send thy darling Baldur down to Hel's domain?"

The Queen of the Ases shrieked, and the gods caught up their weapons. But before they had time to do more, a terrible clap

U

of thunder shook the house, and Thor stood before them swinging Miölnir. The blasphemer turned upon him and sneered at him for having hidden away in the thumb of Skrymir's glove. And when Hlorridi (heat bringer) threatened him with his hammer, he cried :

' I sang to the glory of the Ases in Ögir's halls, and that glory will soon pass away when once the flames of destruction are seen. They have drunk of cool mead here for the last time, for Ragnarök is coming. I shall now hide myself from the fury of strong Thor, who would willingly strike me down."

And immediately he took the form of a salmon and swam away into the rushing waters that surrounded the crystal palace of Ögir.

The Ases sought everywhere for Loki. They went through Asgard and Midgard, they searched in Jotunheim and in the Home of the Black-Elves, but he was nowhere to be found. They were miserable at the thought that the author of evil might escape their vengeance.

Odin seated himself on his throne Hlidskialf and looked down upon the nine worlds ; he saw a lonely house situated on the other side of a high mountain, and in this house was he whom they sought. So Allfather descended from his throne, and calling the Ases about him, told them where they would find Loki.

The fugitive had made himself a peculiar dwelling in a cliff overhanging a wild mountain torrent. This dwelling consisted of one large room with four doors, all of which were kept open. There he sat day and night gazing out at the four quarters of the heavens to see whether his pursuers were on his track. He felt no remorse, no pricks of conscience—he had long conquered all such weaknesses—he only feared the vengeance that he had called down upon himself. He often swam about in the stream in the form of a salmon, comforting himself with the thought that none could re-

LOKI IN CHAINS.

cognise him. And yet his fears gave him no rest ; he trusted no one, not even his wife Sigyn, who loved him in spite of all his sins.

For whole days he sat in his airy dwelling, keeping a sharp lookout in every direction, while he busied himself in making all sorts of useful things, and amongst others, a fishing-net, which until then was absolutely unknown. He grew so interested in making this net that he quite forgot the danger that threatened him. Suddenly the flames of the fire on his hearth rose in a column, as though to call his attention to something that was going on. He looked up and saw the Ases marching towards him. He threw the net into the fire, and hastened to the water-fall, where he hid himself.

Cunning and treachery are often caught in their own net. The Ases did not find the slanderer in his airy dwelling. The fire had burnt out. But the place where it had been was still warm, and showed that some one had been there lately. One of the gods, who was learned in wisdom and in the runes, examined the ashes, and discovered what no human eye could have seen, the form and use of the net.

" Found ! " he exclaimed ; " the wily enchanter's thoughts have been full of the idea of fish and fishing. He has been making a net, then he burnt it, and is now hiding in the stream in the form of a fish."

Gefion looked at the net, and soon found out how it was made, and, with the help of the others, got a second net ready in a very short time. This they dipped into the water just under the fall. Thor held one side and the rest of the Ases held the other, so that the net stretched across the stream. After dragging the water for some distance, a gigantic salmon was discovered and caught with infinite difficulty. Thor held on by the fish's tail in spite of its struggles. A blow, a knock with a stone, would have killed it ; but it suddenly changed its form, and the blasphemer, the instigator of murder, false Loki, was in the hands of Hlorridi.

The Ases rejoiced to have their enemy in their power. They bound the arch-fiend's legs and arms together and dragged him away to a cave in the mountain. There they prepared for him the bed of misery that had been foretold for him. Three sharp-pointed masses of rock were placed, one between his shoulders, the second under his loins, and the third under his knees. Then his two sons, Wali and Narwi, were brought to him, followed by their weeping mother, Sigyn. Wali was changed into a fierce wolf, and he immediately tore his brother in pieces. The Ases now bound the guilty father to the rock with the sinews of his murdered son, and when this was done the bonds were converted into heavy iron chains.

Skadi carried out the last part of the judgment that had been pronounced upon Loki by fastening a poisonous adder over the head of the evil-doer in such a way that the poison exuding from its jaws should drop upon his face, and this caused him unspeakable torment. After this was done, the Ases returned to Asgard, which was no longer the green home it used to be, for eternal spring reigned there no more, and the mark of change was upon everything.

One creature alone had compassion on the sinner, and that was Sigyn, the wife he had so often treated with cruelty and contempt. She would not desert him, but remained by his side, and, holding a dish above his head, caught the poison as it dropped from the adder. When the dish was full, and she had to remove it to empty it, the horrible slime fell upon Loki's face, and made him howl with agony, and turn and twist himself, till Mother Earth shook to her foundations. That is what ignorant men call an earthquake.

The crime was now punished, and the gods, who here showed themselves as moral powers, carried out the sentence pronounced upon the criminal. But they themselves were not unsullied by sin. Many of the accusations, with which the blasphemer had overwhelmed them, were well-founded, and every sin brings down its own punishment in heaven and on earth. And so the day of destruction drew near, when the tempter, who was at the same time the author of evil, should be freed from his bonds and the world should come to an end.

In this myth Loki appears as the cause of all evil. He is the tempter who makes the innocent fall into sin, although he knows that he thereby destroys them. If in primæval times he had been the sworn brother of Odin and the god of the domestic fire, he was now a consummate villain and threw the brand into the house in which he was to be burnt together with the guilty and the innocent. The principle of vengeance for bloodshed was deeply rooted in ancient Scandinavia. " He who has injured me must pay for it, even though I know that I shall perish with him," was the idea on which both noble and serf acted.

In this tale we have smoothed over a good many discrepancies that appear in the myth, but not all. We let Bragi and Iduna appear, although they dwelt in the depth of the earth. Perhaps they were allowed to rise once more that they might take part in the festival. But we have left out about Kwasir, who, according to the myth, discovered the net in the ashes, because his appearance was unnecessary. It is very curious that Loki, the fire-god, should have hidden in the water; but the belief that fire takes refuge in water is to be found amongst other nations, and is perhaps founded on the reflection of the sun, moon and stars. sunrise and sunset, that are to be seen in the water.

PART FOURTEENTH.

RAGNARÖK, THE TWILIGHT OF THE GODS.

THE tempter, the author of evil, was firmly bound to the cold rock, but the evil seed he had sown grew and flourished, and even the gods, the moral powers, whose duty it was to uphold universal law, were no longer pure and free from guilt; the wholesome bonds of law were broken, and the destruction of the world approached. Neither truth nor faith was to be found in heaven or on earth, and love, which had formerly bound friends, parents, children, brothers and sisters to each other, had lost its power. Self-seeking, self-interest and grasping covetousness became the guiding principles of life ; murder, incendiarism and bloodshed were everywhere to be found.

The sun still continued its course through the heavens, but it shone mistily as through a veil, and gave no warmth in summer. Winter set in early, and it was a Fimbul-Winter, a winter of horrors. The snow-storms were such as had never been known before, and the frost was terribly hard. Many houses and villages were buried in the snow, and their inhabitants perished. The Fimbul-Winter seemed as if it would never end ; it lasted for three years, without any summer to break its fury. Trees and bushes, grass and plants perished, men died of cold and hunger, and yet they did not cease from their lies and murders and other deeds of violence.

Meanwhile Fenris's children, the wolves, grew into horrible monsters, for the old giantess in the forest fed them with marrow taken from the bones of murdered perjurers and breakers of the marriage bond, and gave them to drink of the blood of dead poisoners, parricides and fratricides, and there was abundance of such food.

Wala, the prophetess, was asked what all this meant, and she said, that the sun, moon and Mother Earth were sorrowing over the fall of man, that the wolves and other hostile powers would soon be free, and then the destruction of the universe would begin.

Many signs and wonders were to be seen during that time, as we read in the Lay of Wala.

The glory of the sun was darkened, wicked Idises were seen flying through the air, Fjalar, the bright-red cock of Asgard, crowed loudly, the dark-red cock in Helheim answered him, and all in the Upper-world heard their crowing. The great wolves Skiöll and Hati rushed up to attack the sun and moon ; they seized and swallowed them, and now darkness reigned in heaven and earth. Then the earth itself shook to its very foundations, and all chains were broken. Thus it happened that Loki was set free, that his horrible son Fenris was able to shake off his bonds and hasten with his children to join his father, and that Garm, Hel's dog, could rise out of the Gnypa cave with the other dark followers of the goddess, to take their share in the work of destruction. The sea was stirred to its depths and overflowed the land. Out of its abyss the Midgard-snake reared her frightful head, and flung herself about with a giant's rage, so much did she long for the struggle to begin.

Heimdal then blew a loud blast on the Giallarhorn that sounded through all the homes, wakening Ases and Einheriar, and warning them to prepare for the Last Battle. Odin mounted Sleipnir as soon as he was armed, and rode away to Mimir's Well. The World-Ash was rustling and trembling in the storm, its leaves were falling rapidly, and its roots threatened to snap. The Norns were seated beside it, their heads hidden in their veils. Odin whispered to Mimir's head ; no one heard what he said or how he was answered.

Meanwhile Thrym, the king of the Jotuns, was steering his ship from the east over the everlasting sea. The Hrimthurses, armed with clubs and javelins, were on board. At the same time, Nagelfari, the ship of death, was set afloat, and was borne along on the waves. It was built of the nails of the dead which love had not caused to be cut. Love had died in the parricidal wars that prevailed, and the last offices were therefore denied to the dead. Loki steered the vessel. With him were Surtur, swinging his flaming sword, whose blade shone brighter than the sun, and all the sons of Muspel dressed in fiery armour, which blinded all who looked at it. They landed, mounted the horses they had brought with them, and galloped over the bridge Bifröst, which broke under their weight. Loki led his hosts to the plain of Wigrid, that measured a hundred miles on every side. Odin also went there, accompanied by his brave Ases and heroes.

Once more the Giallarhorn was sounded, and then the Last Battle began. The Wolf howled, the Snake hissed and spat out poison, which filled and infected the air. The sons of Muspel, under Surtur's guidance, rushed on their enemies like flames of fire. The Einheriar, headed by Freyer, withstood them bravely, and they fell back. Thor fought gallantly, and slew numbers of the Hrimthurses and other monsters. Odin sought out the Fenriswolf, and the battle between them began.

No seer or bard has made known to us how that terrible struggle

RAGNARÖK, THE LAST BATTLE.

between the Father of Victory and the Wolf was fought. Even
Wala covers the whole affair with the veil of silence; she only
says that he, the omnipotent Father, was slain by the Wolf.
Freyer's fate was the same when he fought against the sons of
Muspel. He met black Surtur in their ranks and fell dead at a
blow from his flaming sword. Thor slew Jörmungander, but died
himself from the pestiferous breath she had breathed upon him
when dying. Heimdal and Loki fought hand to hand, and each
slew the other. Fenris fell under the sword of Widar. Tyr and
Garm wrestled and struggled together, and at last Tyr was victorious. The leaders of the Ases and their enemies were all dead,
but still the battle raged.

The earth quaked, mountains fell, abysses yawned, and reached
down even to the kingdom of Hel. The heavens split open and
threatened to fall. The ash Yggdrasil groaned and moaned like a
living creature. And now Surtur, the dark, the terrible, began to
draw himself up. He grew taller and taller, till he reached the
heavens

Before him and behind him was fire, and his flaming sword shone
in the darkness in which he was wrapped. He flung his fire-brand
over heaven, earth, and all the worlds, and at once everything that
existed, animate or inanimate, was plunged into a lake of fire.
The fire raged, Yggdrasil was surrounded by flames, the storm-
wind howled, heaven and earth and the nine homes were no more;
Surtur's flames had destroyed them all.

When the fire went out, the unquiet sea overflowed the scene of
desolation. No creature, no life, moved in its depths; no mer-
maid floated on the dark waves; no star was reflected on its
surface.

Years passed, perhaps centuries—there was none to count them—
and again the morning star bathed its head in the calm waters.
Dawn once more flushed the sky. A new sun arose, the blooming,

glowing child of the old. At length a new earth appeared above the waters. At first it was bare and desolate, but the rays of the sun touched it, and soon it was covered with grass and herbs and the well-flavoured leek. Trees and shrubs grew up, and flowers of various colours filled the air with their perfume. In the quiet valley where the Fountain of Urd had flowed of old, and where Odin used to talk with Mimir about the past and the riddles of the future, a youth and a maiden, Lif and Lifthrasir, came out of Hoddmimir's wood.

They were beautiful and loving, pure and innocent as the sweet flowerets around them, and, like them, they had been awaked out of a long dream by the rays of the sun. They had hidden themselves in the wood in the olden days and had lived on dew. Then they had fallen asleep, and were sunk in childhood's dreams while the Last Battle raged. Allfather had preserved them from Surtur's flames by a last miracle.

Ignorant of the terrors that threatened them, as a sleeping child borne in its mother's arms out of a burning house, they had rested safely in the arms of Allfather, and now they looked in astonishment at the new fair world in which they found themselves. They were very happy. There was abundance of fruit; the fields were full of yellow corn ripe for the harvest, which no human hand had sown, and the vines were laden with grapes. Animals of all kinds were grazing in the fat pastures, and many-hued snakes glided harmlessly in the grass, but none of Fenrir's race were to be seen.

Lif and Lifthrasir built themselves a roomy dwelling, and saw children and grandchildren grow up about them, and then make new homes for themselves. From these are descended the numerous races of men that inhabit the earth.

Over the place where Asgard's glorious palaces had stood was a wide plain. This was the Field of Ida, and it was far more beautiful than the green home of the gods. There the holy Ases were

FREYA IN HER CHARIOT.

(See page 209.)

assembled; for they, like the world, had been purified by fire, and were now fitted to dwell in Ida in eternal peace. The bonds of Hel could bind them no more, for the kingdom of evil had passed away, and night had been changed into day. Baldur and Hödur walked there arm in arm, reconciled to each other through love. They were joined by Widar and Wali, the avenging Ases, who no longer thought of vengeance. Surtur's flames had not destroyed them, nor yet had the raging waters. There were also Magni and Modi, the sons of Thor. They brought Miölnir with them, not as a weapon of war, but as the instrument with which to consecrate the new heavens and the new earth.

On the Field of Ida, the field of resurrection, the sons of the highest gods assembled, and in them their fathers rose again. They talked together of the Past and the Present, and remembered the wisdom and prophecies of their ancestors which had all been fulfilled. Near them, but unseen by them, was the strong, the mighty One who rules all things, makes peace between those who are angry with each other, and ordains the eternal laws that govern the world. They all knew he was there, they felt his presence and his power, but were ignorant of his name. At his command the new earth rose out of the waters. To the south, above the Field of Ida, he made another heaven called Audlang, and further off, a third, known as Widblain. Over Gimil's cave a wondrous palace was erected, which was covered with gold and shone brighter than the sun. There the gods were enthroned as they used to be, and they rejoiced in their restoration and in the better time.

From Gimil's heights they looked down upon the happy descendants of Lif and signed to them to climb up higher, to rise in knowledge and wisdom, in piety and in deeds of love, step by step, from one heaven to another, until they were at last fit to be united to the divinities in the house of Allfather.

This was what our forefathers believed about Ragnarök, the

X

Twilight of the gods or the Divine Judgment; it was no contemptible faith, and in our opinion it deserves more reverence than the teaching of the Greeks and Romans, whose gods eternally drank nectar and ambrosia on the heights of Olympos, while mortal men descended into dark Hades, or perhaps to the Elysian Fields.

Ragnarök means the Darkening of the Regin, *i.e.*, of the gods, hence the Twilight of the Gods; some, however, explain the word Rök to mean Judgment, *i.e.*, of the gods. The gods sinned, evil gained the upper-hand amongst gods and men, and when the god of holiness and righteousness was taken away, they all sank into a deep abyss of guilt; murder, fratricide and convulsions of nature portended the destruction of the universe. Ragnarök followed. Then a new and more beautiful world appeared, in which Ases and men, purified by fire, could now live in peace and good-will.

It is true that in the Younger Edda and in the Lay of Wala we find allusions to places of punishment in the realms of Hel; but, in our opinion, these descriptions have been introduced from other poems and are at variance with the leading idea which we have just given.

The Aryans, like all other people living in a state of nature, had at first a vague indefinite consciousness of God; they felt that there was a Being who had created everything and who guided and governed the universe. In the ancient records, in which this idea had already grown dim, this Being was called Zerwana-Akarana, *i.e*, everlasting time and immeasurable space, and was perhaps essentially Eternity. According to later concepts this Being took no part in the direction of the world or in the doings of man.

Two other beings, Ormuzd (Ahura-Mazda) and Ahriman (Agramainyus) fought for the supreme power; but neither they nor their spiritual hosts entered into personal collision with each other ; instead of this, they sought to bring the human spirit and earthly things under their dominion : the latter by cunningly planned temptations, icy cold snow-storms and darkness ; and the former by good deeds, fine weather, and especially by the light that conquers darkness and evil. At the end of days Ormuzd and all the righteous were to enjoy blessedness and peace, while Ahriman had to undergo a painful purification by · fire before he could attain a similar condition.

The modern theory is that the belief in Zerwana-Akarana, and the dogmas respecting the end of the world and the purification of Agramainyus are of later origin, and that they first arose through the influence of the Western Iranian and Semitic races ; but traces of these beliefs are to be found in the Zend-Avesta of Zoroaster and in the Indic Vedas, and the relationship with the Norse belief in Allfather, the Last Battle, and the Renewal of the World, seems to be founded on this Aryan belief.

We must allow something for the influence of Christianity on the Germanic races especially with regard to Ragnarök, and the Resurrection of the world, the Ases and men, and also in reference to Allfather, to the description of the realm of Hel, and of the places of reward and punishment. It is a mistake to deny this influence, to make so much of the fact that the heathen had a foreboding of the existence of the one God, that the Edda possessed a water-hell and the Christian myth a hell of fire, and lastly to maintain that a knowledge of the Christian faith was impossible to the Scandinavians. Why may not the indefinite foreboding, the misty conception of something divine, have first received a distinct form in the consciousness of the heathen through Christian influence? And if the Teutons had ever heard of the Christian idea of punishment in hell, would they not have conceived this hell after their own fashion and according to the conditions, climatic and other, that surrounded them? We have already shown how not only the Germans, but also the Scandinavians, early came in contact with Christianity, and this was the case even before the Wiking raids of the ninth and tenth centuries. The Jutes, and perhaps the Danes and Norwegians as well, went to Christian Britain in the fifth century and conquered it after a struggle that lasted for a hundred years. There these wild people were brought into contact with the Britons and even with their Christian priests, who gladly told the warlike and musical skalds about their own faith. These seeds of a purer religion took form and life in the poems of the skalds, which however retained their old Northern colouring and were not changed into hymns of victory in a foreign faith.

The myths exist in the present like the stately ruins of a past time, which are no longer suitable for the use of man. Generations come and go, their views, actions and modes of thought change ; and yet as the poet says :

> " All things change ; they come and go ;
> The pure unsullied soul alone remains in peace."

Thousands of years ago our ancestors prayed to Waruna, *i.e.* the Father in heaven ; thousands of years later the Romans entered their sanctuary and worshipped Jupiter, the Father of heaven, while the Germanic races worshipped Allfather. We, after the lapse of centuries, now turn in all our sorrows and necessities to Our Father which is in heaven. Other thousands of years may pass, and we shall not have grown beyond this central point of religion. But as everything that our forefathers added to this has passed away, so the systems that we have built up round it may also pass away. No man ever yet has seen the full truth, or can see it. " For now we see through a glass darkly, but then face to face."

This " then " can never be on earth.

> Our little systems have their day ;
>   They have their day, and cease to be :
>   They are but broken lights of Thee,
> And Thou, O Lord, art more than they.

> We have but faith : we cannot know ;
>   For knowledge is of things we see ;
>   And yet we trust it comes from Thee,
> A beam in darkness : let it grow !

LAY OF WALA.

We here annex one of the most interesting poems of the Elder Edda, the Wöluspa or Lay of Wala, the prophetess. It is the translation given in Pfeiffer's " Visit to Iceland," and we think it will be of value to our readers.

LAY OF WALA.

To attention I invite all the holy generations,
The sons of Heimdal, great and small ;
Of the Father of the Elect I would proclaim the mysteries,
The antique traditions of heroes which I have formerly learned.

I remember the Jotuns born at the commencement ;
They formerly taught me.
I remember the new worlds, the new forests,
The great tree in the midst, upon the earth here below.

It was the commencement of the ages when Ymir established himself :
There was neither shore, nor sea, nor cool waves ;
Neither earth nor heaven above was found ;
There was the yawning gulf, but vegetation nowhere.

Then the sons of Buri raised the firmament ;
They formed the great enclosure of the middle ;
Sol will enlighten, from the south, the rocks of the Aboae ;
The earth immediately became green with tufted verdure.

Sol scatters from the south her favours upon Mani,
On the right of the gate of the Celestial courser.
Sol knew not where she had her abodes,
The stars knew not where are their places,
Mani knew not what was his power.

Then the Great Powers all went to the elevated seats ;
The most holy Gods deliberated upon that ;
To the night, to the new moon they gave names ;
They designated the dawn and the middle of the day,
The twilight and the evening, to indicate the time.

The Ases met together in the Plain of Ida,
They built very high a sanctuary and a court ;
They placed furnaces, fashioned jewels,
Forged nails, and fabricated utensils.

They played at the tables in the enclosure ; they were joyous,
They were in want of nothing, and everything was in gold.
Then the three Ases of this band,
Full of power and of goodness, descended towards the sea
They found in the country some wretched beings,
Ask and Embla, needing destiny.

They had no soul, they had no understanding,
Neither blood, nor language, nor good exterior ;
Odin gave the soul, Hönir gave understanding,
Lodur gave the blood and the good exterior.

Then arrived three Virgin Thurses
Very powerful from the land of the Jotun.
I knew an ash, it is called Yggdrasill,
A hairy tree, moistened by a brilliant cloud,
Whence proceeds the dew which falls in the valleys ;
It raises itself, always green, above the Fountain of Urd.

Thence arose the three Virgins with much knowledge,
From this lake which is below the tree ;
Urd one is called, the other Verdandi ;
They engraved upon tablets ; Skuld was the third ;
They consulted the laws, they interrogated fate,
And proclaimed destiny to the children of men.

Then the Great Powers all went to the lofty seats,
The most holy Gods deliberated upon that ;
" Who would form the chief of the Dvergues,
From the blood of Brimir, from the thighs of the livid giant?"

Then Modsognir became the first
Of all the Dvergues, but Durin the second ;
They formed of earth the multitude of the Dvergues
In the human figure, as Durin proposed ;

Nyi and Nidi, Nordri and Sudri,
Austri and Vestri, Althiofr, Dwalin,
Nar and Nain, Nipingr, Dain,
Bifurr and Bafurr, Bumburr, Nori.

Anarr and Onarr, Aï, Miodvitnir,
Veigr, Gandalfr, Vindalfr, Thorinn,
Fili and Kili, Fundinn, Nali,
Hepti, Vili, Hanarr, Sviorr.

Frar, Fornbogi, Frœgr, Loni,
Thrar, and Thrainn, Thror, Vitr, Litr,
Nyr, and Nyradr.—Behold, I have enumerated exactly
The Dvergues powerful and intelligent.

It is time to enumerate the human race,
The Dvergues of the band of Dwalin, as far as Lofar :
These latter have sought, far from the Abode,
Habitations at Aurvangar, as far as Joruvellir.

There was Draupnir and Dolgthrasir,
Har, Haugspori, Hlævangr, Gloînn,
Skirvir and Virvir, Skafidr, Aï,
Alfr, and Yngvi, Eikinskialdi.

Fialarr and Frosti, Finnr and Ginnarr,
Heri, Haugstari, Hliodolfr, Noinn :—
As long as there shall be men, they will always exalt
The great number of the descendants of Lofar.

She knows that the horn of Heimdal is concealed
Under the sacred and majestic tree :
She sees that they drink with hasty draughts
In the pledge of the Father of the Elect—Know you it ? But what ?

She was seated without, solitary, when he came, the oldest,
The most circumspect of the Ases, and looked in her eyes :—
"Why sound me? why put me to the proof?
I know all, Odin ; I know where thou hast concealed thine eye,—
In that great fountain of Mimir ;
Every morning Mimir drinks the sweet beverage
In the pledge of the Father of the Elect."—Know you it? But what?

The Father of the Combatants chose for her rings and jewels,
The rich gift of wisdom, and the charms of vision :—
Then she saw far, very far into all the worlds.

She saw the Walkyries hastening from afar,
Eager to repair near the race of the Gods ;
Skuld held the buckler, Skogul followed her,
As well as Gunrr, Hildur, Gondul, Giruskogul :
There are enumerated the servants of the Combatant,
The Walkyries in haste to plunder the country.

She recollects this first war in the world,
When they had placed Gullweig upon the pikes,
And had burned her in the dwelling of the Most High ;
Three times had they burned her ; three times was she born again ;
Burned often, frequently, she lives, however, still.

Heidur is called to her in the houses she has entered ;
She despised the charm of the visions of Wala ;
She knew magic, she magic abused ;
She was always the delight of the wicked race.

Then the Great Powers all went to their elevated seats,
The very holy Gods upon this deliberated :
" The Ases should they expiate their imprudence,
Or else shall all the Gods have authority ?"

The exterior wall of the Ases was overthrown ;
The Wanes knew how, by stratagem, to break down the ramparts ;
But Odin darted his arrow, and drew upon the enemy—
Such was the first war in the world.

Then the Great Powers all went to their elevated seats ;
The very holy Gods deliberated upon this :
" Who had filled with disaster the plains of space,
And given up the affianced of Odur to the race of the Jotuns?"

Thor alone rose, inflamed with anger;
Rarely does he remain seated when he learns such a thing :—
Oaths were violated, promises and assurances,
Every valid treaty that had passed on one side or the other.

I foresaw for Baldur, for that bloody victim,
For that son of Odin, the destiny reserved for him :
He was raising in a charming valley
A tender and beautiful mistleoe.
From that stalk, which appeared so tender, grew
The fatal arrow of bitterness which Hödur took upon himself to dart.

The brother of Baldur had only just been born ;
One night old, he was taken to fight against the son of Odin.
He neither washed his hands nor combed his hair,
Before that he carried to the funeral pile the murderer of Baldur ;
But Frigg wept in Fensal
For the misfortunes of Walhall.—Know you it ? But what ?

She sees lying down near Hveralund
A wicked creature, the ungrateful Loki ;
It is in vain he shakes the fatal bonds of Wali ;
They are too stiff, those cords of catgut.
There is seated Sigyn, who at the fate of her husband
Does not much rejoice.—Know you it ? But what ?

Towards the north, at Nidaföll, was raised
The hall of gold of the race of Sindri ;
But another was built at Okolnir.
The drinking-hall of the Jotun who is named Brimir.

She saw a hall situated far from the sun,
At Nastrendr ; its gates are turned to the north ;
Drops of venom fall into it through the windows,
The hall is a tissue of serpents' backs.

A river rushes on the east into the venomous valleys,
A river of slime and mud ; it is called Slidur ;
Wala saw dragged in it in the muddy waters,
Perjured men, the exiled for murder,
And him who seduced the partner of others :
There, Nidhögg sucked the bodies of the departed,
The wolf tore men.—Know you it ? But what ?

In the east she was seated, that aged woman, in Jarnvid.
And there she nourished the posterity of Fenrir ;
He will be the most formidable of all, he,
Who, under the form of a monster, will swallow up the moon.

He gorges himself with the life-blood of cowardly men,
He stains with red drops the abode of the Great Powers ;
The rays of the sun are eclipsed in the summer following,
All the winds will become hurricanes.—Know you it ?   But what ?.

Seated quite near upon a height he tuned his harp,
The guardian of Gygur, the joyous Egdir :
Not far from him, in Gagalvid, crowed
The beautiful purple cock which is called Fialar.

Near the Ases crowed Gullinkambi ;
He awoke the heroes in the house of the Father of the Combatants ;
But another cock crowed below the earth,
A black-red cock, in the dwelling of Hel.
Garm howls frightfully before Gnypahall.
The chains are going to break ; Freki will escape :
She pauses much, the prophetess : I see from afar
The twilight of the Great Powers, the Fighting Gods.

Brothers are going to fight against each other, and become fratricides ;
Relations will break their alliances ;
Cruelty reigns in the world, and a great luxury ;
The age of axes, the age of lances, in which bucklers are cleft,
The age of north-winds, the age of fierce beasts succeed before the world
      falls to pieces ;
Not one dreams of sparing his neighbour.

The sons of Mimir tremble, the tree in the middle takes fire
At the startling sounds of the noisy horn ;
Heimdal, horn in air, loudly sounds the alarm ;
Odin consults the head of Mimir.

Then the ash raised from Yggdrasil,
That old tree, shivers : the Jotun breaks his chains :
The shades shudder upon the roads to the lower region,
Until the ardour of Surtur has consumed the tree.

Hrym advances from the east, a buckler covers him :
Jörmungander unfolds himself in his giant rage :
The serpent raises the waves, the eagle beats his wings,
The yellow beak tears the bodies of the dead : Nalhfar is pierced :

The ship sails from the east, the army of Muspel
Approaches over the sea, Loki holds the rudder :
The sons of Jotun sail all with Freki,
The brother of Bileist is on board with them.

Surtur starts from the south with disastrous swords ;
The sun glitters upon the blades of the hero-gods :
The mountains of the rock are shaken, the giants tremble,
The shades press the road to hell.   Heaven opens !

What are the Ases doing?   What do the Elves?
All Jotunheim bellows ; the Ases are met together ;
At the gate of the caverns groan the Dvergues,
The sages of the sacred mountains.—Know you it?   But what?

Then the affliction of Hline is renewed,
When Odin set out to combat the Wolf ;
Whilst the glorious murderer of Beli is going to oppose himself to
     Surtur ;
Very soon the cherished hero of Frigg will fall.

But he comes, the valiant son of the Father of Combats,
Widar, to struggle against the terrible monster :
He leaves in the mouth of the scion of Hvedrung
The steel plunged even to the heart.   Thus the father is avenged.

Here comes the illustrious son of Hlodune,
He goes, the descendant of Odin, to fight the Serpent ;
The defender of Midgard strikes him in his anger.
The heroes go all to stain with blood the column of the world.
He draws back with a new step, the son of Fiorgune,
Bitten by the adder, intrepid with rage. . . .

Behold coming the black flying Dragon,
The adder, soaring above Nidafiöll :
Nidhögg extends his wings, he flies over the plain,
Above the bodies of the dead.   Now she will be swallowed up.

The sun begins to be dark ; the continent falls fainting into the Ocean ;
They disappear from the sky, the brilliant stars ;
The smoke eddies around the destroying fire of the world ;
The gigantic flames play against heaven itself.

She sees rising anew,
In the Ocean, an earth with a thick verdure.
Cascades fall there ; the eagle soars above it,
And from the summit of the rock he espies the fish.

The Ases are found again in the plain of Ida,
Under the tree of the world they sit as powerful judges :
They recal to mind the judgments of the gods,
And the antique mysteries of Fimbultyr.

Then the Ases found again upon the grass
The marvellous tables of gold,
Which the generations had, in the beginning of days,
The chief of the gods and the posterity Fiölnir.

The fields will produce without being sown :
Every evil will disappear : Baldur will return
To inhabit with Hödur the enclosure of Hropt,
The sacred abodes of the hero-gods.—Know you it ?　But what ?

Then Hönir will be able to choose his part,
And the sons of the two brothers shall dwell in
The vast abode of the wind.—Know you it ?　But what ?

She sees a hall more brilliant than the sun
Arise, covered with gold, in the magnificent Gimlir :
It is there that shall dwell the faithful people,
And that they will enjoy an everlasting felicity.

Then there came from on high to preside at the judgments of the Great
　　　Powers,
The powerful sovereign who governs the universe :
He tempers the decrees, he calms dissensions,
And gives sacred laws inviolable for ever.

INDEX.

V

THE ABERDEEN UNIVERSITY PRESS LIMITED

CPSIA information can be obtained at www.ICGtesting.com
Printed in the USA
LVOW081612251011

252041LV00004B/41/P